ESSAYS
IN
BIOGRAPHY

BY
CHARLES WHIBLEY

Essay Index Reprint Series

BOOKS FOR LIBRARIES PRESS
FREEPORT, NEW YORK

First Published 1913
Reprinted 1968

LIBRARY OF CONGRESS CATALOG CARD NUMBER:

68-57343

MANUFACTURED
BY
HALLMARK LITHOGRAPHERS, INC.
IN THE U.S.A.

ESSAYS

IN

BIOGRAPHY

CONTENTS

SIR THOMAS OVERBURY

SIR THOMAS OVERBURY—I

RISE AND FALL

THOMAS OVERBURY, whose haggard ghost still walks in the secret places of the Tower, was born a squire's son, in 1581. He was educated in grammar-learning at Compton-Scorfen in Warwickshire, and at the age of fourteen entered Queen's College, Oxford, as a gentleman commoner. There he devoted himself to the study of polite letters. He cultivated his brilliant talent with assiduity, and when, in 1598, he took his degree by right of birth, he had won the golden praises of his contemporaries. A finished scholar, a poet of just pretension, a wit whose fame far outran his years, he left Oxford with high hopes of preferment, and, like many another youth of promise, took up his abode in the Temple—not to unravel the mysteries of law, but to conquer London. For this conquest an acquaintance with foreign countries was still necessary, and Overbury for a while deserted the tranquil courts of the Temple to learn what lessons of elegance France and Italy might teach him. The Grand Tour of Europe inculcated in his facile nature a knowledge of the arts of life. But it was a journey to Scotland, taken near the time of King

James's coronation, that had the deepest influence on his career.

'When Sir Thomas Overbury was a little past twenty years old,'—it is thus that his father, Sir Nicholas, told the tale many years afterwards,—' he and John Guilby, his father's chief clerk, were sent (upon a voyage of pleasure) to Edinburgh, with £60 between them. There Thomas met with Sir William Cornwallis, one who knew him in Queen's College at Oxford. Sir William commended him to divers, and among the rest to Robin Carr, then page to the Earl of Dunbar : so they two came along to England together, and were great friends.'[1] It is easy to imagine the spirit of raillery with which Overbury described the rough life and uncleanliness of the Scottish capital : these were the commonplaces of English travellers, and assuredly the young Templar found them a whetstone for his merry wit. But wit and raillery are as nothing if we set them by the side of the meeting with Robin Carr, whose rise to wealth and glory Overbury shared, and whose ruin followed the disgrace and murder of his friend with tragical swiftness.

[1] In a manuscript in the British Museum is a set of notes to which the following memorandum is affixed : 'that I, Nicholas Oldisworth, who wrote this book, . . . did deliberately read it over, on Thursday the IXth of Oct. 1637, in the hearing of my old grandfather, Sir Nicholas Overbury, &c., who affirmed the truth of its contents.' It is from these notes that I have cited the testimony of Sir Nicholas Overbury.

'So they two came along to England together,' and it was not long before they found at Court a theatre worthy their design. Nor could any twain be better fitted to play there a foremost part. The talent of the one marvellously supplemented the enterprise of the other. Carr was endowed with the very genius of success. He was born for prosperity and advancement. He had been bred in France, and had there learned those tricks of manner and address which win the favour of kings and ministers. None possessed in larger measure than he the tact of presentation. His handsome face and stately figure were embellished by the natural grace of his movements. He understood the niceties of ruffs and frills. He showed an equal taste in the cut of his doublet and in the colour of his hose. In brief, he was master of all those qualities which should easily endear him to the wisest fool in Christendom. His deficiencies, cunningly disguised, were as conspicuous as his gifts. He had as little talent for affairs as for scholarship. In any other Court, save that of James, he would have remained a mere gentleman of the household, and done his best to still the voices of ambition and avarice.

So ill-educated was he, that at his first promotion the king himself taught him Latin, thus flattering his own vanity and ensuring the rapid triumph of his pupil. His insensitive ear was never attuned to the English speech, and he spoke broad Scots unto the end of his life. But his vivid temperament lifted him high above his faults. He stood in need of one thing only—a brain, and that was supplied him by Thomas Overbury. Already the fame of the young Templar had spread beyond the Inns of Court. The friend of poets, he could boast of his acquaintance to the young lawyers about him. Early was he sealed of the tribe of Ben, and though he presently fell out with that magnanimous tyrant of letters, time was he lived with him on terms of easy familiarity. 'Ben Jonson, the poet,' wrote Manningham in his Diary in 1602, 'now lives upon one Townsend, and scornes the world. So Overbury,'—a simple statement, which proves that the Templar spoke with authority, even then, of his mighty friend.

But it was not merely Overbury's culture that stood Carr in good stead. Overbury's sense of affairs and aptitude for politics were yet more valuable to the favourite of the king. Well skilled in the expedition of business, he was able to shield the idle Carr from failure and detection. It was not for him to play the sycophant ; his pride stood in the way of that adventure ; it amused him vastly to aid and abet the sycophancy of his ally. Pride, indeed, was Overbury's dominant quality. Friends and foes alike bear witness to his haughty temper, which forbade him to stoop even to a king, and which persuaded him, while he undervalued others, to overvalue himself. Bacon, in throwing discredit upon him, says that he was 'of an insolent and thrasonical disposition,' and Aubrey's gossip goes beyond the censure of the King's Attorney. 'Old Sir Robert Harley of Brampton-Brian,' he wrote, 'would say 'twas a great question who was the proudest, Sir Walter Raleigh or Sir Thomas Overbury, but the difference that was was judged on Sir Thomas's side,' and the mere coupling of the two names is the highest possible tribute to Overbury's arrogance.

And Overbury was at no pains to conceal his sense of superiority. He had learned from Ben Jonson, together with a fine taste in poetry, the fatal lesson that it was better to lose a friend than a jest, and not a few men and women at Court were scarred by his mordant tongue. Moreover, there went with his insolence that cynicism that is bred of contempt. He put but a light value upon human morals and human intelligence. A set of maxims, ascribed to him, and published after his death, sufficiently explain the philosophy of his life. Every man, he held, is weak in his own humours, and a little beyond himself is a fool. The loves of men were for him their afflictions. Titles of honour, he thought, were no better than rattles to still ambition ; and he put down man, woman, and the devil, as the three degrees of comparison. It is not strange, therefore, that, looking down from this altitude of scorn, he made for himself an eager band of enemies, and that when he tumbled from his high estate few friends were found to break his fall.

The alliance knit between Carr and Overbury seemed at the outset irresistible, and the society in which they lived eagerly ministered to their ambitions. A sudden change had overtaken the English capital. With the death of Elizabeth had died the spirit of austerity and empire which had placed upon her reign the laurel wreath of renown. London was packed with an eager crowd of adventurers, resolved to succeed by the easy paths of flattery and chicane. Money was the universal quest, and those who sought it cared little what means they used. When the name of 'beggarly Scots' was thrown at the favourites of James I., 'Content yourselves,' he cried, 'I will soon make the English as beggarly as you, and so end that controversy.' A vulgar magnificence, a squalid recklessness, seemed the proper end and aim of life. The chain of tradition was snapped in twain, and whatever was new seemed praiseworthy for no better reason than that it was new. The upstarts about the Court flung away their easily gathered gains with a careless hand; they shod their horses with silver; they hung precious jewels about their necks, thinking to please their monarch by an ill-bred extravagance of attire. Those who missed their mark, and incurring vast expense found not where-withal to discharge their debts, formed themselves into sects of Roaring Boys, Bonaventers, and

Bravados, who were no better than highwaymen, and who plundered the peaceful citizens with so shameful an effrontery and with so small a chance of punishment, that after nine at night scarce any durst walk the streets. Gulls and gallants brawled in taverns, dicing-houses, and ordinaries, and, as an eye-witness said, there were 'as many ways to spend money as the windings and turnings in towns and streets.' It was, moreover, the first and general article of faith that all difficulties might be resolved by witchcraft. Sorcerers were ready at a word to cast spells or fling figures, and it is characteristic of the time that when Sir Edward Coke examined in court the papers of Simon Forman, he found his wife's name at the head of the necromancer's list. Yet, ' like a fool that laughs when he is putting on her fetters,' London was merry in the height of her misfortunes, and of this sinister merriment none had a greater share than Overbury.

The gaiety of his temper was a pleasant contrast to Carr's more sombre ambition. He turned to scorn the serious things of statecraft, and he fitted the gravest of the Ministers with nicknames of contempt. Once upon a time, at Greenwich, his humour led him into disgrace. He and Carr were walking in the garden, and the queen, espying them, said, 'There goes Carr and his governor.' Presently Overbury laughed, and the queen, thinking that he laughed at her, had him committed to jail. For whistling in the presence of Marie Antoinette, a hapless Frenchman passed forty years cloistered in a *maison de santé*. Overbury was more fortunate. He swore that he did but laugh at a jest of the king's, and was instantly set at liberty. The queen, forced to forgive, did not forget, and presently made the affront, in which she still believed, one excuse for his ruin. But for Overbury life, death, and the State were food for laughter, and he laughed though the shadow of the Tower hung over him. And, if we may believe the voice of adulation, he taught the king and his favourites to think as well as to laugh. He carried to the Court the appreciation of poetry and the trick of criticism, which he had picked up from Ben Jonson and his compeers in the taverns of Fleet Street. Before he became his mortal enemy, Jonson dedicated some lines to Overbury, in which praise outran even the behests of friendship. 'I think,' he wrote—

> 'I think, the fate of court thy coming crav'd,
>   That the wit there and manners might be sav'd:
>   For since what ignorance, what pride is fled!
>   And letters, and humanity in the stead!'

But whatever the Court craved, Overbury's real purpose in coming thither was to be in earnest, what the queen called him in jest, Carr's governor. He wrote the letters for which the young Scot got credit; he despatched the business which the courtier whose fortunes he followed was powerless to despatch. And Carr's fortune was indeed worth following. From the day when, in the king's presence, he rode in the tiltyard with Lord Dingwall and fell under his horse, his progress was ominously rapid. James's solicitude drew all men to the minion's side. All the great ones of the nation flocked to see him. Henceforth to win his favour was the first step on the road of ambition, and as in those days nothing was achieved that was not paid for, few men obtained any office in Court or Parliament without paying toll to Carr. And from the very outset Overbury played Phintias to Carr's Damon. He shared his influence and emoluments, as was but just, since, united, the two men were all-powerful, divided they would have been naught. His father was made a judge at the son's demand, and there were those who did not disdain to pay obeisance to the father that they might win the favour of the son. Sir Nicholas, indeed, did himself confess 'that Sir Fran. Bacon used heretofore to stoop and crouch to Sir Tho. Overbury, in hope of Carr's favour to be Master of the Court of Wards : for which place he offered much ; and Sir Thomas his father might once have had £1000 if he would have spoken effectually to his son. But Sir Thomas knew Bacon to be corrupt.'

What a dark picture is here painted of bribery and intrigue ! Bacon stooped and crouched, though not for long, and then took a bitter revenge upon Overbury, whose favour he had asked in vain. Sir Thomas knew him to be corrupt, and doubtless Bacon well remembered the rejection of his suit when, as King's Attorney, he prosecuted Sir Thomas's murderer. 'Overbury,' said he, 'was naught and corrupt; the ballads must be mended for that point.' Thus by chance the two men imputed to one another the same vice, and both were in the right of it. For a while, however, the adventurers, Carr and Overbury, suffered no check, and looked upon the great affairs of which they had the conduct as a profitable joke. 'They made a play of all the world besides themselves,' said an enemy, 'so as they had cyphers and jargons for the king and queen and the great men of the realm.' From Carr no matter of State was concealed by his doting master, and Carr hastened to reveal all the mysteries of the council chamber to his eager friend. Is it strange, then, that their arrogance increased, that they believed themselves the sole repositories of the king's power and the king's favour? Of the two Overbury's position seemed the stronger. He enjoyed influence without responsibility, and firm in the conviction of his intellectual superiority, he thought he had Carr's head under his girdle, since Carr had never scrupled to betray to him the secrets of State, or, as he called them in his pleasant jargon, 'the secrets of nature.'

The king rewarded them for the services he supposed they had rendered him after his kind. Carr was first knighted, then made Viscount Rochester, was presently appointed private secretary to his majesty, and received the Garter. Overbury was granted the honour of knighthood in 1608, a year later than his friend, and obtained the office of Sewer to the King.   His father, with the pride of memory and old age, treasured up a story of this office whose pointlessness is its point.   'When Sir Thomas was made Sewer to the King,' said he, 'his Majesty walking in the privy garden, showed him to the Queen, saying, Look you, this is my new Sewer ; and Queen Anne answered, 'Tis a pretty young fellow.'   The pretty young fellow had died in misery and disgrace five and twenty years before the trivial tale was told, and the father could still look back proudly and without anger at his son's superb career. If he lacked Sir Thomas's humour, he had a fair share of his haughty spirit.   He could even take pleasure in the reflected glory which shone about his own head.   'Himself,' said he, 'being of the Middle Temple, was often pointed at by way of honour in the streets : There goes Sir Tho. Overbury's father.'

The lofty humbleness of this confession not merely proves the amiable temper of Sir Nicholas, but shows to what a pinnacle of power and notoriety Sir Thomas had attained.   From this pinnacle he was thrust with a suddenness which, if it appalled, should not, as it did, have surprised him.   His shrewd intelligence might long before have recognised the truth that he who rises by fortune, falls by fortune. He had gratified a vaulting ambition not by the exercise of his own conspicuous talent, but by taking advantage of the shifts and chances which perplex the life of a courtier. Nevertheless, he did not expect ruin, least of all from that quarter of the sky whence it was hurled upon him like a thunderbolt. At any rate, he believed the friendship of Rochester secure, and overlooked in that security the vengeful cunning of such a woman as rarely disturbs the course of history.

In 1606, Frances Howard, a Messalina in temper, if not in enterprise, was married to the Earl of Essex with all the pomp and splendour that belonged to the time. James smiled approval on the union. Ben Jonson, with the aid of Inigo Jones, devised the finest masque that ever had been seen at Court. Though the bride was thirteen, the bridegroom but a year older, the marriage seemed to be made under the happiest auspices and with the best hopes of felicity. The children parted, and some five years later returned to Court, still children, as we should account them to-day. But no sooner had Lady Essex beheld her husband again than she refused to live with him. He neither flattered her eye nor ministered to her ambition. Determined to rid herself of an encumbrance at all costs, she followed the habit of her age and consulted the sorcerers. And first of all she asks counsel of Mistress Turner, 'sweet Turner' she calls her, a monster of profligacy, from whom the art of science and poisoning held no secrets. The widow of a disreputable doctor, she had been bred to a knowledge of drugs and magic, and she was ready for any enterprise which would bring her fame and profit. By a strange perversity she was of a haunting beauty. 'It seemed that she had been some gentle dame,' says the poet of 'Overbury's Vision,' who praises most eloquently her crystal eye, her ivory brow, her globe-like head, her hair like threads of gold; indeed it is clear that, with all her crimes, she had not forgotten the practical value of coquetry and display. She it was who first set the fashion of stiffening with yellow starch the frills and ruffs then worn, a fashion presently killed by the scandal of her life and death.

Such was the woman into whose hands Lady Essex wilfully confided her destiny, and Mistress Turner did not fall below the occasion. Calling in the aid of Simon Forman, whom Antony à Wood calls 'a very able astrologer and physician,' and whom others knew by worse names, she set herself by the black arts of sorcery to do the bidding of Lady Essex. And first by her enchantments she must alienate Essex from his wife and so bewitch him out of his manhood. To this end she bade Forman make many pictures of wax, crosses, and other uncouth things, and at last the couple seemed to achieve their purpose by sticking a thorn from a tree that bore no leaves into a waxen image. Meanwhile Lady Essex had fallen in love with Rochester, at the encouragement of her kinsman, Lord Northampton, the most sinister figure in a sinister age, and either by the magic of Mistress Turner or by her own charm had inspired him with a passion as violent as her own.

To Northampton, an ancient courtier, who thought no villany incompatible with his rank, and whose hands had long been stained with Spanish gold, the intrigue promised nothing but advantage. Its success would bind Rochester to him with the bonds of gratitude, and at the same time might remove from his path the dangerous rival that Overbury was fast becoming. Therefore he set no hindrance in the path of the lovers, and so well did his plot prosper that nothing but an annulment of the former marriage and a legal union would please either Rochester or the Lady Essex. Overbury behaved himself with the honesty and indiscretion which he had never been at the pains to check. So long as the intrigue remained an intrigue, he uttered no protest. When he saw his friend drifting to the hapless marriage which a divorce would make possible, he did what he could with speech and pen to save him from the pit. With all his eloquence he urged him not to cast away his honour and glory on a woman ; he told him roundly that he might expect no better requital at her hands than she had shown her husband ; and when Rochester answered him harshly, he gave him back angry word for angry word, demanding at last what portion of money was due to him, and declaring that he would no longer endure his quarrels and insults.

He did more than this. With a simplicity of

mind admirable and unexpected, he attempted to turn
Rochester aside from his purpose by writing the
poem—'A Wife'—which with his 'Characters' is
his best title to literary fame. His father's evidence
is clear enough on the point. 'Sir Thomas,' says he,
'wrote his poem called "A Wife" to induce
Viscount Rochester to make a better choice than
of the divorced Countess.' So little it seems to
achieve so much! It is like attempting to stem a
torrent with a withered leaf. Nevertheless, the
poem, published after Overbury's death, with many
sets of commendatory verses, the best of them from
the hand of John Ford, in which poets and
Templars conspired to do him honour, is packed
with good, sound commonplace. The poet asks of
a perfect wife neither birth nor beauty. As to
portion, 'nor will I shun,' says he, 'nor my aim it
make.' Indeed, 'rather than these the object of my
love,' he writes,

> 'Let it be good ; when these with virtues go,
> They (in themselves indifferent) virtues prove,
> For good, like fire, turns all things to be so.
> God's image in her soul, O let me place
> My love upon ! not Adam's in her face.'

It is, in truth a prudent rather than a lofty view
of matrimony that Overbury expounds. Though
he gives the best advice he can to his friend, he is
no idealist. He asks understanding, not knowledge,
of a woman. 'Domestic charge,' he is sure, 'doth

best befit that sex,' and he would grant it neither
leisure nor books.   Learning he deplores :

'Learning and pregnant wit in womankind
What it finds malleable makes frail,
And doth not add more ballast, but more sail.'

Above all, of woman's frailty he holds a harsh
opinion.   She is to blame, he thinks, who has been
tried without consent.   'He comes too near,' he
says in the best-known line, 'who comes to be
denied.'   For the rest the poem may boast a kind of
epigrammatic elegance.   It suggests Donne at a
discreet distance and in an interval of studied plainness.   It presents the complete antithesis of the
society in which its author lived, and if it be sincere
it throws a strange cross-light upon a wayward
character.   That Overbury thought well enough of
it to wish it brought before the woman he loved, we
are assured by Ben Jonson.   'The Countess of
Rutland was nothing inferior to her father, Sir P.
Sidney, in poesie,' Jonson told Hawthornden.
'Sir Thomas Overbury was in love with her, and
caused Ben to read his "Wife" to her, which he with
an excellent grace did, and praised the author.   The
morn thereafter he discorded with Overbury, who
would have him intend a suit that was unlawful.   The
lines the lady kept in remembrance : "He comes too
near who comes to be denied."'

'Tis a strange story this of Overbury's love for
the Countess of Rutland and of his sending so un-

couth a ruffler as Ben Jonson on an embassy of adoration. But in the dark tragedy of Overbury's life it is a mere interlude. If the poem were read to Sir Philip Sidney's daughter, who was well able to appreciate its beauties, it was read also to the Moabitish woman who was filling the Court with evil thoughts and the promise of evil deeds. Lady Essex took fire at the simple verses, which she thought designed to rob her of Rochester's affection. As before she had been intent to bewitch Essex, so she was now resolved upon the ruin and murder of Overbury. Not only had he written a persuasive poem—he had done far worse than that ; he had taxed her with a name of plain Saxon sound, which is not acceptable to polite ears. Up and down she denounced him, calling him 'that negro, that scum of men, that devil incarnate.' Her first plan was to hire a ruffian to kill him outright, or with the mere pretence of a duel ; and the ruffian she elected to do her bidding was Sir David Wood, whom Sir Nicholas Overbury calls 'a boisterous and atheistical soldier.'

The plot was made, the amount of blood-money agreed upon, and then the wayward Countess changed her mind. Her enemy should be removed by a more subtle contrivance, and again she sought the aid of her familiar friend, Mistress Turner. For this queen of poisoners to think was to act. The means and the instrument were speedily devised. There was one Weston, a rope-ripe

scoundrel who shrank from no crime, and was bold
to encounter the last danger. Once a servant of
Dr. Turner, he also well understood the practices,
and was eager to obey the behests, of the sorceress.
His outward look betrayed the cold cruelty of his
temper. A meagre fellow, with a bloodless face
pallid as death and a grisled beard, he was cast by
nature for the part he was called to play. His price
was more modest than his intent, and he promised
that he would put Sir Thomas out of the way for a
poor £200. There remained only to appoint to the
Tower a governor pliant and sympathetic, and to find
a good excuse for sending the victim thither a close
prisoner. The plan was less hazardous than it
appears to-day. Few obstacles lay in the path of
Rochester and Northampton. Their baleful influence was enough to drive Sir Thomas Waad, an
honourable gentleman, from his office, and to
replace him in the governorship of the Tower by
Sir Gervase Helwes, a grave and trusted friend of
the conspirators.

The arrest of Sir Thomas was a masterpiece of
calculated treachery, in which the king himself
most certainly had a hand. With all the pomp and
circumstance of honour, an embassy was proposed
to Overbury. He could go, as a free choice led
him, either to France, where the Ambassador was
soon to be changed, or to the Archduke's Court,
where the office was even now vacant. The
proposal might well have flattered an older and

more distinguished man than he. But life at Court had thrown its spell upon him, and made him loth to leave his friends, or to lose in foreign exile the chance of a higher preferment at home. Even in this matter a solace was given to his ambition. If he would accept the mission, he was promised the Treasurership of the Chamber on the death of my Lord Stanhope. Still he hesitated, and at last took the fatal step of consulting Rochester. The favourite outwardly amiable, yet now resolved upon the ruin of Overbury, gave him the advice of a false friend. Reject the offer, said he in effect, and stay at home. Overbury, blinded by pride, did as Rochester bade him. He refused to go abroad, and his answer was interpreted by the Council as 'pregnant of contempt.'

In excuse for Overbury it may be said that he was ignorant of the conspiracy which had been made against him. The plot had been framed with so profound a secrecy that even Sir Henry Wotton, an accomplished man of affairs, knew not 'whether this were done without the participation of my Lord of Rochester,' and the bird is always the last to see the fowler's net spread before him. By this time too, as I have said, Overbury was friendless and alone. King and Court were alike weary of him and his bitter tongue. The parasites of the favourite had long been irked by the too stiff carriage of his fortune. James himself was determined to be rid of this turbulent counsellor, not merely for his own sake but for the sake of Rochester. He had not forgotten 'the scandalous offence of the Queen at Greenwich, which was never but a palliated case,' and it was commonly rumoured that Sir Thomas Overbury had vented some stinging sarcasms upon the Court, which came to the king's hearing. So great an evil is a sharp and thoughtless wit. The many jests, which, when Sir Thomas spoke them, had raised a laugh, were now remembered to the discredit of the falling star. Northampton, too, had his reasons, and very cogent ones, for wishing the ruin of Overbury. Old in years, he was yet young in hope; nor could he easily forgive the slur that had been thrown upon Lady Essex, his kinswoman and a Howard.

As for Lady Essex, her acrimony needs no explanation. How could she do other than hate the man who had scorned her pretensions and cast a slur upon her honour? And Rochester, now confident that he could stand alone, made no scruple of kicking down the man upon whose intelligence he had climbed to power. Resentment, rather than gratitude, is the common reward of unrequited service, and Overbury did but pay the debt exacted of those who in making the career of others foolishly believe themselves indispensable. There was another reason, also, why Rochester had turned him from love to hatred. Overbury was the repository of all his secrets. No intrigue, no dispu-table bargain had been hidden from the favourite's

Governor. One or other of them, then, must die, and Rochester was resolved that his should not be the blood that was spilt.

Thus the trap was set; thus the victim was snared. Overbury disdained the ambassage, and his disdain, as one of the craft said, was thought 'an eternal disgrace to their occupation.' The king, in ignorance of the baleful part played by Rochester, ordered Overbury's arrest, and on 21st April 1613 he was 'from the council chamber conveyed by a clerk of the council and two of the guard to the Tower, and there by warrant consigned to the lieutenant as a close prisoner.' Sir Henry Wotton, who has left us an account of this memorable episode, describes it as 'both by the suddenness like a stroke of thunder, and more by the quality and relation of the persons, breathing in the beholders (whereof by chance I was one) very much amazement.' And upon none did the thunderclap come more suddenly than upon Overbury himself. He stood in the second degree of power at Court; only Rochester was above him; and two hours before the catastrophe he had described himself as 'never better than at the present of his own fortunes and ends.'

And when he was gone, one wonder possessed all the world. Had Rochester a hand in it? That was the question murmured on every side. If the arrest were made without Rochester's knowledge, said the gossips, then we must expect of himself

either a decadence or a ruin.   If he were participant
in the affair, then was the future dark indeed.
To Sir Henry Wotton's optimism a few days seemed
sufficient to clear the doubts away.   Two weary
years were to pass before any light was cast upon
the sinister drama of poison and death.   In the
meantime, said Wotton, 'I dare pronounce of Sir
Thomas Overbury, that he shall return no more to
this stage.'   Here the ambassador was in the right
of it.   Sir Thomas Overbury returned to this stage
no more.   The Court was governed by no new
philosophy, and the old principles would not bear
his restoration.   Thus the gates of the Tower were
shut upon the hapless prisoner, for whom nothing
was left, as we shall see, but desertion, torture, and
a creeping death.

SIR THOMAS OVERBURY—II

IMPRISONMENT AND DEATH

NO sooner was Sir Thomas Overbury safely
locked up in the Tower, no sooner was the
inflexible Sir Thomas Waad replaced by the greedy,
complaisant Sir Gervase Helwes, than the hapless
man's enemies began to devise their dark and dismal
plot for his destruction. Once more Mrs. Turner,
'the lay-mistress of the poisons,' was summoned to
weave her spells. Though Forman, her ancient ally
and gossip, was dead, she found in Thomas Franklin
of Tower Hill an instrument yet readier to her hand.
Now, Franklin was monstrous alike in fame and face.
He looked ill-favouredly as though he could raise
a devil. Withal he was not without a certain vanity.
He took a pride in his ruddy beard, and he grew
a wanton curl, which fell upon his back, and which
he called his 'elf-lock.' It was the only elfish thing
about him. For the rest he was a ruthless sorcerer,
so well skilled in the compounding of powders, that
he could hasten or protract the death of his victim
as he would. To a contemporary he 'appeared to
have been a professed atheist, drenched with disease
both bones and marrow, and to have poisoned his
own wife.' And this was 'the groom who had

access to the Countess's bed-chamber at all hours, though she was in bed.'

Such were the plotters. The plot was worthy of them. Mrs. Turner and Franklin procured the drugs, Weston, the suborned jailer, administered them, and the Countess eagerly paid the bill. Many were the poisons they employed, at first without effect—roscetre, arsenic, and mercury sublimate. These failing, the Countess bade Franklin purchase some powder of diamonds, and gave him four angels to that end, which, said he, to him proved to be four devils. Sometimes the poison was concealed in tarts, sometimes in jellies, sent to the captive by sympathetic friends without. As the days passed, the conspirators grew in courage and recklessness. ' I was bid to tell you,' wrote Lady Essex to Helwes, ' that in the tarts and jellies there are *letters*, but in the wine none. And of that you may take yourself, and give your wife and children ; but of the other not. Give him these tarts and jelly this night, and all shall be well.' It seems that *letters* signified poison, and so thin was the word of disguise that it was scarcely worth using.

To Lady Essex, Lord Northampton, and other sharers in the plot, Overbury was known as 'the scab,' and openly discussed. ' This scab,' said Sir Gervase, ' is like the fox, who the more he is cursed the better he fareth' ; and so well did Sir Thomas fare that for awhile his strength baffled all the evil designs of his enemies. Either he was proof against poison, or the *aurum potabile* which he took as an antidote saved him from death. At any rate, he lingered on alive in his prison, until Weston was roundly told that he would get no more pay until Overbury was dead. 'I have already given him as many poisons,' he retorted, 'as would poison twelve men.'

While the wizard and sorceress were doing their utmost to compass his ruin, Overbury was not idle in the Tower. There he sate in his chamber and wrote letters to his family, and to those whom he vainly thought were his friends. Silence would have profited him better, and he was not without warning. 'As you love me, burn this,' wrote his brother-in-law Lydcote, 'and forbear writing all you can, for it never was so dangerous.' Alas! he could not forbear. Condemned to inaction, stripped of companions, he found his only solace in writing, and his indiscretion will appear the less if we remember that he knew not what was being contrived against him, nor that his former friends were most eagerly bent upon his death. A bundle of his letters, still preserved, marks the sad progress of his tragedy. There is not a line of them all that is not written in agony and distress. As you read them you seem to be looking over the dying man's shoulder, as his shaking hand pens the bitter words. 'Good my Lord,' he says in one place, 'excuse my blotting by reason of my weakness at this time.' It is the last expression of pathos, and hard, indeed, must have been the hearts of those who read, and who, having read, left a gallant gentleman to die, whose worse faults were pride and indiscretion.

At the outset he enjoins cunning and secrecy upon his friends, and shows something of his ancient spirit in devising nicknames for those whose aid he entreats. 'Look well to your seals and mine,' he writes, 'and mark them well. My letter yesterday was sealed with soft wax ill-favouredly three seals ; this is sealed with hard wax and my little seal. Never write but upon some hope coming, then darkly and shortly. Call Rochester hereafter Similis, because he is like Henry VIII. ; call the King Julius. Remember these two changes. Call Pembroke Niger.' With the eloquence of despair he implores that he may be sent into the country to save his life, ' for,' he tells Rochester, ' 'tis not the close air but the apprehension of the place that hurts me.' Again and again he lifts up his voice to the same purport. ' If you leave me here,' he writes to Rochester, ' I shall never see you more, and that I fear my enemies understand well enough, and hope so to come by my office, but do not you be accessory to my death, though you could not conceive my body should have over-lived thus much.'

Then he promises that if ever he be restored he will never engage in faction again, and still believing Rochester his ally, prays him to use his influence with the king. ' Thursday is a month close prisoner !' he exclaims. ' Since the reason he keeps

me close so long is to try all ways upon you alone,
whether he can' work your consent to a separation,
for after the doors are open, then he thinks we will
mingle thoughts again. . . . Therefore lose no hour
to declare your resolution that God forsake you if
ever you forsake me for any hope or fear. . . . For
me I shall be reformed according to his instructions,
never to transgress, which he cannot but accept.'
And if all this fail, he adjures Rochester, feigning
illness, not to recover till he be out, and to be so
dangerously sick that he much desires to speak with
him before he dies, or to fall in talk about him at
Windsor, that the king may know his suffering
and his loyalty. Weston, the cynical jailer, well
knew the vanity of his purpose. 'They say Sir
Thomas Overbury hath wit,' this he confided to
a friend, 'but I think he is not so wise as the world
takes him to be, for he sues only to my Lord of
Rochester to get him his liberty, and I know that
Lord does but mock him, and means never to effect
it for him.' Scrupulously he hid the truth from his
victim, and every line that Overbury writes proves
his complete ignorance of what was done outside the
walls of the Tower. He was punished, he thought,
for the jealousy of the king, who brooked not, it
should be said, that he ruled Rochester and
Rochester the king, or for the malice of those
who were angry that he should have made a stranger
so great an actor in the State.

Thus, emboldened by his faith in a dead friendship,

he demands not merely enlargement but a warranty that he shall not go abroad. If the king would have him go overseas for two or three months, the answer to that is, 'that nothing helps the spleen so much as our native air, and foreign, though better, hurts it.' He gravely cites the case of Mr. Burges, the famous preacher, who 'having the spleen though otherwise of a strong body, was fain to leave his charge at The Hague, only to come to London, his native air, for the ease of his sickness,' and he declares that he himself 'whiles he was abroad was never well one hour, as Mayerne knew, which made him return so soon.' This, then, is the constant burden of his prayer : obtain the king's forgiveness, let him know ' the intent of my letter both before and now, which was to desire his pardon, that my heart was far from offending him.' And to all his plaints and prayers he receives no answer but deceits, no hope but promises made to be broken.

And then the agony of increasing sickness drives him to despair. 'This morning,' he writes, 'notwithstanding my fasting all day yesterday I find a great heat continue in all my body and the same desire of drink and loathing of meat.' He is consumed with heat ; he can endure no clothes on him ; his thirst is unquenchable. 'This distemper,' he writes, ' contrary to my constitution, makes me fear some fever at the last, and such disease, meeting with so weak a body, will quickly I doubt end it, and in truth I never liked myself worse.' He feels that his end approaches, and demands that he may have leave to go to his own chamber after nine o'clock this very night, in the Lieutenant's carriage, unknown and unseen. Then by neglect the first of many threats is wrung from him : 'This is my last request to you, which if you will deny me you will tempt me far.' Still not a word of help ; still either contemptuous silence or a subtle treachery. One more attempt he makes to move Rochester's pity and to invoke their ancient friendship. 'My fever grows so upon me anew,' he exclaims, 'that by God if you leave me here a week longer, I think I shall never see you more, for the fever will never leave me while I am here.' Full well did Rochester know that he would never see him again. He was deaf to threat and entreaty alike. Why should he fear the enmity of one whose words he confidently believed would never reach the eye or ear of king or friend ?

So Overbury grew daily worse and worse. His hand is weak, and he writes in much pain. There is not a letter, to friend or foe, which does not prove his agony and distress. Then a few broken words come as a cry from the heart : 'I was let blood Wednesday ten o'clock, to the Friday morning my heat slackens not ; my thirstiness the same, the same loathing of meat, having eat not a bit since Thursday was sennight to this hour, the same seworring and vomiting, for yesternight about eight o'clock after Mr. Mayerne was gone I fainted and vomited : the very same dryness . . .' Then it ceases suddenly, as though the poor wretch's strength failed it, and the words, which might have melted a stone, did but increase the vengeance of Rochester and the cunning treachery of Northampton.

The fever which destroyed his body broke his pride, and in this tragedy of blood and tears there is no episode so grimly tragical as the proud man's surrender of his arrogance. He who had stooped to no man now fell upon his knees in abject supplication to Lord Suffolk, who had promised his mediation with the king. 'If it would please your Lordship,' he writes, 'to add again your Lordship's hand, to perfect this work so successfully begun,'—there is a great irony in these words—'and to be a means first for my present liberty and after for the recovery of his Majesty's favour, I protest before the living God I will ever hereafter be as faithful to you as your Lordship's own heart, and when I digress from this protestation let this letter be a testimony to convince me of dishonesty to all the world.'

He is still but weak, he says, 'which will make the benefit for his liberty more precious'; yet the very thought of Suffolk's intercession cheers his mind. For a while his letters assume a tone of sanguine humility which is doubly sad—sad because it implies a wavering spirit, sad also because it was unrequited. In his buoyancy he promises Suffolk the friendship of Rochester, which he declares he will continue firm and inviolable. With all the eagerness of reviving hope he implores Suffolk to

hasten the hour of his freedom for his health's sake.
He complains that the piercing air and solitariness
of the Tower will not suffer his strength to grow,
and he looks forward with impatience to the moment
when he shall speak with his lordship in any private
place he may appoint.   He concludes his letter with
such words as he could have written to none before
his captivity.   'This request I was bold,' he says,
'to impart to your Lordship, knowing that your
noble nature would have some care of a weak man
added to that of a prisoner.   So with all taking leave
I rest yours faithfully to death.'   His fidelity was
not long tried.   Even as he wrote the words the
hand of death was upon him.

There was one further step in humility which he
was destined to take.   It still remained for him to
ask the pardon of Lady Essex, the woman who was
sending him by the path of torture to the grave, and
he asked it in a letter addressed to her kinsman and
accomplice, Lord Northampton.   Truly his adversaries were determined that he should taste the
bitterness of shame as well as of death.   'Right
Honourable and my very good Lord,' thus runs the
letter, 'I received an advertisement yesterday from
your Lordship by Mr. Lieutenant that my Lady of
Essex had been informed of some speeches of mine
wherein I should wrong her in her honour.   'Tis
true, my very good Lord, that I have heard from
many, yea from my Lord Rochester himself, with
what bitterness her Ladyship would often speak of

me, and out of the sense of that 'tis possible I may
have spoken with less respect of her than was fit,
but that ever I touched her in point of her honour,
far be it from me. For I protest 'twas never in my
words nor in my belief, and this I will profess to all
the world. And if either my Lady of Suffolk or the
Lady herself shall rest unsatisfied, I will be ready to
tender as much to their Ladyships and to say the
same which now I write to your Lordship; and for
my Lady of Essex, if I might be only freed from her
ill-will for time to come, there shall be no man
readier to respect and honour her than myself.' In
this passage there is a true and bitter irony. Overbury prays to be delivered from the ill-will which in
the very moment of his prayer was compassing his
death, and promises to honour and respect the implacable woman whose hatred neither pity nor
suffering could appease.

Once and once only did his ancient courage revive,
his ancient insolence break out again. Stung by
the desertion of Rochester, enraged by the complaint
that he had addressed him in an irreverent style, he
let loose the flood of his fury and overwhelmed the
false friend with a torrent of vituperation, which
even to-day it is good to contemplate. In words of
pitiless logic he reminded Rochester that it was to
him he owed his fortune, his understanding, and his
reputation. He tells him that he has no more
human affection or compassion than the colt in
Enfield Chase, and he promises him that he will bring

him to a public trial before all the friends he has.
He pictures him visiting Lady Essex, frizzling his
hair, solicitous about his clothes, while he himself is
lying miserably upon the rack.   He shows the ruin
that has been brought upon him and upon his family
—his father and mother languishing, his brother
Lydcote overthrown ; and then describes the author
of it all, who should perish rather than see him perish,
as losing not a jot of anything that concerns him.
Fiercely he insists that he can no longer conceal the
bitterness of his spirit ; and boasts, as he is not free
to speak his last words to his friends, that he has
spent his leisure in writing the story betwixt
Rochester and himself from the first hour unto this
day—how he found him, how many hazards he ran
for him, what secrets passed between them, and how
when Rochester had won that woman by the letters
which he wrote, he caught him mercilessly in a
trap.

'So then,' he says in the last words that ever he
penned, 'if you will deal thus wickedly with me, I
have provided that, whether I die or live, your name
shall never die, nor you leave to be the most odious
man alive.' [1]   That which Overbury prophesied has
come to pass, though not by the road the hapless
victim intended.   The story, as he wrote it, is lost,
but the hand of justice has stripped the disguise of
friendship from the dishonoured Rochester, and sent

[1] This letter is printed in full in Winwood's ' Memorials,' vol.
iii. p. 478.

him down the ages in the dark colours of shame and treachery.

When Overbury wrote this last letter, he must have known full well that his end was approaching. His weakness increased upon him. He passed his tedious and sorrowful hours with many discontents, suffering and alone. For the last fortnight of his life, says his cousin Rawlins, he was not to be seen as usual at his window. Yet his ardent spirit was not easily extinguished, and the governor records that, receiving a hopeful message from Suffolk, 'he could not contain himself for joy.' This was written eight days before his death, and the very obstinacy with which he clung to life did but fill his enemies with the greater fury. It was even feared that the king might be persuaded to a premature clemency, and, lest so untoward an accident should interrupt the course of vengeance, on 14th September 1613 Overbury received his *coup de grâce*. A poisoned clyster, administered by an apothecary's boy, drove the last breath from the worn-out body, and Lady Essex's purpose was achieved.

Sir Gervase Helwes sent the first news of the welcome event to Lord Northampton, as in duty bound, and his lordship's replies are an eloquent proof that, as Bacon said, he was deep in the business. In one letter, meant for publication, he assures Sir Gervase that Rochester, desiring to do the last honour to his deceased friend, would have the body of Sir Thomas Overbury delivered to any friend of

his that claims it, and declares that Rochester pro-
claims the constancy of his affection for the dead,
and the intention which he harboured at this time of
procuring his liberty when the king was at Tibbald's.
So much was written for the public eye.   In Sir
Gervase's private ear he had another tale to tell.
'Worthy Mr. Lieutenant,' said he, 'let me intreat
you to call Lydcote and three or four of his friends,
if so many come, to view the body. . . . If they have
viewed, then bury it by-and-by ; for it is time, con-
sidering the humours of that damn'd crew, that only
desire to move pity and raise scandals.   Let no man's
influence move you to make stay in any case, and
bring me these letters when I next see you.   Fail
not a jot herein, as you love your friends.'   Here is
no shadow of uncertainty.   The Lieutenant did as
he was bid ; the poor wretch's body was buried with
haste in the chapel of the Tower, and then for many
months was silence.

The death of Overbury was well timed by the
conspirators.   Ten days after he had been hurried
into his tomb Lady Essex triumphantly procured
an annulment of her marriage.   That which the
sorceries of 'sweet Turner' failed to achieve was
easily compassed by the sycophancy of bench and
bar.   Four bishops and three doctors of law were
found ready to obey the king and to do the behests
of the favourite.   The Archbishop of Canterbury
and the Bishop of London, to their great glory,
refused to bow the knee at the bidding of an unjust

monarch, and are absolved from complicity in the
most cynical act of a cynical age.[1]

No obstacle now remained in the path of her who
was once Lady Essex. Overbury, whom his enemies
had paid him the compliment of believing an in-
superable impediment, was removed. Rochester,
raised, as Earl of Somerset, to a rank equalling the
adventurous lady's own, was impatient until he might
protect her with the ægis of his name and fame.
The king, delighted in the pleasure of his favourites,
eagerly mistook a squalid intrigue for a pure romance
of joyousness and youth, and resolved that the ceremony which united the lovers should be of a noble
and ingenious splendour. Never before had the
court, well used as it was to brilliant spectacles,
witnessed so fine a display. The bride, to emphasise
the virginal purity of her mind, was married 'in her
hair.' The king, the queen, and Prince Charles
witnessed the union in the chapel of Whitehall

---

[1] The letter which James I. wrote to the Archbishop, who
had refused to sacrifice his conscience to the humour of his king,
is so intimately characteristic of the time and the man that it is
worth quoting. 'I will conclude therefore with inverting the
argument,' wrote James, 'that if a judge should have a prejudice
in respect of persons, it should become you rather to have a
kind of faith implicit in my judgment, as well in respect of some
skill I have in divinity, as also that I hope no honest man
doubts of my conscience; and the best thankfulness that you,
that are so far my creature, can use towards me, is to reverence
and follow my judgment, and not to contradict it, except where
you may demonstrate unto me that I am mistaken, or wrong
informed, and so farewell.   JAMES R.'

Palace. Courtiers and poets vied with one another
in heaping flatteries upon the handsome couple.
Donne himself did not disdain to compose an
epithalamium in the loftiest strain of adulation.
'Blest pair of swans,' he wrote—

> 'Blest pair of swans, O may you interbring
> Daily new joys, and never sing:
> Live till all grounds of wishes fail,
> Till honour, yea, till wisdom grow so stale
> That new great heights to try,
> It must serve your ambition to die.'

The unconscious irony of this poem gives it an
interest, unconnected with the ingenuity of its
images and the elegance of its expression. Nor is
it necessary to bring charges of insincerity against
Donne. Though he had eagerly sought preferment
from Rochester, and had done his best to further the
suit of nullity, he wrote in complete ignorance of
Overbury's murder, an ignorance which he shared
with the vast majority of his countrymen, and he
exercised his gracious art for those whom he believed
a beautiful woman and a brave courtier. He was
not alone in this ardour of flattery. Thomas
Campion made a 'Gallant Masque of Lords' which
was given on the wedding-day. And Ben Jonson,
who some seven years before had with his eloquence
added lustre to the nuptials of Lady Frances Howard
and Lord Essex, devised two Masques—'A Challenge
at Tilt' and an 'Irish Masque'—for this more
august occasion.

But it was Bacon who with the ease of genius outpaced all flatterers. His exquisite 'Masque of Flowers,' in which with a pompous lack of humour the learned and bewigged gentlemen of Gray's Inn transformed themselves into dainty blossoms, was designed for the pleasure of Lord and Lady Somerset. That it was a beautiful spectacle there is no doubt. Bacon, whose vigilance nothing escaped, was curious about Masques and Triumphs. 'These things are but toys,' he said, '. . . but yet since Princes will have such things, it is better they should be graced with elegancy than daubed with cost.' The cost wherewith this particular masque was daubed was no less than £2000, a sum which one is sure did not disgrace its elegancy. It is possible, indeed, to surmise from the learned lawyer's own words the fair effect of his dainty device. If he followed the dictate of his own taste, it was all brilliance and gaiety. 'The colours that show best by candle-light,' said he, 'are white, carnation, and a kind of sea-water green,' for the use of which his procession of flowers was very apt.

Thus it was that youth and gravity, princedom and learning, did honour to bride and bridegroom. Nothing was omitted from the ceremonies which might win the favour of the fortunate courtier. It is as though time and history stood still for the joy of these happy souls, and yet it was less than three months ago that the miserable and tortured Overbury had paid the brutal penalty of pride. That poets and attorneys should be lavish in the praise of those who basked in the smile of chance is not surprising. We cannot but wonder whether the murderers, as they climbed the topmost pinnacle of courtly fame, were haunted by the emaciated spectre of him who had once been his friend, and was the victim of them both.

For a while Lord Somerset and his wife sunned themselves in the royal pleasure. The king still confessed that he took 'more delight and contentment' in Somerset's company than in any man's living. But presently there began murmurings of suspicion. It was whispered to Somerset's discredit that Overbury did not come honestly by his death. The flattery lavished upon the favourite seemed to the colder eye of reflection somewhat exaggerated. No man can keep the first place in a jealous court by the cut of a doublet and the mere exercise of the grand manner, and Somerset, if he delighted in his escape from thraldom, missed the counsel of Overbury, who had been not merely his governor, as they said, but his brain. A yet heavier blow was struck at his power and influence by the sudden rise of Villiers. James had neither place nor inclination for two favourites at once, and the triumph of Villiers meant nothing less than the ruin of Somerset. When, therefore, the half-forgotten name of Overbury was mentioned, it fell upon the ears of those whose policy chimed with the discovery of the truth. How the secret was first revealed is uncertain ; possibly it was never very profound, and when its betrayal seemed expedient there were not a few who could speak with a knowledge of the foul deed.

Sir Ralph Winwood was the channel whereby the strange story reached the royal ears, and Sir Ralph heard it from Lady Shrewsbury, who, herself a prisoner, had picked up the gossip of the Tower. Presently another rumour came from Trumbull, the British Minister at Brussels, that an apothecary's boy, one Reeve, had related the whole history to his servant.[1] The gossip spread up and down the city. Everywhere there was a reaction in Overbury's favour. Those, who had been the loudest in denunciation, now insisted most clamantly upon vengeance. The king would not lift a hand to shield Somerset. With a fine show of justice he declared that the evil-doers should be punished. 'Lord, in what a miserable condition shall this Kingdom be (the only famous nation for hospitality in the world) if our tables should become

[1] There is a strong and undesigned piece of evidence that Reeve told the truth out of his own knowledge. Lobell was an apothecary, who prepared the prescriptions of Dr Mayerne, the famous physician to the king, who attended Overbury in the Tower, and doubtless knew far more of the tragedy than he thought it prudent to acknowledge, and the fatal clyster is said to have been of Lobell's making. A witness called Edward Ryder says that he saw Lobell in October 1615, and 'told him that it was now manifest Overbury was poisoned by an apothecary's boy in Lime Street. Madame Lobell explained to her husband, "That must be William, whom you sent in to France "; on which he trembled violently, and said that as William was leaving his master he gave him a letter of recommendation to Paris.'

such a snare as none could eat without danger of his life,' said he, and thus saying called down God's curse upon himself and his posterity for ever if he spared any that were found guilty.

The sword of justice fell first upon the heads of the guilty hirelings, against whom the prosecution was conducted with a zeal and energy inspired by the king himself. Weston went to the gallows, having expressed a hopeless hope that 'they would not make a net to catch the little fishes, and let the great go.' The infamous Franklin murmured so many confessions in jail that none would give them credit. At the tree he behaved with a strange levity, boxed the hangman's ears, and persuaded all present that he was either mad or drunk.[1] Mrs. Turner was

---

[1] An unsigned letter, printed in the Egerton Papers, describes Franklin's demeanour at Tyburn. 'His Doctor Whiting told him,' says the unknown writer, 'he should do well to give the world some testimony of the manner of his death : No says he, I'll testimony nothing (I use his own words) ; my confessions are all true that are under my hand : I did not know of this bloody act at the first, but afterwards (I cannot deny) but I had my hands very deep in it. There are some yet left behind, and great ones too with whom (and then he clapped his hands twice or thrice upon the coffin that lay upon the cart before him)— but let that pass. . . . He was put in mind that it was his own desire to have his confessions put in print. . . It is true, (said he) I desire indeed that it may be put in print; . . . and then the cart was driven away and thus he died, never heard to pray one word. The best word he used was that he hoped to sup with Christ that night.' For the rest when he was told he was to die he danced corantoes up and down his chamber, and talked in agony of 'three great ones.'

accompanied to Tyburn by a vast concourse of courtiers and their ladies, and died most decently, as became so elegant a sorceress. It is said that she spent the last days of her life in denouncing the errors of papistry, and by wearing a yellow-starched ruff on the fatal day put an end for ever to an ugly fashion. Helwes, whom Somerset ungratefully described as the worst deserver in this business, followed her to the scaffold. In the meantime the chief criminals set their wits at work to avert suspicion. Lady Somerset did her best to destroy the traces of her guilt, while her lord, in Bacon's memorable phrase, instantly began to 'sew fig-leaves.' He had already asked and obtained a general pardon. Now he searched Weston's house; now he bade his servants lay hands upon Mrs. Turner's papers—and all in vain. The king, firmly set upon justice, left his haughty favourite to his fate; and if we may believe Weldon, took fare-well of him with as fine a treachery as ever Somerset had shown to his friend. It was at Royston, whence, as the king well knew, Somerset was summoned to arrest and doom. '"For God's sake," asked the king, "when shall I see thee again? On my soul, I shall neither eat nor sleep until you come again." The Earl told him on Monday, this being Friday. "For God's sake let me," said the king; "shall I, shall I?" Then lolled about his neck; then, "for God's sake, give thy lady this kiss for me;" in the same manner at the stairs' head, at the middle of the stairs, and at the stairs' foot.   The Earl was not in his coach when the king used these very words (in the hearing of four servants), "I shall never see his face more."' It is true that Somerset deserved no better at the hands of his king ; but so sudden and callous a forsaking can hardly be found within the scope of history.

On 24th May 1616 the Countess of Somerset was called in Westminster Hall to answer the charge of having murdered Overbury. It was not much more than two years since her marvellous beauty had dazzled the beholders in the Royal Chapel. Now she was bidden to play another part, and she assumed a becoming modesty of garb and demeanour. She was dressed in ' black tammel, a cypress chaperon, a cobweb lawn ruff, and cuffs.' She had come thither to confess her fault and to ask for mercy. She pleaded guilty 'with a low voice, but wonderful fearful,' and when asked why the sentence of death should not be pronounced on her, 'I can much aggravate,' she answered, 'but cannot extenuate my fault.   I desire mercy, and that the lords will inter- cede for me to the king.'   The Earl, who was tried on the following day, assumed a prouder carriage. Refusing to put in a plea of guilty, he maintained his innocence with an obstinate fortitude.   He turned a deaf ear to the eloquent persuasion of his sovereign.   The king was in a fever of apprehension and anxiety.   So many secrets had he shared with Somerset, so openly had he abandoned him, that he

feared betrayal even in Westminster Hall. He
believed unto the last minute that Somerset would
cast some aspersion upon him, that he was in some
sort accessory to his crime, and some days before
the trial was held he wrote such a letter to the
Governor of the Tower as plainly shows the sleep-
less timidity of his mind. 'You know Somerset's
day of trial is at hand,' said he, 'and you know also
what fair means I have used to move him by confessing the truth to honour God and me, and leave
some place for my mercy to work on.'

The note of unconscious humour which is heard
in these words does not silence the murmurings of
fear. Some have assumed, therefore, that James
was indeed accessory; it is far more probable that
his natural nervousness had got the better of him,
and that he saw in a plea of guilty the only sure
method of avoiding scandal. But Somerset was
obdurate. He was resolved to assert his own
innocence at all costs, and never in an unworthy
career did he bear himself with so fine dignity as
when he fought for his life before his peers. He
brought no charge against any one; he was content
to defend himself. The sense of drama, which was
always his, did not desert him in the supreme crisis.
He put upon him all the marks of honour: he wore
the cloak, the George, and the other insignia of the
Garter, as if to prove that he still held himself
worthy of the noble order to which he belonged.
Imprisonment and dread had already set their mark

upon him. His pale visage, his long beard, his eyes sunk in his head, demanded the sympathy of all beholders. He was dressed, with a severity which became the occasion, 'in a black satin suit, laid with two white laces in a seam, a gown of orient velvet, lined with unshorn, all the sleeves lain with satin lace, a pair of gloves with satin tops, his hair curled.'

Such was the guise in which he presented himself to the court, and when by the flickering light of many torches, at the end of a long and weary day, he rose to address his peers, there was none present who was not moved by the tragedy and picturesqueness of the scene. All the forces of chance and nature were arrayed against him. His wife had mournfully confessed her guilt, and it seemed (and seems) impossible to the impartial mind that he should not have shared it.[1] He was fighting single-handed against the serried ranks of bench and bar, with no practice in the law and no lawyer to aid him. And truly an unlettered courtier, opposed by Sir Edward Coke upon the bench, and by Francis Bacon, the King's Attorney, had no more chance

---

[1] If Simcox, a friend of Weston's and 'a man of fashion and of some understanding,' is to be believed, then Somerset's guilt is clear. For Simcox declared 'that in the league of friendship that was between Weston and him, Weston told him that the Earl of Somerset did often give him money with his own hand, and bade him keep Sir Thomas Overbury safe, for, says he, if ever he get out, he or I must die for it.'

of escape than a rat in a trap. Somerset did not escape, and yet he spoke with a strength and clarity which surprised his hearers. His hearers were surprised, and not persuaded. By a unanimous verdict he was adjudged guilty and sentenced to be hanged.

As was but natural, Lord and Lady Somerset escaped the gallows. There was still place, though Somerset had not confessed, for the king's mercy to work upon. They were committed to the Tower, where they spent many weary years, and they were stripped of all the wealth and lands which were the fruit of the royal bounty. How lavish was this bounty the inventory of their possessions is an eloquent testimony. We read of bedsteads with gilt pillars, and purple velvet furniture; of large Persian, Turkey, and Egyptian carpets; of pavilions of cobweb lawn, embroidered with silk flowers; of tapestries representing the wars of Troy and Roman story; of many pictures, described as 'great tables,' and whole-length portraits. The jewels and plate, with which they embellished their courtly lives, were of a splendour which might well have lit the spark of jealousy even in a royal breast, and it is easy to imagine what was their destiny. Not even the Earl's horses were forgotten. A list of them was made by the groom of his stable, and the best distributed according to the king's command. Bay Minion was delivered to his Prince's Highness, Black Denny to Lord Danvers, and White Steward to Sir Charles Howard.

The partition was pitiless and complete. And the popular verdict followed the king's displeasure. Lord Somerset, once the favourite, presently became the mock of the balladmonger.[1] He was scoffed and laughed at in many a halting rhyme, until he suffered what is worse even than contempt—forgetfulness. Buried alive in the Tower, he was as dead as Overbury, the victim of his perfidy. He makes but one or two furtive reappearances, as one speaking from the grave. The last letter that has come down to us from his hand is addressed to King James, and is an ardent appeal that his estate should be returned to him. He fell, he declares, rather for want of well defending than by the force and violence of any proofs, and he urges that he, like the family of Helwes, might be given his estate—a greater gift than life, because it extends to posterity.

Was he conscious, I wonder, in writing to James,

---

[1] The ballads, songs, and doggerel verse which describe the death of Overbury and the rise and fall of Robin Carr, Lord Somerset are many and various. The following passage, taken from a manuscript at Belvoir Castle, clearly shows the contemporary opinion of the disgraced courtier :—

> 'Thou wast a man but of compounded part ;
> Nothing thy own but thy aspiring heart ;
> Thy house Raleigh's, Westmoreland's thy land,
> Overbury's thy wit, Essex' thy wife.   So stand
> By Æsop's law, each bird may pluck his feather,
> And thou stript naked art to wind and weather.
> Yet care of friends, to shelter thee from cold,
> Have mewed thee up in London's strongest hold.
> Summer is set, and winter is come on,
> Yet Robin Redbreast's chirping voice is gone.'

that he was using the same argument which Sir Walter Raleigh, whose house and lands he had usurped, had once urged to him ? 'After many losses, and many years' sorrows,' wrote Raleigh to Carr, . . . 'it is come to my knowledge, that yourself (whom I knew not but by an honourable favour) hath been persuaded to give me and mine my last fatal blow, by obtaining from His Majesty the Inheritance of my Children and Nephews, lost in Law for want of a word. This done, there remaineth nothing with me but the name of life.' With a better eloquence than Somerset's he pleaded to Sir Robert Carr the cause of his descendants. 'And for you, Sir,' said he, 'seeing your fair day is but in the dawn, mine drawn to the setting . . . I beseech you begin not your first building upon the ruins of the innocent, and let not my sorrows and theirs attend your first plantation.' Raleigh spoke to a deaf ear, and had the grim satisfaction, before his death, of seeing the despoiler despoiled. Intent upon his own misfortunes, Somerset forgot, perchance, how deeply he had wronged others.

'It is not I who thus put your Majesty in mind importunely,' he wrote, full of self-pity. 'It is he that was your creature, it is Somerset, with all your honours and envious greatness, that is now in question'; and even in the extremity of disgrace he confesses to the king that he is 'the workmanship of his hands, and bears his stamp deeply imprinted in all the characters of favour.' The letter availed him nothing.   He died a landless and unhappy man.

Though, when they emerged from the Tower, he lived beneath the same roof which sheltered his wife, the two accomplices are said never again to have exchanged a word of amiable greeting. And to prove that in this drama of Greek intensity the hand of Nemesis was far-reaching, the daughter whom Lady Somerset bore in the Tower did not escape the curse.   Brought up in complete ignorance of her mother's crime, she grew to womanhood in beauty and innocence, and was wooed by the Earl of Bedford.   Despite the opposition of his friends, he married her, and still she knew nothing of Overbury's death.   Then one day, not long after her son had perished on the scaffold, she discovered, by an unhappy chance, a time-worn account of the trial, and the reading of it broke her heart.   Surely Overbury was avenged.   Surely his bitter prophecy was fulfilled that Somerset's name should never die, nor he himself leave to be the most odious of men.

BEFORE Sir Thomas Overbury was sent to the Tower he had never suffered, said his servant, from any disease save the spleen, caused by too much study; and true it is that his 'Characters,' to which his tragic fate has given a sinister interest, smell pleasantly of a well-trimmed lamp. They are but a faint reflection of his romantic life and of his dissolute age. There is not the bustle of court or camp in their quiet pages. Though their author is clearly a man of the world, he is also a scholar, prevented by the natural timidity of learning from betraying his thoughts and sensibilities too wantonly. After the chastened expression of his malice, his dearest ambition is the perfection of his phrase. He looks at the world through a minifying glass, and sees no one at greater length than two pages. In the modest scale of his portraiture he reveals a natural reaction. He could not match the spacious masterpieces of Shakespeare and Ben Jonson. They planned their heroes of a larger size than life, and hewed them out of colossal blocks of marble. He was content to carve cherry-stones.

But Sir Thomas Overbury's 'Characters' claim our interest on other grounds than the scandal of his life or the deftness of their handling. For well-nigh a century they exercised a wide and deep influence upon our writers. They form a chapter in the history of literature as well as in the history of manners. If they were not the first of their kind to be composed in English, they were the first to win a general popularity, and it is from Overbury, and not from Hall, his one English predecessor, that we must mark the beginning of the 'Character' as a literary convention. Though Theophrastus was the father of them both, Overbury speedily became an inspiration to many who had no Greek, and to whom the gravity of Hall seemed austere and forbidding. Nor will it detract from his merit, if before we examine his work and its effect we look back for a moment upon its origins.

The 'Character,' as understood by Theophrastus, is of an engaging simplicity. The author chooses the victim of this vice or that weakness, and explains, with a humour which never galls, what the victim will do and say in the circumstances of a homely life. Each phrase is an independent example of a generalised quality. The Flatterer is a person 'who will say as he walks with another, "Do you observe how people are looking at you?"' The Complaisant Man will assert 'that foreigners speak more justly than his fellow-citizens.' The Late-Learner 'will study passages for recitation when he is sixty and break down in repeating them.' When a servant has smashed a jug or a plate the Penurious Man 'will

54 SIR THOMAS OVERBURY

take the value out of his rations.' Thus will these
men behave in all times and under all skies. Theophrastus deals not in differences but in similarities.
He writes not of individuals, but of classes. He
drives mankind into separate pens, according to the
temper and complexion of each bunch. And his
' Characters' are as true to-day as they were in the
day when they were written, because he is careful
always to choose for comment the bare, plain facts of
life, and never loses himself in subtle distinctions.
The background of his tale is as shadowy as the
appearance of his victim. Were it not for a reference here and there to the market-place and the
gymnasium, you might be in some doubt as to
where he chose his examples of vice or folly. And
these accidental touches of local colour do not disturb his air of detachment. He reflects : he does
not observe. He is drawing men, not Athenians.

The first deviser of 'Characters' in English, Joseph
Hall,[1] was a faithful disciple of Theophrastus. Not

---

[1] *Characters of Vertues and Vices* : In Two Bookes. By
Jos. Hall. London : 1608. There are two books, earlier in
date than this, which look like books of ' Characters,' and are
not. One is Harman's *Caveat for Commen Cursetors, vulgarly
called Vagabones* (1567); the other is *The Fraternitye of Vaca-
bondes* (1575). The purpose of these books is the same : to
warn the honest man against the rogues that lie in wait for him,
and to explain to those who understand not Pedlar's French the
names by which the rogues know one another. Both authors
tell us what is an Abraham Man and what is a Ruffler, what is
an Upright Man and what a Whip-jack. Neither is concerned
with character as Theophrastus and Overbury understood it.

merely does he prove on every page that he holds
imitation better than invention, but he frankly and
freely acknowledges his debt. He has trod in the
paths of the ancient philosophers, he says, 'but with
a higher and wider step.' Especially he follows
Theophrastus, 'that ancient master of morality,
who thought this the fittest task for the ninety-
and - ninth year of his age, and the profitablest
monument that he could leave for a farewell to
his Grecians.' Thus, in consonance with the
master's theory, Hall's characters are mere abstractions. He does not write with his eye upon this or
that specimen. He attributes to each virtue and
to each vice the qualities and manifestations which
he thinks each ought to reveal. His Wise Man and
his Busy-Body, his Hypocrite and his Malcontent
are the same, wherever he found them. They were
the same in the time of Theophrastus ; they are the
same to-day—the same in essence, different only in
phrase.

Though he speak of Cales and Nieuport ; though
he speculate of Holland's peace and the Guiana
voyage, Hall's personages, good or ill, inhabit a
shadowland of morality, not the England of his
day. And Hall reveals other ambitions, of which
Theophrastus knew nothing. Before all things he
is a man of letters, not writing with the careless ease
of the Greek, but striving busily and consciously
after a literary effect. Here he is in the right of it.
Brilliant finish and a fine surface are the essentials

of work composed on so small a scale as is the 'Character,' and in Hall's pages you will never find a wry or ill-considered word. He delights in imagery, like the artist that he was. 'He is a lowly valley,' he says of the Humble Man, 'sweetly planted and well-watered: the proud man's earth, whereon he trampleth; but secretly full of wealthy mines, more worth than he that walks over them: a rich stone set in lead: and lastly a true Temple of God, built with a low roof.' He replaces the just and commonplace humour of Theophrastus with a kind of mysticism. He is metaphysical, like Crashaw and Donne. He enwraps his simple virtues in phrases of fantasy. Of the Faithful Man he says: 'He walks every day with his Maker; and talks with Him familiarly. . . . If his own parents lie on his way to God, his holy carelessness makes them his footsteps. . . . He hath white hands and a clean soul, fit to lodge God in; all the rooms whereof are set apart for his Holiness.' Even at his plainest, he has the tact to choose the right word, to fashion a comely sentence. What can be better than this of the Valiant Man: 'He hath often looked death in the face, and passed it by with a smile'? Or of the Honest Man, who 'scorneth to gain by orphans, or ransack graves: and therefore will be true to a dead friend, because he sees him not'? All the resources of antithesis and epigram are his. He has a grave wit, and thinks it no shame to set a fine point even on moral exhortation. The Patient Man, he tells us, 'goes with the same mind to the shambles and the fold.' And again, 'Superstition is godless religion, devout impiety.' The few flashes of humour which light up the book are turned upon the vices. In describing the Vainglorious Man he steps down from his pedestal. 'A bare head in the street'—thus he writes—'doth him more good than a meal's meat. He swears big at an ordinary; and talks of the Court with a sharp accent. . . . He picks his teeth when his stomach is empty, and calls for pheasants at a common inn.' In brief, though Hall's book is made up of moral generalisations, it is yet a mirror in which every man may find his counterfeit. And happy is he, or vain, who seeks it among the virtues.

That Hall's book escaped notice is not wonderful. It came, modest and inobtrusive, into the heyday of our literature. But Overbury knew it, and with Hall and Theophrastus—whom he read in Latin, if not in Greek—as examples, he sat him down to sketch characters for himself. From his masters he borrowed not much more than a technical process. He, too, got his effects by an accumulation of traits and habits. And there he left them. Their cold abstractions did not satisfy his quick eye and ardent soul. It was not for him to classify and arrange. Even though he could not pack into words all that he did and thought; even though, being better adapted to intrigue than to letters, he wrote as an amateur,—he did not shut out from his book the fruits of his experience. He replaced the reflection

of Hall and Theophrastus by a vivid observation of
his own. He drew always from the life, and fixed his
gaze upon concrete examples. At his book's end
he set down his own definition of a character. 'It
is a picture (real or personal),' said he, 'quaintly
drawn, in various colours, all of them heightened
by one shadowing. It is a quick and soft touch of
many springs, all shutting up in one musical close:
it is wit's descant on any plain song.' Thus he lets
us into his secret. His pictures are real or personal.
There was not one of his models with whom he had
not an intimate acquaintance. They are one and all
of his own time and place, and they light up for us
those darker corners of the past which serious history
holds still in obscurity.

That the 'Characters' are the work of a scholar
and a courtier writing to amuse his friends is evident
in every page. As I have said, it was not for Overbury wholly to express the life that he had led. The
faculty of expansiveness was not his. It is equally
evident that he castigated his prose with the greatest
severity. His sketches are models of concision and
economy. He aims at producing an effect in every
sentence, and he does not often fail. He devises
phrases and constructs epigrams with a zeal and
artistry which cannot elude his readers, and as he
was the first to paint the 'Characters' of individuals
he may claim all the credit which belongs to originality. Moreover, despite the impersonality of his
style, despite the reticence of his method, Overbury

and his friends emerge now and then from the measured prose, and for those who know his story it is impossible not to detect the traces of auto-biography. His Courtiers, his Glory-Hunters, his Flatterers are the men whom best he knew, and as you contemplate their portraiture you think instinctively of Overbury himself and of Rochester. When he calls the Flatterer 'the shadow of a fool,' was he not thinking of the ungrateful part he had taken for his own? By accident or design, that which follows is surely Rochester delineated : ' He knows no man that is not generally known. His wit, like the marigold, openeth like the sun, and therefore he riseth not before ten of the clock. He puts more confidence in his words than meaning, and more in his pronunciation than his words. He follows nothing but inconstancy, admires nothing but beauty, honours nothing but fortune. Loves nothing.'

Look at the 'Amorist' and picture to yourself Rochester's intrigue with Lady Essex, the intrigue which for a while Overbury assisted : 'Her favour lifts him up as the sun moisture; when she disfavours, unable to hold that happiness, it falls down in tears. . . . He answers not, or not to the purpose ; and no marvel, for he is not at home. . . . His imagination is a fool, and it goeth in a pied coat of red and white; shortly he is translated out of a man into folly; his imagination is the glass of lust, and himself the traitor to his own discretion.' If this and other

portraits were recognised in the manuscripts, which we
may suppose Overbury handed from friend to friend,
there is another clear reason for his unpopularity, for
they are drawn with a truth and bitterness which
would at once enrage and disconcert his victims, and
they help to explain though not to condone the indifference wherewith his friends looked upon the
fallen courtier.

But it is not only upon the Court that Overbury
showers his invective. He expected more of life
than life had to give, and thus was constantly out
of humour with his surroundings. He contemned
always that which was nearest to him, and detected
with the quick eye of criticism the weakness and folly
of his intimate companions. The University, which
lay not far behind, seemed to his memory a place of
desolation and pedantry. For him 'the mere fellow
of an house' was rescued from shame neither by
virtue nor by intelligence. He represents him as
small-minded, greedy, improvident, and penurious,
as one who commits more absurdities in maintaining
talk with a gentleman than a clown in the eating
of an egg, who 'thinks himself as fine when he is
in a clean band, and a new pair of shoes, as any
courtier doth, when he is first in a new fashion,' who,
in brief, 'respects no one in the University, and is
respected by no man out of it.'

Earle, Overbury's successor in this craft of characters, was of another and a better mind. If he was
not blind to the scholar's faults he did not close his

eyes to the scholar's virtues. 'Practise him a little in men,' said he, 'and brush him over with good company, and he shall outbalance those glisterers as much as a solid substance does a feather, or gold gold-lace.' The Inns of Court came off no better in Overbury's esteem than the University. His sojourn in the Temple had not softened to his heart the traits of his colleagues. He saw little difference between the Inns of Court of Man and the Scholar, save a pair of silk stockings and a beaver hat. He thought the Templar was as far behind the Courtier in fashion, as the Scholar is behind the Templar; and he despised the meanness, which bade him forget his acquaintance, and his shame to be seen in any man's company that wore not his clothes well.

Like many another satirist, Overbury, scorning thus the society which he knew best, pretended an admiration for the amiable simplicity which was beyond his reach. By temperament and habit he was fitted to live in the great world. The intrigue and trappings of the court were essential to his happiness. His quick brain and ready tongue gave him a confident superiority in the battle of the wits. He felt that he was born to shine in splendid assemblies, and he was not one to hide his light under the bushel of obscurity. But he followed the ancient models in affecting a love of the golden mean and a country life. If we may believe his words, he found nothing that was noble and of good report within the boundaries of London. So Horace,

constant in his love of Rome, would have us know
that he was never happy save in the seclusion of his
Sabine farm. It is a pleasant weakness to vaunt
simplicity and to cultivate elegance—a weakness
which inspired Overbury to his best pages. This
haunter of courts, this favourite of favourites, writes
with the keenest zest of 'a fair and happy milkmaid,
who makes her hand hard with labour and her heart
soft with pity,' all whose care is that 'she may die
in springtime, to have store of flowers stuck upon
her winding-sheet'; or of an honest Franklin, the
pattern and example of plain and decent living, an
ancient yeoman, who 'with his own eye doth both
father his flock and set forward all manner of
husbandry.'

For such simple folk as he had known in the
Gloucestershire of his boyhood, and as still lingered
in his memory, Overbury kept a sentimental corner
of his heart. His sentiment did not excuse the
country gentleman, who, in his view, was an ignorant
bumpkin, insolent to his tenants, amongst his equals
full of doubt, out of his element at court, and with
no more eloquence than would save him twopence.
On the other hand, his loftiest panegyric is reserved
for the Noble and Retired Housekeeper, whose
bounty is limited by reason, not ostentation, whose
word and meaning never shake hands and part,
whose great houses bear in their front more durance
than state, and whose mind is so secure that thunder
rocks him asleep. Thus by his preferences you may

detect the theory, not the practice, of his life. Thus by the variety of his portraiture you may measure the breadth of his curiosity. Though he is seldom impartial, he excludes from his survey little that is human. His sympathy, it is true, was never as wide as his interest, but he is not guilty of narrow-mindedness who gravely sate him down to delineate a Buttonmaker of Amsterdam or a Drunken Dutchman resident in England.

The 'Characters,' published a year after their author's cruel murder, achieved a large and rapid popularity. In 1614 no less than five editions were demanded, and the book was reprinted twenty times within half a century. The scandal of its author's life and death no doubt excited a general curiosity, but we must look beyond the tragedy in the Tower if we would find a reason for the book's success. It chimed with the temper of the moment. The artifice of its style, which he who ran could imitate, made it acceptable to the Temple, the Tavern, and the Court. A world overwhelmed with the splendour of the drama sought to express its intelligence after a more modest fashion, to escape as far as possible from a hopeless competition. And the 'Character,' widely as it was separated in manner and method from the drama, touched the art of the theatre at one essential point. It also aspired to delineate man, not at his full stature nor with the courage of creation, but with a minute analysis and quick introspection. In other words, a book of 'Characters' was the drama reduced to its lowest terms. The playwright set men and women on their feet and bade them speak for themselves. Overbury and his imitators put men and women on the dissecting-table and described their features and their qualities. The object was the same, though the process was reversed, and it was Overbury's insight or good fortune to hit upon a kind of literature which his century could understand with sympathy and turn to its own purpose with imitative zeal.

Indeed, no better vehicle for the criticism of life, which is the grave business of prose and poetry alike, than the 'Character,' as Overbury designed it, could be found, and there is no end which it was not destined to serve. The satirist found in it a means of invective, the politician a means of argument, the idealist a means of expressing the hope that was in him. Characters tumbled from the press in hundreds. There were characters of plain men and women, characters of statesmen—magnanimous and servile, characters of cutthroats and pick-pockets, characters of states and countries. And perhaps, if the seventeenth century had not worn the artifice to detrition, we might still express our-selves by the same method that seemed good to Sir Thomas Overbury.

The authors of 'Characters' were of many kinds and many ambitions. Nicholas Breton and Henry Parrott, Wye Saltonstall and Lord North all tried their hands at the new craft. The common hack vied with the person of quality in explaining his fellow-men. The Projector and the Trimmer, the Reformado and the Fanatick, the Tory and the Prince, were one and all put under the microscope. The titles of the books are some measure of their nature and eccentricity. *The Good and the Bad, Cures for the Itch, Picturæ Loquentes,*—these are some of them. The most are mere echoes. Many who had nothing to say could still learn the trick of characterisation, and hope with the sanguine temper of the imitator that they would not be found out. One of them, gravelled for matter, thought it worth while to travesty the noble prose of Hall in heroic verse, to destroy a masterpiece that he might build a trivial monument for himself.[1]

But among them are a few who knew well how to profit by a good example, and who could put some substance of their own into a borrowed form. Here, for instance, is Geoffrey Mynshull, turning a bitter experience to the best account. Who and what he was is still uncertain. We know little more of him than that he belonged to a good family in Cheshire, that in 1617 he lay in the King's Bench Prison in

---

[1] This was Nahum Tate, whose *Characters of Vertue and Vice . . . Attempted in Verse from a Treatise of the Reverend Joseph Hall, Late Lord Bishop of Exeter,* is a marvel of ineptitude. Here is a specimen of his misplaced zeal :—

> ' The Hypocrite to sadness can convert
>   His looks, while Mirth is Rev'lling in his Heart,
>   Then Jugler-like with Pleasure does retreat,
>   To think how smoothly he has pass'd the cheat.'

Southwark, and that his *Essayes and Characters of a Prison and Prisoners* (1618) ill merit the oblivion into which they have fallen. It is a brave and tragic little book, the work of an ingenious scholar and a high-minded gentleman. The author does not tell us by what misfortune or improvidence he was brought within the rules, but clearly he bore his punishment with a quiet courage, and he wrote of the underworld into which he had been thrust with a vividness of style and imagery that never fails. For him, 'a prison is a grave to bury men alive, it is a microcosmos, a little world of woe, it is a map of misery, it is as intricate a place as Rosamund's Labyrinth, and it is so full of blind meanders, and crooked turnings, that it is impossible to find the way out, except he be directed by a silver clue, and can never overcome the Minotaur without a golden ball to work his own safety.' Such is the place, and what are the inhabitants? 'A prisoner,' says Mynshull, 'is an impatient patient, lingering under the rough hands of a cruel physician; . . . he is fortune's tossing-ball, an object that would make mirth melancholy : to his friends an abject, and a subject of nine days' wonder in every barber's shop.' Then he pictures him as 'a poor weather-beaten bird, who, having lost the shore, is driven by tempest to hang upon the sails and tacklings of a prison.'

But in whatever likeness you see him, the prisoner lies in his dungeon, neglected and forgotten, the victim of a rascal creditor, 'who hath two pairs of hands, one of flesh and blood, and that nature gave him; another of iron, and that the law gives him: but the one is more predominant than the other, for mercy guides the one and mammon the other.' And if the creditor gives no hope, little solace may be got of visitants, who are men, for the most part ' composed of all protesting promises, and little or no performance; who are like your almanacks, which, when they prognosticate fair weather, it is a million to a mite if it prove not contrary.' Thus he sketches, with the eloquence of anger, the jailers, the lockers-up of nights, and the other masters of cruelty, who made the life of a debtor's prison intolerable. Yet, though he rise to the height of Juvenal's invective, he knows that his duty is to preserve a tranquil mind in the bitterest adversity, and when he draws the character of a noble, understanding Prisoner, he shows to his reader the ideal of life, which he himself would hope to realise.

'A noble understanding Prisoner,' says he, ' is a book so truly printed that Fortune (with all her mistakings) cannot find in him any *errata*. He comes to prison, as a great ship in a storm to shore, showing more noble emblems of constant sufferings than the seas could stick upon it of their tyranny. He beholds jailers as a valiant soldier looks upon his wounds, which how dangerous soever, yet he smiles upon his surgeon, and will endure dressing with an undaunted countenance, because he knows it is to fetch him off from danger.' Above all, though

he does not underrate the miracle of his freedom, he
knows that good and evil come alike from himself,
that oppression cannot break his magnanimous soul.
He asks, in one of his loftiest passages, why the
name of prisoner is distasteful. 'Is it because thou
art cooped under lock and key? Is it because
thou feelest wants? . . . Is it because thy friends
look strangely on thee, or forsake thee? Is it
because thou art disgraced and holden in scorn?
. . . Yet let not all these dismay thee, for hadst
thou the whole country to walk in, yet thy soul is still
imprisoned in thy corrupted body. . . . Look into
thy own bosom, and learn but a short rule, yet very
difficult, viz. *Nosce teipsum*, and thou shalt find that
it is not imprisonment that afflicts thee, but the evil
that is in thyself.' From all which it is clear that
Mynshull mingled reflection with his portraiture,
and showed us not merely what manner of men
infected a prison, but how a hero might bear
himself though he lay fast bound under lock and
key.

To Mynshull's exotic purpose the convention of
Overbury was perfectly adapted. Artifice well
becomes that which lies outside our commonplace
experience. The poor Cheshire gentleman shows
us but one corner of life, and that a dingy corner,
but he shows it us with a gravity and a verisimilitude
which none will contest. John Earle, whose *Micro-
cosmographie, or a Piece of the World Characteriz'd*, was
published in 1628, had an ampler design. He set out to

paint the personages whom he had encountered on his earthly journey, and the colours and the brushes which he employs are Sir Thomas Overbury's. In some respects he is superior to his master. While his observation is as keen as Overbury's, he shows a finer sense of impartiality and a happier sentiment. He does not see his subjects either all black or all white. He does not make characterisation an excuse for invective, nor attempt under a general head to castigate a particular enemy. He was content to look about him, and write down his impressions. If his world was circumscribed, he knew it all the better for that, and it is the University, the Church, and the countryside which inspire his happiest efforts.

When he touches the court, and the rufflers who frequented there, he does but echo the voice of the dramatist. His gallant is the gallant of convention, 'one that was borne and shaped for his clothes,' whose 'main ambition is to get a knighthood, and then an old lady, which, if he be happy in, he fills the stage and a coach so much larger. Otherwise himself and his clothes grow stale together, and he is buried commonly ere he dies in the gaol, or the country.' That is the gallant of many a comedy, who has wandered into Earle's notebook, not by observation, but by accident. Nor can we accept as sincere his vision of Paul's walk, the land's epitome, the lesser Isle of Great Britain. If we would find its stale knights and captains out of service, its men of long rapiers and long breeches, we would rather seek them in the plays of Jonson and Dekker, who knew them well, than in the book of this amiable country parson, who viewed them from the pit of a theatre.   On the other hand, Earle paints those that inhabit his own world with a rare tact and rarer humour.   He gives them their right professions, and he decks them out with the trappings that belong to each.   You may know his young raw Preacher, as he knew him, 'by his narrow velvet cape, and his serge facing, and his ruff next his hair, the shortest thing about him.' His plain country fellow stands before you, house and all.   'His habitation is some poor thatched roof, distinguished from his barn by the loopholes that let out smoke, which the rain had long since washed throrow, but for the double ceiling of bacon on the inside, which has hung there since his grandsire's time, and is yet to make rashers for posterity.'   Is it any wonder that such a man should think 'Noah's flood the greatest plague that ever was, not because it drowned the world, but spoiled the grass?'

The chief lesson of Earle's book also is the uniformity of human nature, and nowhere does he teach this lesson more clearly than in his sketches of the University.   How well we know the mere young gentleman 'who comes there to wear a gown, and to say hereafter he has been at the University, whose companion is ordinarily some stale fellow that has been notorious for an ingle to gold hatbands,

which he admires at first and afterwards scorns'!
With how kind a sympathy does he show us an old
college butler, who is 'none of the worst students in
the house, for he keeps the set hours at his book
more duly than any,' and who 'domineers over the
Freshmen when they first come to the hatch'!
And the University Dun, is he not the same to-day
as when he sat for his portrait to the ingenious
Earle? 'He is very expensive of his time,' we are
told, 'for he will wait upon your stairs a whole
afternoon, and dance attendance with more patience
than a gentleman usher. . . . He grumbles at the
ingratitude of men that shun him for his kindness,
but indeed it is his own fault, for he is too great
an upbraider. No man puts them more to their
brain than he, and by shifting him off they learn to
shift in the world.' With equal justice Earle
describes the hangers-on of scholarship—the Antiquary, who loves all things as Dutchmen love cheese,
'the better for being mouldy and worm-eaten';
the Pot-Poet, the dregs of wit, 'a man now much
employed in commendation of our Navy, and a
bitter inveigher against the Spaniard'; and best of
all, the Pretender to Learning, that gentleman
whom we all know, a great nomenclator of authors,
which he has read in the catalogue, 'who never
talks of anything but learning, and learns all from
talking.' In conclusion, when Earle writes of that
which comes within the circuit of his experience,
he writes with a truth, a humour and a skill of

phrase which few of his rivals surpass, and which, if
we forget the claims of invention, entitle him to
as high a place as Overbury's in the history of the
'Character.'

As I have said, the drawing of 'Characters' was
for the idealist a means of expressing the hope that
was in him. Nor did George Herbert disdain to
employ, for his own purpose, the literary form
handled with equal skill and to another end by
Overbury and Mynshull. *A Priest to the Temple,
or the Country Parson, his Character and Rule of
Holy Life* (1632), is a sanguine sketch of what the
Parson's Character should be. It is a vision of
excellence, not a picture of reality, and it is seen
by a devout and simple soul. Different as Herbert's
aim was, his method is precisely the method of his
predecessors. His sentences have the same arrange-
ment ; they rise and fall to the same cadences.
Each chapter begins with a brief enumeration of
qualities, and if it ends in exhortation, that is exacted
by its subject. For instance : ' The Country Parson
is full of all knowledge. They say it is an ill Mason
that refuseth any stone : and there is no knowledge,
but, in a skilful hand, serves either positively as it is,
or else to illlustrate some other knowledge. He
condescends even to the knowledge of tillage and
pasturage. . . . But the chief and top of his knowledge consists in the Book of Books, the storehouse
and magazine of life and comfort, the Holy Scrip-
tures. There he sucks and lives.' And again :

'The Country Parson, as soon as he wakes on Sunday morning, presently falls to work, and seems to himself so as a Market man is when the Market-day comes, or a shopkeeper when customers use to come in. His thoughts are full of making the best of the day and contriving it to his best gains.'

In these two passages it is not difficult to recognise the technical processes of other and secular writers, and George Herbert's adoption of the 'Character' best proves its elasticity. And no more violent contrast could be found, in matter, though the manner is the same, to Herbert's quiet idealism, which calls up before our eyes the tranquil places of the earth, the grave church, the homely parsonage, the yew-shadowed churchyard of a remote and pleasant village, than the 'Characters' of Samuel Butler, which are full of strife and violence, and which on every page provoke discussion and challenge to the fray. It was not for the author of *Hudibras* to use any other than a boisterous humour. He was a fighter who never shrank from the field, and who struck at his foes as fiercely in the prose of his 'Characters' as in the inspired doggerel of his verse. Their wit is as turbulent as their temper, and if in the end we find them tedious, that is because we cannot dine off sauces, and because Butler refuses to mitigate his bitter seasonings with a morsel of bread or a plain piece of beefsteak. Nevertheless it is a curiosity of literature that George Herbert and Samuel Butler, each in a single work, should confess a common ancestry, that Hall and Overbury should divide the credit of having been examples to talents so diverse as these.

Butler was neither the first nor the last to see the value of the 'Character' in political controversy. The pamphleteers of a militant age took it in hand, and fashioned it valiantly to their use. The ardent discussions of the seventeenth century found in the unconscious following of Theophrastus the quickest outlet for their malignant humours. There was scarce a statesman who was not pilloried in the name of the class to which he was supposed to belong. And from the hustings the fashion of character-drawing passed into history. Clarendon and Burnet, to give but two instances, were not content to record events, to cite the mere names of soldiers and politicians. They must fit each hero, each villain, with an appropriate character; and so well did they practise the art, that we know their contemporaries as well as we know our own. Thus it is by an irony of chance that they too owed something to the ingenuity of a poor hapless courtier, who fell a victim many years before their time to the fierce passions of love and hate. As he lay dying in the Tower, Sir Thomas Overbury thought only of that last letter, which he prayed would involve Northampton in the net of eternal shame. And by one of the accidents which defeat the settled purposes of men, the letter was speedily forgotten, to be remembered long after only by the curious, and the

book of *Characters* which doubtless their author
thought scattered to the winds of heaven, was
sent down the stream of Time to make him famous
in the eyes of those, who knew not the scandal of
his life, and to be an example to a vast number of
writers and pamphleteers, hardly conscious of the
debt they owed.

GEORGE BUCHANAN

GEORGE BUCHANAN

I

GEORGE BUCHANAN was the type and exemplar of the wandering Scot. He was of the adventurous band which once made its country's name glorious for arms and arts from one end of Europe to another. If the hard life of an inhospitable land sent forth the many profound scholars and brave soldiers who taught and fought wherever there was a professor's rostrum or a field of battle, the kindlier soil of France or High Germany encouraged the growth both of learning and courage. The Scots abroad proved themselves as nimble with their swords as with their brains. They were as ready to enter a quarrel as to begin an argument. *Fier comme ung Escossois* passed into a commonplace; and it is not surprising, when we remember how quick to anger and valiant in combat were the heroes of the sixteenth century. There was Thomas Dempster, for instance, who not only professed the humanities at Toulouse and Paris, at Pisa and Bologna, but who was so stout a man of his hands that he once made prisoners three soldiers sent to castigate him. And there was Francis Sinclair, who fought mathematically, and

mathematicised like a soldier. And there was
James Crichton, *Scotus Admirabilis*, whose prowess
in the schools and in the tourney has been celebrated
by the most eloquent of his compatriots, and who
for three centuries has inhabited the gracious realm
of romance.

Thus from the Netherlands to Muscovy the
Scots met the scholars of all nations on equal terms.
The world, sharply divided by politics, knew no
boundaries of intelligence, and as Latin was the
universal language, human intercourse was not
hindered by diversity of speech. There was no
essential difference, save in the quality of the
professors, between the colleges of Scotland and
France. And George Buchanan, in leaving his
own land, changed neither his tongue nor the
course of his instruction. Born in 1506, of a family
that was more ancient than rich, he lost his father in
early youth, and was sent by an uncle to Paris in
1520 ; and thus he began the life of a wandering
scholar, which ceased only with his final return
to Scotland after forty adventurous years. The
Paris to which he came was the last stronghold
of scholasticism. The new learning had not yet
crossed the Alps, and the study of Greek, which
Erasmus had carried to Cambridge twenty years
before, was still regarded in Paris as pestilent and
heretical. But Buchanan was not checked on the
road of scholarship by the scruples of faith. Already
profoundly versed in the reading and writing of

Latin, he presently taught himself Greek, and, when the years had matured his talent, his knowledge of the classical tongues was unrivalled in France.

Meanwhile his ardour for learning had suffered a check. In 1522 his uncle died, and poverty sent him back to Scotland for a while. Here he took part in the Duke of Albany's hapless expedition against England, and won that acquaintance with warfare which well became the scholars of his time. A year later he visited St. Andrews, that he might sit at the feet of John Major, who, to cite Buchanan's own words, 'tum ibi dialecticen, aut verius sophisticen, in extrema senectute docebat.' That Buchanan ever had much sympathy with the system of John Major, the last and greatest of the schoolmen, is unlikely, and before long he became one of the old professor's bitterest opponents. But his sojourn at St. Andrews taught him the worst of the ancient method, and inspired the lines which, together with Rabelais' contemptuous reference, keep alive the fame and name of Major. Among the books which Pantagruel found in the library of St. Victor was Major's treatise *De modo faciendi boudinos.* Buchanan is more highly elaborate in his satire than Rabelais. Here is his epigram :

> 'Cum scateat nugis solo cognomine Major,
>   Nec sit in immenso pagina sana libro :
> Non mirum, titulis quod se veracibus ornat :
>   Nec semper mendax fingere Creta solet.'

Buchanan, however, did not remain long in Scotland. In a few years he was back in Paris, living the hard life of a beggar-student, picking up a crust where he might, and engaged in a fierce tussle with fortune. And then increasing renown brought him prosperity. Not merely was he Regent at Ste. Barbe, the most highly enlightened college in Paris, but he held the honourable office of Procurator in the German Nation. Yet none knew better than he the penalties of scholarship. In the sixteenth as in the eighteenth century the reward of learning and poetry was 'toil, envy, want, the patron, and the jail.' The deepest erudition was not enough to save a professor from neglect. Devotion to the classics was powerless against the indifference of loafing students. In an elegy on the miserable lot of those who taught the humanities in Paris, George Buchanan has described with much feeling the hardships which he himself suffered. At four o'clock a watchman aroused the college from a tardy and broken slumber. At five a bell summoned the scholars to their work. Then there enters the master in cap and gown, his cane in one hand, his Virgil in the other: in vain he insists upon silence; in vain he expounds the text of the poet; the scholars sleep or look about them, complain of sickness or write their letters home. Then the master must needs use his rod, and the day, begun in sloth, is passed in tears.

So the foolish round of sleep and toil is complete,

with hardly an hour for dinner. And, even if the master ensures a moment's tranquillity, he is soon disturbed by a racketing crowd of idlers from the city, under whose iron-bound shoes the very earth trembles. And how is the wretch repaid ? By the ingratitude of scholars, the discontent of parents, and by grinding poverty :

> 'Denique quicquid agis, comes assidet improba egestas,
>   Sive poema canis, sive poema doces.'

Buchanan both sang and taught, with small profit to himself, and his farewell to the Muses, said when he left the college of Ste. Barbe, was doubtless sincere, despite its formality. 'Ite leves nugæ,' said the poet in bitterness of heart,

> 'Ite leves nugæ, sterilesque valete Camœnæ,
>   Grataque Phœbæo Castalis unda choro.
> Ite, sat est : primos vobiscum absumpsimus annos,
>   Optima pars vitæ deperiitque meæ.'

Nevertheless, Buchanan's vocation was loud and imperious. Like many a college don before and since, he clung to the office which he affected to despise. Born to scholarship, he could not avoid his destiny ; and his happiness was complete if only he were permitted the privilege of complaint. After all, were there not compensations in a life of study ? What mattered it that he got up early, sat up late, and ate the bread of sorrow, if he might surprise the secrets of the past and echo in his numbers the voice of Virgil and Horace ? Nor must it be forgotten

that Buchanan's profession summoned him to the
land he loved best in the world. To him, indeed,
as to countless others, France was at once a solace
and an inspiration. Three centuries after Buchanan,
Thackeray paid his tribute of respect. 'I never
landed at Calais pier,' said he, 'without feeling that
a load of sorrow was left on the other side of the
water.' And when Buchanan had deserted the arid
wastes of Lusitania and the pasturage fertile only in
poverty, he sang so noble a pæan to France as proved
that the horror of the watchman's bell was not
always in his ear. In his best iambics he greets the
happy land of Gaul, 'bonarum blanda nutrix artium.'
He celebrates her nimble air and fertile soil,
her wooded glades and sheep-covered downs, her
mountain streams, her stately rivers, and her
hospitable ports. He pays homage to her splendid
cities, her modest life, her easy converse, her polished
manners. But, declares he, if she be amiable in
peace, she is unconquerable in war—an amiable
friend and a gallant enemy. What wonder, then, if
he pay the allegiance of a son? 'Ni patrio te amore
diligam,' he writes,

> 'et colam
> Dum vivo, rursus non recuso visere
> Jejuna miseræ tesqua Lusitaniæ,
> Glebasque tantum fertiles penuriæ.'

His fidelity to France severed him for many a
year from his native land. But in 1535 he returned
thither with the Earl of Cassilis for a pupil, and, as

is proved by the Treasurer's Accounts,[1] was closely bound for some years to the Court. On 16th February 1535, by the king's gracious precept and special command, George Buchanan received so many ells of 'paries blak' for the making of a gown and other liveries—viz. hose, bonnets, hocquetons, and doublets. And three years later the munificent gift was repeated. But, confident in the friendship of the Court, Buchanan had grossly offended the rulers of the Church. Inspired, one likes to think, by the example of Rabelais, he had attacked the Franciscans in a set of bitter, rasping satires. He had held up to the general ridicule their sloth, their greed, their ignorance. His verses, courageous as they were sincere, won the approval of the king; but not even the king could save the poet from punishment, and he was thrown into prison under suspicion of harbouring Lutheran doctrines. On his enlargement nothing remained save flight, and after a brief sojourn in England he once more found refuge in the kindly city of Paris.

Here a bitter disappointment awaited him. The worst of all his enemies, Cardinal Beaton, was there on an embassy, and lost no time in stirring up the French Government to avenge the insulted Franciscans. Unwilling to offend the Scottish Ambassador, Paris threatened Buchanan with expulsion or imprisonment; and he, like many another

[1] These are quoted in Mr. Hume Brown's erudite *Life of George Buchanan*.

persecuted scholar, bowed to the storm. Discreetly leaving the capital, he made his way to Bordeaux, where his friend, André de Gouvéa, presided over the Collége de Guyenne, and where a chair was speedily found for him. Fortunate in his colleagues, he was fortunate also in his pupils. Among them he numbered Montaigne, who amply repaid the debt of gratitude he owed his master by such a meed of praise as was sufficient of itself to confer immortality. 'The famous Scottish Poet'—thus he described him, and after this handsome tribute we cannot grudge the Essayist the trifling boast, wherewith he capped it. George Buchanan and his other domestic tutors often told him, said he, 'that in his infancy he had the Latin tongue so ready and perfect that themselves feared to take him in hand.' Nor was this all : he further declared that when Buchanan—whom afterward he saw attending the Mareschal de Brissac—was about to write a treatise on the instruction of children, he took the model and pattern from him. For this statement there is no support, yet it matters not, since Montaigne has explained his own method with a fulness of eloquence and illustration after which Buchanan, his master, might have limped in vain.

Such was Buchanan's good fortune, even in times of stress, to be honoured in the honour of his pupils. And his sojourn at Bordeaux, by knitting more closely the ties of friendship which bound him to André de Gouvéa, persuaded him to the adventure which he regarded as the unhappiest of his career, but which the eye of romance may contemplate without displeasure. In 1547 King John of Portugal desired to restore the University of Coimbra to eminence, and he invited André de Gouvéa to undertake the task. De Gouvéa, consenting, enrolled such of his ancient colleagues as were willing to teach humane letters and the rudiments of Aristotle's philosophy. Buchanan, as he tells us, needed little inducement to accept de Gouvéa's proposal. The whole of Europe was at war or on the verge of war ; and the scholar, who had now passed his eighth lustrum, confesses that he saw in Portugal the one corner likely to remain undisturbed. Moreover, he was invited not so much to travel as to live among friends and neighbours, and so hopefully did he view the prospect that he asked his brother Patrick to be of the party.

Alas, for human hopes ! Within a year de Gouvéa was dead, the College of Coimbra had closed its doors, and Buchanan and his colleagues were handed over to the Inquisition. Upon Buchanan the misfortune fell most heavily. The Church had an ancient score to settle with the scourger of monks, though the king had promised to overlook the offence ; and the voice of detraction was soon busy. He had eaten meat in Lent, said one, which, in fact, was the general habit of Spain. He had declared, said another, that Augustine's views on the Eucharist were heretical. It was affirmed by more than one witness that he was not a sound Catholic. And his persecutors, in zeal for their faith, shut him up in a monastery, that he might be taught the true doctrine by a set of monks who, as he confesses, were not inhuman nor evilly-disposed, but merely ignorant. That the scholar chafed at the impertinence is plain enough. But he solaced his leisure by turning the Psalms into Latin verse, and he took the first chance, offered by a Cretan ship, to make his way to England.[1]

II

Such are some of the adventures which befell this travelling Scot on his journey through the world.

[1] Buchanan's hardship, great as it was for a sensitive scholar to bear, was not unprovoked nor wholly unjust. It has been involved by partisans in a mist of prejudice. The truth is simple enough, if we remember the state of opinion and Buchanan's own love of free speech. He was clearly treated with consideration, and he himself made no complaint. Neither Cardinal Beaton nor the Franciscans had a hand in the prosecution as has been pretended. Beaton was dead, and the chief witness against Buchanan was a Dominican. The Inquisition does not seem to have acted harshly. Buchanan at his trial confessed that he had vacillated and had been persuaded at one moment to embrace Lutheranism—a confession which could not in the Portugal of the sixteenth century be lightly passed over. His conduct throughout the discussion was absolutely correct, and he showed both wisdom and courage in confronting his judges. His imprisonment was never close, and he was soon put on his parole and 'permitted to quit the monastery in which he was, and go to the city.' See *George Buchanan in the Lisbon Inquisition*, by G. J. C. Hennriques, Lisbon: 1906.

With Latin for a key to unlock the gates of learning, he taught and lectured wherever his destiny
placed him. And all the while he had pursued his
true craft of letters with zeal and success. During
his sojourn in France the triumph of Humanism had
been complete, and few scholars had made themselves better masters of the New Learning than
George Buchanan. Wherever scholasticism found
an enemy, Buchanan found a friend. He fought
against the folly of Duns Scotus and the superstitions
of the monks with as keen a blade as any of them.
His literary fame made him a citizen of the whole
world. Nor is it a wild conjecture to suppose that
he lived on terms of easy friendship with the leaders
of the school. Guillaume Budé and Vinet were his
intimates, and surely Budé must have made him
acquainted with the great Rabelais himself. That
Rabelais frequented the society of Scots has been
proved by the fact, ingeniously demonstrated by
Professor Ker, that Panurge, in displaying his
knowledge of the English tongue, used the dialect
of North Britain.[1] Nor was Budé the only link

---

[1] Is it too fantastic to suggest that Rabelais learned the
little English (or Scots) that he had from Buchanan himself?
The careers of the two men were parallel, and the legendary
Buchanan owed not a little to Rabelais. All the chapbooks
describe George Buchanan's encounter with a French or Italian
professor of signs, and it is clear where he came from. If
Buchanan was not Rabelais' master of Scots, then surely it was
Florence Wilson, another friend and secretary of Cardinal du
Bellay.

which might have united Buchanan and Rabelais. Briand de Vallée was the friend of both, and while Buchanan addressed to this Senator of Bordeaux a witty and characteristic elegy, *pro Lena Apologia*, to Rabelais he was ' le tant bon, tant vertueux, tant docte et équitable président Briand de Vallée, Seigneur du Douhet.' There remains Cardinal du Bellay, who knew them both, and doubtless extolled to each the virtues of the other.

But there is a yet graver reason why Buchanan and Rabelais should have been well acquainted. The end and purpose of their writings was the same. They assailed the same abuses, they preached the same gospel. If you may compare dissimilar things, it might be said that Buchanan was the Scottish Rabelais. His early works were designed, like *Gargantua* and *Pantagruel*, for the encouragement of sound learning and good-humour, and for the discomfiture of idle friars and other squint-minded persons. Though nothing could be farther apart than Buchanan's trim Latin and the coloured, authentic speech of Rabelais, *Somnium*, *Palinodia*, and *Franciscanus* are a genuine, if frugal, rendering of Pantagruelism. Buchanan was as little devoted to a cloistered life as Rabelais. He, too, lived freely in the world ; he, too, enjoyed the sounds and sights of the open air ; he, too, refused to pass his days in the idle mortification of the flesh ; and it is difficult to believe that the two evangelists of learning and merriment, sharing the same friends, did not also frequent the same taverns.

And during his many years of wandering, Buchanan met with all the respect that is shown to a master. He was poor ; perhaps he was hungry ; but he always preserved the dignity of his calling. If literature was not lucrative, at least it was distinguished ; and if the writer's pockets were empty, his profession skilled him in the writing of begging-letters. Though he was no rival to Erasmus in the delicate art of extracting money from the rich man's pocket by cunning words, he was not without proficiency, as many an epigram remains to show. It was his amiable practice to flatter his patron in verse, and to hide the serious object of his quest beneath the sheltering cloak of humour. On one occasion he suggests to Lennox that he will gladly receive anything he may give him except his gout ; and it is thus that he persuades Mary to benevolence, in the days before he assailed her with bitter words :

> ' Do quod adest : opto quod abest tibi : dona darentur
>   Aurea, sors animo si foret æqua meo.
> Hoc leve si credis, paribus me ulciscere donis :
>   Et quod abest, opta tu mihi : da quod adest.'

To-day the patron is dead, and the client is despised. It is not surprising, therefore, that Buchanan's importunity has appeared disgraceful to many. But without reason. In the sixteenth century there was no eager public to dictate what should be written for its amusement, and the man of

letters thought it as little shame.to ask for money as
kings and nobles to give it. And who should demand
these honourable alms, if not George Buchanan?
By common consent he was regarded as the first
poet of his time. Montaigne's tribute has already
been quoted—'ce grand poëte escossois,'—and it
does not stand alone. Estienne, in a preface to the
poet's version of the Psalms, described him as 'poet-
arum nostri sæculi facile princeps.' Guy Patin,
using the very language of hyperbole, declared that
Virgil wrote no better verses than Buchanan, and
that it took fifteen centuries to make another Virgil.
And Joseph Scaliger, not to be outdone, composed
an epigram of equal happiness and extravagance to
the one poet who, as he said, left all others in Europe
behind :

> 'Namque ad supremum perducta Poetica culmen
>   In te stat, nec quo progrediatur habet.
> Imperii fuerat Romani Scotia limes :
>   Romani eloquii Scotia finis erit.'

In these four lines are all the qualities of the lapidary
style. They are not too long to be cut upon stone,
and it is evident that Scaliger, in writing them, was
not upon oath.

III

Thus the chorus of praise was swelled, and we
cannot but ask, Was it justified? At the outset, let
it be said that we must not judge the poets and
critics of the sixteenth century by the standards of

to-day. Latin was then the universal language of cultivated Europe, and scholars wrote, as they thought, in what is now a dead language. Where Erasmus, the greatest man of letters among them all, led the way, why should not Buchanan follow? By avoiding his own vernacular he put the polish of culture on his verse and immeasurably increased his audience. He knew not that thus he was bartering the chance of immortality for an immediate fame. Great in his own age, he is but the shadow of a name in ours. He added nothing to the sum of human expression. He did not extend the boundary stone of poetry by a single hand's-breadth. He put on the style of others, as a man may wear a borrowed overcoat, and though the style fitted him it was not his own.

Now, convention is the essence of all the arts. Conventionality, which is the vice of convention, as sentimentality is the vice of sentiment, is their bane. Poets, like runners, 'vitaï lampada tradunt.' And Buchanan did not take the lamp from him who went before; he rummaged in the dust-heap of antiquity for an ancient lantern. Though the lantern which he found had once been bright, the choice was arbitrary. In other words, he used phrases, the coinage of a broken and revived tradition, which were more nearly allied to the lecture-hall than to literature. His poems were written not because Buchanan was forced to write them, but because somebody else had written something which he thought worthy of imitation. Such is the road not of life but of death, and he who follows it is an antiquary rather than a poet. And thus it is that two lines written in the white heat of inspiration by Robert Burns are worth the complete works of him who, in Scaliger's eyes, had reached the top and pinnacle of poetic eminence.

It is, therefore, not among the authentic poets of the world that we must rank Buchanan. He did but compose exercises of unrivalled wit and elegance. Not even his *Calendæ Maiæ*, which won the admiration of Wordsworth, entitles him to wear the bays. But his Muse, as he called her, was apt for every enterprise, grave or joyous, complimentary or satiric. Her ease was as conspicuous as her variety. Wherever Horace or Virgil, Seneca or Martial, gave the lead, she followed with spirit and address. As a Latin versifier, indeed, Buchanan deserved all the praise that has been heaped upon him by the lavish hand of Scaliger and others. Though he was not guiltless of false quantities, the fact that he allowed himself certain freedoms forbidden to schoolboys proves that he handled his material like a man of letters, and not like a pedant. Whether he excelled in satire or in drama, in epigram or in elegy, in epic or in song, the curious may dispute. It is the dead level of excellence which appears ominous to the critic.

His mastery of many forms is equalled by his skill in the treatment of the classic metres. Hexameters,

elegiacs, hendecasyllabics, iambics, sapphics, alcaics,
asclepiads,—he uses them with licence and facility.
He was an adept in all the arts of honour and
compliment. Of the many kings who ruled in his
time, there are few at whose feet he did not lay the
tribute of his praise. Charles V., 'Vasconidis reg-
nator aquæ'; Mary Stuart and Francis, 'fortunati
ambo, et felici tempore nati, et thalamis juncti';
Elizabeth, 'regina, princeps optima principum';
Henry VIII., whom 'virtus Diis immortalibus æquum
efficit,'—he hymned them all in terms of elegant
extravagance. It need not be supposed that in these
exercises Buchanan's loyalty was deeply engaged.
It is the man of letters, not the patriot, who speaks
in their well-turned lines. And he was as eloquent
in satire as in encomium. It has already been said
how he followed the same road as Rabelais in denouncing the monks : his *Franciscanus* and his *Fratres
Fraterrimi* will remain models of their kind so long
as they find readers. In his tragedies *Jephthes* and
Baptistes he set himself to rival Seneca; in his
translations from Euripides, wherein Montaigne
acted a part, he broke a lance with Erasmus himself.
That he did all these things well is beyond cavil or
dispute. Were they worth doing ? Time has given
a melancholy answer to the question.

When Buchanan was imprisoned in Portugal, he
beguiled his leisure, as has been said, by making his
celebrated paraphrase of the Psalms, the best-known
and in some respects the most skilful of his works.

It is not a translation in the literal sense, but a collection of poems, composed in various metres, on the themes of the Psalms. Read wherever the Latin tongue was understood, Buchanan's paraphrase gave him a universal fame, and it is only a growing ignorance of the dead languages that has thrust it back into the bundle of literary curiosities. And, by a coincidence that has surprised some, Buchanan was addressing verses to Neæra, Leonora, and the rest at the very moment that he was composing his version of the Psalms. The coincidence is not surprising. As Paul Verlaine, a poet of our own times, has insisted, man is a duplex creature, whom it amuses to express both sides of his genius at the same time. So Verlaine himself wrote *Parallèlement* as a relief to the austerity of *Sagesse* and *Bonheur*. So Buchanan took refuge from the Psalms in such love-poems as his rugged temper could devise. And the conjunction is less remarkable in Buchanan, because Leonora and Neæra were no more to him than were Julia and Anthea to the author of the *Hesperides*.

His Muse, like Herrick's, was doubtless more jocund than his life; and the biographer who has been at the pains to clear him of a moral taint is merely ploughing the sands. Had not Catullus reproached his Lesbia with infidelity in sincere and immortal verse, Buchanan would have found no fault with the ladies of Portugal. But he was not one to shrink from his duty, and without diffidence he

attempted to rival the greatest poet of them all.
His courage, indeed, outran his discretion. Catullus
puts no word upon paper at which he has not
writhed and bled. Buchanan, in obedient pupilage,
turns the armoury of rhetorical abuse upon Leonora,
who was bred and lived in his fancy. With her for
excuse, he exhausts the terms of obloquy and reproach.
'Matre impudica filia impudicior,'—thus he addresses
her, conscious, as you are, of the phrase's origin.
With the candour of one who has never known or
respected women, he catalogues her imperfections :

> 'Miniata labra, sordidæ creta genæ,
>   Hiatus oris indecens
>   Rictu canino.'

And so on with wearisome iteration. He declares
that she is as false as her painted face, her lying
tongue, her brazen ring, and her gem that is but
glass. And the declaration is made with so frank
a brutality, that she is obviously no more than an
exercise in Latin versification. Neæra is the invention of a finer subtlety. Though she, too, is
the child of letters, not of experience, she is nearer
to human life than her erring sister. One epigram
there is, dedicated to her name, which should hold
a place in every anthology :

> 'Illa mihi semper præsenti dura Neæra.
>   Me quoties absum semper abesse dolet ;
>   Non desiderio nostri, non mæret amore,
>   Sed se non nostro posse dolore frui.'

Ingenious as they are, these lines have been

turned into English with equal ingenuity by James Hannay :

> ' Neæra is harsh at our every greeting ;
> Whene'er I am absent, she wants me again ;
> 'Tis not that she loves me, or cares for our meeting—
> She misses the pleasure of seeing my pain.'

And Neæra has yet another claim to our gratitude. Did not the tangles of her hair suggest to Milton an exquisite phrase ?

IV

In 1561 Buchanan, after many years of absence, returned to Scotland. He returned in an evil hour. Hitherto he had lived the tranquil life of a scholar and poet. It was now his destiny to mingle in the bitter fray of politics and theology. That he should have come badly out of it was foregone. As he had not been bred to affairs, so he had escaped, with a single bruise, the religious persecutions which had disgraced the continent of Europe. He was made of the same stuff as Erasmus and Rabelais, who thought that scholars might better serve the cause of learning than by being burnt alive. And he came to a country devastated by the passion of fanatical divines. His humanism could not endure the strain of Knox's friendship. He descended from the professor's chair to the stool of the pamphleteer, and ever since his reputation has suffered. At first fortune smiled upon him. He found employment about the Court. He became a favourite of Queen

Mary, with whom he read Livy, and to whom he addressed verses of ecstatic adulation. And then Darnley was murdered, and for Buchanan all was changed. Turned in an instant to a bitter partisan, he dipped his pen in the gall of gossip and slander, and in his famous *Detectio* he assailed Mary without ruth or scruple. For so doing his enemies have reproached him with ingratitude and inconsistency, and they have reproached him, it seems, unjustly.

No man is compelled to hold with unwavering tenacity the opinion which once he thought prudent. A crime may absolve the blandest courtier from the duty of continued devotion. The death of Darnley may have been for Buchanan a sufficient reason for opposing Mary and her policy with all his strength. We cannot blame him for transferring his allegiance. What is unpardonable in Buchanan is the method of his attack. A scholar and a humanist should not stoop to collect the tittle-tattle of the kitchen. He should not listen with an avid ear to the voice of malice. It is consonant neither with learning nor chivalry to insult a woman and a queen. The guilt or innocence of Mary does not palliate or enhance the crime of Buchanan. Whoever was right, he was wrong ; and he may not even plead the poor excuse of religious fanaticism. Nevertheless, as we read the *Detectio*, we cannot but admire the skill of its author. It is a masterpiece of violent, calculated invective. So well arranged is it, so faithfully does it obey the laws of controversy, that Buchanan's head seems more deeply engaged than his heart. And the kindest view to take of the episode is that Mary was to his imagination as unreal a personage as the shameful, shameless Leonora herself.

But while the manner of the work is an evident disgrace, it did no violence to the author's political creed. Now, Buchanan, who believed in the pagan world as devoutly as his pupil Montaigne, derived his opinions concerning governors and government from the same source as the Essayist. It was Plutarch and the classics from whom he learnt the familiar lesson of liberty and of the popular control of kings. He was no believer in the doctrine of divine right. Harmodios and Aristogeiton were doubtless among his heroes, and he, too, would have approved by word, if not by deed, the supreme act of tyrannicide. He held, in brief, that a king might rule only so long as he retained the confidence and respect of the people ; and if his point of view was philosophic rather than political, he did not change it in the course of a long life. In verse and prose he taught the same lesson. A king, said he, must be wise, or his subjects have the right of vengeance : and it is interesting to note that, while he himself trained the most foolish king that ever sat upon the throne, his treatise *De Jure Regni* helped to prepare the way for the Great Rebellion and the Deposition of Charles I.

Buchanan's attack upon Mary was rewarded by more than thirty pieces of silver. Though wealth escaped him, he lived henceforth in dignity and esteem. He was of the Commission which carried the indictment against Mary to London. He was appointed tutor to James VI., and thereafter he held many distinguished and honourable posts. As Director of the Chancery and Keeper of the Privy Seal, he could exert an influence which never had been his in the Universities of Europe. But his career lay not in the field of politics. Being a theorist and a man of letters, he was more at ease in making the best of King James's intellect, and in composing his last work—*Rerum Scoticarum Historia*,—a vast tome, which is shut off from the general reader by its excellent Latinity, and which, composed before the days of historical criticism, does not carry a heavy weight of authority.

V

It is not easy to discover the essential character of George Buchanan. This one episode in his career —the attack upon Queen Mary—has aroused so thick a cloud of controversy, that the man himself has been obscured. But it was a mere episode, and though it has coloured the popular opinion with prejudice, it cannot diminish Buchanan's services to humanism and literature. When he wrote the *Detectio* he had passed his sixtieth year, and he may fairly be judged by what he achieved before ever he soiled his hands with politics. As has been said, he was a scholar of liberal understanding and vast

erudition.   If he was neither so witty as Erasmus nor
so humorous as Rabelais, the spirit of those great men
breathed within him.   Though he did not possess
the same originality of mind which persuaded
Master Alcofribas to discard Latin and to discover a
noble, genuine prose of his own, though he erred in
believing that classical Latin was the universal
language of scholarship, he erred with Erasmus and
Boccaccio and many another greater man than himself.

And assuredly he was all untainted by the sin of
pedantry.   No man was ever more fitted by temper
and breeding to live in the larger, fresher air of life.
Ronsard, a witness of truth, said that there was
nothing of the pedant in him save the cap and
gown ; and had it not been for the strife of politics
the charge of pedantry would never have been
brought against him.   As he bitterly opposed John
Major and the Schoolmen, so for the greater part of
his life he kept aloof from the murderous quarrels
of the theologians.   He was neither Catholic nor
Lutheran.   While he fortified himself with reasons
why he should not become a Franciscan, he had
never even a momentary intention of taking the
vows.   His portraits suggest that he was a man of
a dry, sardonic humour, contemptuous of fools, and
absolute in courage.   Yet in the ruggedness of his
unkempt features there is a touch of kindliness, an
evident love of banter, which make us regret that
we know little of him that is not revealed in his

work. How shall elegy or epigram be a true index of character? The rarest humanist may be forgiven if he cannot express his soul in classical Latin.

And for the most part Buchanan's contemporaries are silent concerning him. James Melville in his 'Diary' gives us a sketch, which we gladly accept in default of a better. Now, Melville visited him with some friends a year before his death, when his History was under the press. 'When we cam to his chalmer'—thus writes the diarist—'we fand him sitting in his chaire, teatching his young man that servit in his chalmer to spell a, b, ab; e, b, eb. Efter salutation, Mr Andro sayes, "I sie, sir, yie are nocht ydle." "Better this," quoth he, "nor stelling sheipe, or sitting ydle, quhilk is als ill." Therefter he schew us the Epistle Dedicatorie to the King; the quhilk, when Mr Andro had read, he tauld him that it was obscure in some places, and wanted certean words to perfyt the sentence. Sayes he, "I may do na mair for thinking on another mater." "What is that?" sayes Mr Andro. "To die," quoth he; "bot I leave that and manie ma things for you to help."'

It is not much, but it is the sole authentic utterance of George Buchanan, and if it does nought else, it proves him to have been abrupt in utterance and parsimonious of speech. Another Melville—Sir James—has drawn a character of Buchanan which is at once truthful and ingenious, and which is perhaps the justest estimate left us by a contemporary.

'Mester George,' says he, contrasting him with Peter Young, 'laith till offend the King at any tym,'

'was a stoik philosopher, and looked not far before the hand; a man of notable qualities for his learning and knawledge in Latin poesie, mekle maid accompt of in other contrees, plaisant in company, rehersing at all occasions moralities short and fecful, whereof he had aboundance, and invented wher he wanted. He was also of gud religion for a poet, bot he was easily abused, and sa facill that he was led with any company that he hanted for the tyme, quhilk maid him factious in his auld dayes; for he spak and wret as they that wer about him for the tym infourmed him. For he was become sleperie and cairles, and followed in many thingis the vulgair oppinion, for he was naturally populaire, and extrem vengeable against any man that had offendit him, quhilk was his gretest fault.'

Here are summed up the diverse qualities of the man. Here, also, is explained the sorry figure he cut in the political strife of his day. He spoke and wrote as he was told to write and speak by those about him. Surely that is the kindest construction to put upon the *Detectio*. 'He was become sleperie and cairles' —is that not a sufficient reason, and a wholly inadequate excuse, for his violence and scurrility? In brief, Buchanan, like all great men, was guilty of mistakes in conduct and policy. But when the death on which he long had pondered overtook him, he might depart with the happy reflection that only one gross sin burdened his soul, and that he had played an honourable part on the stage not only of Scotland but of Europe.

VI

As in life Buchanan most nearly resembled Rabelais of all his contemporaries, so after death he shared the same fate as the author of *Pantagruel*, and for the same reason. He passed into a legend of infamy and contempt. He became the hero of a chapbook,[1] the protagonist in many a foolish farce. That the greater injury might be done to his character, he was endowed by the authors of these scurrilous gibes with a ready understanding and a cunning wit. He is represented not merely as the teacher of King James, but as his private counsellor and his public fool. An adept in the selling of bargains and other kindred sports, he plays his silly games and cuts his coarse jests beneath many a rough woodcut. It may be said that this confusion of learning and folly symbolises the popular view of things. To know is to be an ass. Wisdom is but jesting. But that does not wholly explain the Buchanan of the chapbooks. He was born, as the legendary Rabelais was born, of monkish spite. What Puy-Herbault and the friars did for the reputation of Rabelais, the champions of the Catholic Church did for Buchanan. There was many an old score to be paid off. The satire of *Franciscanus* still rankled, and the attack upon Queen Mary merited revenge. And

[1] The chapbooks containing *The Witty and Entertaining Exploits of George Buchanan* have been popular in Scotland for several centuries, and are doubtless still to be purchased of book-pedlars and others.

it is not difficult to see when and how the infamous legend was constructed.

Buchanan, as Melville tells us, was 'plaisant in company, rehersing at all occasions moralities short and fecful, whereof he had aboundance, and invented wher he wanted.' That was enough for a beginning. Granted a ready wit, the rest was easy. At first he was painted as merely vicious, or as a miscreant, 'convicted of a design to eat the Paschal Lamb, after the manner of the Jews.'[1] But he soon vied with the Rabelais of Puy-Herbault in being 'never praised but for drunkenness.' Garasse, the eminent divine, assailed him while James I. was still upon the throne. 'I will tell our Atheists,'[2] said he, 'the wretched end of a Man of their Belief and Humour, as to eating and drinking. It was George Buchanan, a perfect Epicure during his Life, and a perfect Atheist at his Death.' According to Garasse, then, Buchanan was told by his doctors that if he abstained from wine he might live five or six years, and that if he continued to drink he could hold out three weeks at longest. 'Get you gone,' he exclaimed, 'with your Prescriptions and your course of Diet, and know that I would rather live three weeks and be drunk every day, than six years without drinking wine.' He was as good as his word. 'Having discharged his physicians like

[1] This charge was unfortunate, for, as he said at Lisbon, 'in his country there were no Jews.'

[2] This story and many others to the same purpose are cited in Bayle's Dictionary.

a desperate man, he ordered a Hogshead of *Graves*
Wine to be set at his Bed's-head, resolved to see
the bottom of it before he died, and he carried himself so valiantly that he emptied it to the lees.' And
the worst is not yet told. Having death and the
glass between his lips, he was exhorted to pray.
' "As for me," said he, still in his undisturbed and
perfect senses, "I never knew any other prayer than
this :

> Cinthia prima suis miserum me cepit ocellis,
> Contactum nullis ante cupidinibus."

And scarce had he repeated ten or twelve verses of
that Elegy of Propertius, when he expired among
the glasses and pints.'

It is a good story, and sufficient for a whole library
of slanders. It is vicious, it is valiant, it is quick in
repartee ; and the makers of the legend had soon a
solid foundation whereon to build. But it cannot be
said that the priestly enemies of Buchanan were rich
in invention. Not content with subjecting him to
the process of detraction to which they had subjected
Rabelais, they thought that the same stories might
serve for both. Of Rabelais it is told how once he
wished to get from Montpellier to Paris without encroaching on his own pocket. And so he wrote
upon packets of dust ' Poison for the King,' 'Poison
for the Queen,' and straightway being arrested made
his journey at the public expense. Buchanan, if we
may believe the chapbooks, played the same prank,

and travelled from Cornwall to London under a welcome arrest. These slanders touch Buchanan as lightly as they touch Rabelais. Poor in fancy, they are chiefly memorable because they prove the limits of the human intellect and the unchanging stupidity of revenge. As for Buchanan, so grave a scholar was he, so elegant a poet, that he can wear the fool's cap and jingle the fool's bells in the ears of the people without plucking a leaf from his crown of glory, without besmirching by a single blot the white shield of his fame.

EDWARD HALL

EDWARD HALL

EDWARD HALL, the eloquent panegyrist of Henry VIII., was born in London towards the end of the fifteenth century. His parents,[1] of gentle birth and affluent circumstances, gave their son the best education that the time afforded, and from Eton he proceeded, in 1514, to King's College, Cambridge, where he took his degree in due course. In the spurious edition of Wood's *Athenæ* it is claimed that he also studied at Oxford, but there is no evidence that he visited the other University, and the credit of his nurture is due to Cambridge alone. After leaving Cambridge, he entered Gray's Inn, where he speedily became eminent in the practice of the law. John Bale praises his eloquence and erudition, as well he might, since they were of the same side both in

---

[1] His father was John Hall, of Northall, in Shropshire, while his mother was Catherine, the daughter and heiress of Thomas Gedding. Herbert, quoted in Ames's *Typographical Antiquities*, gives him an august ancestry. 'These Halles,' says he, 'were of Kinnersley and Northall, in the county of Salop, and descended from Sir Francis Halle, a natural son of Albert, Archduke of Austria, King of the Romans, so called from being borne at the city of Halle in Tyrol.' The statement is improbable and unsupported.

politics and theology. 'Edvvardus Hallus,' says the
historian of English writers, 'politioribus a tenera
aetate literis adornatus, ex longo Brytannicarum
legum studio, peritissimus evasit.' Nor did his
industry and learning go without their reward.
In 1532 he was appointed Common Serjeant of
the City of London, and presently became a judge
in the Sheriff's Court. Though, like many a greater
man than himself, he has baffled the biographer, his
name occurs now and again in the records of the
time, and it is safe to conclude that his career was
successful as well as prudent. He was, as Fuller
says, 'well-affected to the Reformation': he ad-
hered, in prosperity as in disaster, to the king's
party; and he was not allowed to suffer for his
faithful allegiance. That the king can do no wrong
was the maxim of his life, as of his book; and he
followed Henry VIII. through the twists and turns
of his tortuous policy with a patient submissiveness
which was safe, if not always creditable. Not
merely did he approve the 'abolishing' of the papal
power and the declaration of the king's supremacy;
he made a speech in the Commons in favour of the
Six Articles, that whip with six strings, as the people
called it, which relentlessly undid the work of reform
His argument was characteristic: 'To be short,' said
he, 'in chronicles it may be found that the most part
of ceremonies now used in the Church of England
were by princes either first invented, or at the least
established; and, as we see, the same do till this day

continue.' Thus he would permit neither the clergy to propound and defend its doctrines, nor his fellow-citizens to exercise their private judgment. Moreover, he closed his harangue with a text wherewith he was ready to justify the last cruelties of his sovereign. 'For it is written,' exclaimed he, 'obey your King.' And he obeyed his king with a zeal, which he esteemed more highly than the truth, and which ensured his employment on many delicate occasions. He was one of the London Commissioners appointed in 1540 for the suppression of heresy; he visited Anne Askew in her cell, in the hope of hearing her recantation; and by way of recompense for his many services he received a grant of Abbey lands, which doubtless was a solace to his later years. We last hear of him as Member of Parliament for Bridgnorth, and in 1547 he died, thus escaping from the vengeance of Mary, which, had he survived, would surely have fallen upon him. The punishment which he avoided fell upon his family and his book. In 1555 his father and mother were in Newgate, receiving letters from John Bradford, ' for the testimony of the gospel,' while in the same year his book was burned by the queen's command, and thus rendered a rarity for ever.

And perhaps it was fitting that the book should be punished rather than the man, for the book is by far the more important. The deeds that were done by Edward Hall are uncertain and fall short of fame. His *Chronicle of England* is a possession for all time.

The title justly indicates the scope and purpose of the book. 'The Union of the two noble and illustrate famelies of Lancastre and Yorke,' thus it runs in the high-sounding terms of Tudor prose, 'beeyng long in continual discension for the croune of this noble realme, with all the actes done in bothe the tymes of the Princes, both of the one linage, and of the other, beginnyng at the tyme of Kyng Henry the Fowerth, the first aucthor of this devision, and so successively proceadyng to the reigne of the high and prudent prince, King Henry the Eight, the indubitate flower, and very heire of both the sayd linages' : such is the true and only hero of his book —King Henry VIII. The lives of this sovereign's predecessors do but lead on to his nobler renown. The deeds which they accomplished are memorable only because they prepared the way for the mighty achievements of the most splendid monarch that ever sat upon a throne. In brief, the Chronicle, so far as the death of Henry VII., is but a preface. And the author has marked the distinction with perfect clarity both in style and measure. He did not handle the facts which he learned from others with the same fulness and circumstance wherewith he described the events of his own time, and *The Triumphant Reign of Henry VIII.*, as Hall proudly styles it, is in all respects a separate and coherent biography.

The twofold nature of the work is illustrated also by the diverse opinions which the critics have held concerning its style. It is Roger Ascham, in his

Scholemaster who put the case against Hall with the greatest ingenuity. He points out in a well-known passage that some kind of Epitome may be profitably used by men of skilful judgment : ' as if a wise man,' says he, ' would take Halle's Chronicle, where moch good matter is quite marde with Indenture Englishe, and first change strange and inkhorne tearmes into commonlie used words : next, specially to wede out that, that is superfluous and idle, not onelie where words be vainlie heaped one upon an other, but also where many sentences, of one meaning, be so clowted up together as though M. Hall had bene, not writing the storie of England, but varying a sentence in Hitching schole.' Thus Ascham ; and then on the other hand we find Hearne, the Antiquary, and many another critic praising the 'masculine style' and direct utterance of the Chronicle. At first sight it would seem impossible to reconcile the opposing judgments, but a little thought will show that both are fair. Until he came to the reign of Henry VIII., Hall ' compiled and conjoyned ' his work out of widely-gathered materials. He overlooked none of the familiar authorities. The French and Latin chronicles, Hector Boetius, Johannes Major, Jean Bouchet, Polydore Vergil, who presently equalised the debt by borrowing from Hall, Trevisa, the author of the *Life of Richard III.*, which, like the rest, he ascribed to Sir Thomas More—he knew and quoted them all ; but, in order to make their matter his own, he marred it with what Ascham rightly calls 'Indenture Englishe.' Restless to contribute something of himself, he tricked out the facts of others in strange terms and bombastic periods. If you compare his *Life of Richard III.* with that called Sir Thomas More's, you will easily discern the process. The history is the same ; the very phrases are echoed; but Hall gives you the impression, in Ascham's excellent words, that he is 'varying a sentence in Hitching schole.' He could, when he chose, compose in pedantic English as well as any of his contemporaries. He could clowt up his sentences with unsurpassed elaboration, and the early part of his *Chronicle* assuredly smells too much of the schools. He had not yet freed his style from the Latin which was spoken and written in Gray's Inn. The opening passage of his book is as good an example as another of the faults which spoiled his narrative. 'What mischief hath insurged,' thus the passage runs, 'in realmes by intestine devision, what depopulacion hath ensued in countries by civil discencion, what detestable murder hath been committed in cities by separate factions, and what calamitee hath ensued in famous regions by domesticall discord and unnatural controversy : Rome hath felt, Italie can testifie, Fraunce can bear witnes, Beame can tell, Scotland may write, Denmarke can shewe, and especially thys noble realme of Englande can apparauntly declare and make demonstracion.' Here, indeed, is work for the writer of Ascham's epitome, who, by cutting away words and sentences, might have left the matter half as much in quantity, and twice as good as it was, 'for pleasure and commodity.'

But Ascham's censure touches but one side of the Chronicler's talent. No sooner did Hall write of what he saw and knew, than his style justifies Hearne's epithet, and becomes 'masculine.' He says good-bye at once to the stale artifices of repetition and decoration. He describes the shifting scenes of life, not in 'inkhorne tearmes,' but in vivid words, which were then, if not now, commonly used. And his style is neither dry nor timid. He can enrich his prose with precisely the true colour, the proper dignity; and he has made the language of pageantry his own. No more do you smell the oft-trimmed lamp; you are in the open air, mingling with the loyal crowd in Chepe, or watching the king's procession, as it passes majestically through Gracious Street. In truth, when once he touches upon his own time, Hall writes like an inspired reporter; not like the reporter of to-day, who shuts his eye, and sees in phrases; but like a man of letters, unperplexed by the tricks of journalism, who goes out into the street to see, and writes down the result with sincere simplicity. Thus he gives you an impression of life and movement, for which you may ransack the most of historians in vain. And his sense of picturesqueness never deserts him. Turn his pages where you will, and you will find a living scene perfectly realised. Thus, in a few lines is described Anne Boleyn's appearance at her coronation: 'Then came the quene in a litter of white cloth of golde not covered nor bayled whiche was led by ii. palferies clad in white damaske doune to the ground head and all, led by her foetemen. She had on a circot of white clothe of Tyssue and a mantle of the same furred with Ermyne, her heere hanged doune, but on her head she had a coyffe with a circlet about it ful of riche stones. Over her was borne a Canopie of clothe of golde with iiii. gilte staves and iiii. silver belles. For bearyng of whiche Canapye were appointed xvi. knightes, iiii. to bear it one space on foote and other iiii. another space accordyng to their owne appointment.' Hall, in truth, has the rare tact of finding the right word, even in the simplest phrases, and of giving an air of distinction to plain facts. In deploring the impertinences of the king's minions, they 'were so familiar and homely with hym,' says he, 'and plaied such light touches with hym that they forgat themselves.' And when the English fleet sets sail against the French, the king, as Hall tells us, 'caused Sir Edwarde Hawarde his Admirall with all diligence to take the sea, whiche, with all spede possible made ready diverse goodly and tal shippes.' The effect is produced not by Latinisms nor fantastic terms, but by the right use of a simple, yet dignified, English, the secret of which was long since lost. Hall, in brief, was the master of two distinct styles, and Ascham's criticism leaves unscathed *The Triumphant Reign of Henry VIII.*

The date of the book's appearance is still a matter of controversy. Tanner declares, in his *Bibliotheca Britannica*, that the first edition was printed by Berthelet, and published in 1542; if that were so, the burning of the book, in 1555, was so effectively performed that no perfect specimen of the first edition survived. A supposed fragment of it, however, has been found in a composite copy belonging to the University of Cambridge, and pieced together from three separate editions.[1] But, with the scanty evidence before us, it is impossible to arrive at a dogmatic conclusion, whether Berthelet's edition ever saw the light or not. On the other hand, concerning Richard Grafton's two editions there is neither doubt nor difficulty. They appeared in 1548 and 1550, being printed in part, not from the finished manuscript, for Hall left his work incomplete, but from the author's notes. Now Hall, as Grafton tells us, was a man 'in the later time of his life not so painful and studious as before he had

---

[1] Another fragment of this mysterious first edition (1542) has been detected in a copy bequeathed by Grenville to the British Museum. The colophon bears the date of 1548, but the main body of the book varies both in text and decoration from the familiar edition of that year, and it has been suggested that Grafton used up some of Berthelet's unfinished sheets. It is possible, indeed, that Berthelet did not complete his edition, and that Grafton acquired, along with Hall's notes, whatever sheets had been struck from Berthelet's press. However, here is a puzzle for the bibliographers, hitherto unsolved, and perhaps insoluble.

been.' But, in spite of Hall's imperfections, the editor did not presume to do more than arrange the Chronicler's own materials. 'For as much as a dead man is the author thereof,' says he, with laudable candour, 'I thought it my duty to suffer his work to be his own, and therefore have altered nothing therein.' And so well has Grafton performed his humble office, that we may detect Hall's hand as easily in the last years of Henry's reign as in the first. There is still the same love of pageants, the same obedience to the royal will, the same ardent protestantism in the pages finished by Grafton, as in those which came fresh from the hand of Hall, and we may acknowledge that for once the editor has not betrayed his trust.

The life of Henry VIII. is a sincere picture of Hall's mind and fancy. The Chronicler reveals himself to his readers as well by his expressed opinions, as by the relative importance which he gives to passing events. Above all he is a hero-worshipper; and, when the necessity of worship is satisfied, he proves himself a student of society rather than of politics. The wars, which were the peculiar glory of the reign, interest him chiefly as they throw a lustre upon the courage and martial ardour of Henry. It is true that, as in duty bound, he describes the taking of Terouenne, and the siege of Tournay; he does not forget 'the old pranks of the Scots, which is ever to invade England when the King is out, or within age'; he relates with some circumstance the intrigues of the emperor and the French king. But his heart is not in battles nor in foreign policy. The trumpet does not stir his blood ; the signing of a treaty does not, in his eyes, decide the destiny of nations. A rabble of citizens, on the other hand, arouses his sympathy at once ; and it is characteristic of him that the military exploit in which he takes the profoundest interest is the raid of the Adventurers in the marches of Calais. Now these Adventurers, or Krekers, as Hall calls them, were a body of wild persons, men out of service and fugitive apprentices, who offered their arms and their lives to the Lord Admiral. ' My lord,' said a tall yeoman, their spokesman, ' here be many good felowes that with your favour would leopard to get or lose, for their mynde is to be revenged on the Frenchemen, enemies to the Kyng and his realme.' And the Admiral gave them a pennon of St. George, assuring them that if they got any booty and brought it to the army they should be paid to the uttermost. Therewith he supplied them also with money and weapons, and for many a long day they harried the French. ' These men,' says Hall, ' were light, hardy, and politike, and by their manhood and hardines had robbed many tounes, and taken many prisoners, with great boties.' Again and again their exploits are commemorated in the *Chronicle*, and their death, for they died together, was yet more glorious than their life. Surrounded at last and outnumbered by the

French, they resolved to die, and each promised his fellow to slay him if he took to flight. 'Then every man cryed God mercie,' thus writes Hall, 'and kneled doune and kissed the earth, and strake handes eche wyth other, in token not to depart, and then made themselfs prest to the defence.' And so stout was their defence that not one escaped with his life, and they deserved, these citizen-soldiers, the immortality magnanimously bestowed upon them.

But they were citizens first, and soldiers after, and therefore claimed Hall's ungrudged sympathy. For in his eyes London was dearer even than England, and whenever the rights of her citizens were threatened, he was their loyal champion. To cite one instance of many : he relates indignantly how in 1513 the fields about Islington, Hoxton, and Shoreditch were enclosed by hedges and ditches, so that neither the young men of the city might shoot, nor the ancient persons might walk for their pleasure in the fields. Whereupon a great number of the city, led by a turner in a fool's coat, went forth with shovels and spades, 'and within a short space all the hedges about the townes were cast doune, and the diches filled, and every thyng made plain, the workemen were so diligent.' Neither king nor mayor could withstand such enthusiasm as this ; and Hall lawyer though he was, not merely applauds the licence of the people, but notes with satisfaction that the access of young or old to the fields was never afterwards hindered by hedge or ditch.

But, it is in describing the fierce warfare, which raged for many years between the city and Wolsey, that Hall most clearly shows his sympathy. The Cardinal's vast enterprises could not be carried to a successful issue, nor the king's lavish expenses be defrayed without money. And where should money be obtained if not in the city? So taxes were levied unrelentingly, now as tithes, now under the more amiable title of benevolences. In 1522 the king demanded £20,000, which sore chafed the citizens, but the money was found: 'howbeit the craftes solde much of ther plate.' Two months later the Cardinal demanded that every man should swear of what value he was in movables, and render a tenth unto the king. The Aldermen protested, as well they might. 'For Goddes sake,' they said to Wolsey, 'remembre this, that riche merchauntes in ware be bare of money.' But bare or not, they paid, and some even declared themselves of more worth than they were from pride. The king and his Cardinal, however, were still unsatisfied, and in the next year they proposed that a fifth part of the substance of the realm should be paid as a war-tax. The murmurings grew louder on every side. If all the coin were in the king's hands, how, it was asked, should men live? Hall, of course, makes no attempt to hide his opinion. He is on the side of the people. 'The Merchaunt that is ryche,' says he, 'of Sylke, Wolle, Tynne, Clothe, and such Merchaundise, hath not the fifth parte in money; the husbande man is ryche in corne and cattel, yet he lacketh of that some.' But the Cardinal was deaf to argument; he detected on every hand the signs of great abundance—rich apparel, servants, fat feasts, and delicate dishes. And thus the dispute increased in rancour and bitterness. On the one hand the Cardinal renewed his exaction; on the other, the people cursed the Cardinal, saying that, if men should give their goods by a commission, 'then wer it worse than the taxes of Fraunce, and so England should be bond and not free.'

At last, in 1525, the quarrel culminated. Lord Cobham, the commissioner of the tax in Kent, handled the men roughly, 'and by reason one Jhon Skudder answered hym clubbishly, he sent hym to the Towre of London.' From Kent the disaffection spread throughout the realm. Women wept, young folks cried, and men that had no work began to rage, and assembled themselves in companies. The Duke of Norfolk sent to the rebellious commons of his shire to know their intent, asking them who was their captain. Then a well-aged man begged licence to speak, which was granted. 'My Lorde,' said he, 'sythe you aske who is our capitain, for soth hys name is Povertie, for he and his cosyn Necessitie hath brought us to this doyng.' The whole of this popular movement is sketched with a fulness and insight which we should seek elsewhere in vain, and it clearly marks the difference between Hall and those historians whose chief interest lies in the movements of opposing armies. That, in truth, is Hall's chief merit: he records the simple episodes of every day, which are too often overshadowed by the intrigues of ministers or parliament. Thus he takes delight in a 'goodly disguisyng' played at Gray's Inn, and set forth with rich and costly apparel, and strange devices of masks and morrises; nor was his pleasure decreased by the fact that the play was an allegory of the quarrel between the people and the Cardinal, and that all men laughed thereat save only Wolsey himself. Thus he notes that the proclamation made in 1526 against unlawful games had an unexpected effect. When the young men were forbidden bowls and such other games, 'some fell to drinkyng, and some to ferretyng of other mennes Conies, and stealing Dere in Parkes, and other unthriftines.' In the same spirit he records the variation of the price of wheat, deplores the rains of 1527 which destroyed both crops and beasts, and, in brief, gives us such a picture of life in town and country as could have been drawn only by an eager contemporary.

Being ever a staunch champion of the citizens, Hall harboured a bitter dislike of all foreigners. He hated a Frenchman as bitterly as did the Duke of Buckingham himself, and looked with a wise suspicion upon any interloper, who threatened the trade of London. In those days the popular policy was not protection but exclusion, and the free entry of foreign goods more than once roused the city to rebellion. In 1517, as Hall tells us, the multitude of strangers was so great in London, that the English artificers could scarce get a living. Worse still, the strangers, not content with ousting the citizens from their crafts, mocked and oppressed them, trusting always in the protection of the Cardinal. At last an accident set the whole of London ablaze. A carpenter, named Williamson, bought two stockdoves in Chepe, and was about to pay for them, when a Frenchman snatched them from his hands, and said they were no meat for a carpenter. The French ambassador defended the effrontery of his countryman, and the carpenter was sent to prison. But the triumph was short-lived. Within a few days John Lincoln, a broker, had persuaded Dr. Beale to preach the Easter sermon at St. Mary's, Spittle, against the aliens, and the Doctor, with *Pugna pro patria* for his text, had no difficulty in inflaming the citizens. Foreigners were buffeted in the streets, or thrown into the canal. A general rebellion was prophesied for May Day, and the Cardinal bade the Mayor set a watch upon all suspected persons. But the watch was set in vain : a trivial incident led to so fierce a riot, that the day was known as Evil May Day ever after.

Two young men were playing at buckerels in Chepe, when by the command of an alderman one was arrested. Instantly the cry was raised of

' 'prentices and clubs,' and out at every door they came, weapons in hand. The rioters marched through the streets, sacking the foreign quarters, and putting the lives of all the aliens in jeopardy. At three o'clock the Lieutenant of the Tower turned his ordnance upon the city, and the rioters, who escaped capture, dispersed with what speed they might. Of those arrested, Lincoln alone suffered death, and some others, 'younglinges and olde false knaves,' as Hall calls them, were brought to trial at Westminster Hall, in their shirts and with halters about their necks. There the king pardoned them all, and when the general pardon was pronounced, 'the prisoners shouted at once, and al together cast up their halters into the hal roffe, so that the King might perceave thei were none of the discretest sorte.' While Hall rejoices that the ringleaders remained undiscovered, he praises both their courage and discretion. The citizens might, had they chosen, have taken a fierce revenge upon the soldiers. 'But like true subjects they sufered paciently.'

The French, however, did not profit by the lesson of May Day, and but a year later the public indignation broke out again. An Embassy, sent to London by the French king, brought in its train a vast mob of pedlars and jewellers with 'diverse merchaundise uncustomed, under the coloure of the trussery of the Ambassadors.' A riot seemed imminent, but once more the people's anger was

appeased, although calm was not wholly restored to
the city until, in 1526, an Act was passed which so
bridled the strangers that they came to 'a reasonable
conclusion.' Nor was it only in commerce that
Hall resented the competition of the aliens. He
had an equally sturdy contempt for the manners
which certain young Englishmen brought back
from the Court of Francis I. When they returned
to England, says he, 'they were all Frenche, in
eatyng, drynkyng and apparel, yea, and in French
vices and bragges, so that all the estates of
Englande were by them laughed at.' Indeed for
exclusive patriotism, it would be hard to find Hall's
match, and no historian has ever uttered the cry of
'England for the English' with more eloquence and
justice.

And he would no more willingly permit the
Church to be trammelled by foreign influence than
the trade of London. In other words he was, as
I have said, an ardent protestant. His dislike of
the Pope is profound and unconcealed, nor does he
ever lose a chance of avowing his antipathy to Rome,
an antipathy which colours his history and intensifies
his alert distrust of Cardinal Wolsey. He notes
with satisfaction the growing disputes between the
'Catholics' and 'Evangelicals,' which he knew must
end in the forsaking of the Pope ; he welcomes the
proclamation against bulls : he proudly hails the
king supreme head of the Church, whereafter, says
he, with undisguised enthusiasm, 'the Pope with

all his College of Cardinalles with all their Pardons and Indulgences was utterly abolished out of this realme. God be everlastyngly praysed therefore.' Where his religion is touched, he does not scruple to interrupt his history with tedious digressions, as when he relates the case of Richard Hun, who, being imprisoned in the Lollards' Tower for heresy, was found hanging by the neck in a girdle of silk. The Bishop of London declared that the man had hanged himself, but it was proved that William Horsey, the Bishop's Chancellor, had murdered him, and Hall, to justify an unfortunate heretic, forgets the king and his pageants, and wearies the reader with long-drawn depositions. His protestantism, indeed, knew only one check: when the king in his arrogance, brought forward the Bill of the Six Articles, Hall, as I have said, supported them against his conscience. Much as he loved the reformed religion, he loved his king more. And he had his revenge in his *Chronicle;* for before it was published the Bill was repealed, and the historian could describe it in the words of the common people as ' the bloody statute,' without incurring the charge of disloyalty.

Yet, protestant as he was, Hall had no love of a dismal life. His delight in the pageantry of the Court, and in the masks and mummeries, which Henry VIII.'s ingenuity designed, is most eloquently expressed. His style was perfectly adapted for the description of splendid processions and imposing spectacles. For once historian and monarch were well met: as Hall had at the tip of his pen all the words of magnificence, so Henry nourished a never-failing joy in dressing-up, and in devising brilliant festivals. Nor would he exclude the people from his pompous revelries, and time was when at Richmond the mob rent and spoiled the pageant, stripping even their sovereign and his companions to their doublet and hose. But the king's good humour was undisturbed. He turned the incident to mirth and laughter, and let the plunderers go off with their booty. Thus in war as in peace the jousts and merrymakings continued. Once upon a time the Scot's Ambassadors were amazed that King Henry should disport himself, when he was at war with France, and were shortly told by a gentleman of the Court that they did not set by the French king one bean. And if the spirit of revelry was unchanging, the devices were as various as cunning and extravagance could make them. Now the pageant was shaped like a mountain, with a tree of gold set upon the top; now it was a castle, garnished after the most warlike fashion, with 'la forteresse dangereuse' written upon its front. Or the garden of Esperance, with roses and pomegranates of silk and gold was presented; or wild men apparelled in green moss rushed suddenly from an artificial wood; or a fair lady sat upon a rock with a dolphin on her lap; or an allegory of ships passed before the king and queen. The gay and joyous Court always found an excuse for a pageant. Christmas and Twelfth Night each had their gorgeous festivals, while on May Day, his Grace, 'beyng yonge, and wyllyng not to be idell,' would rise in the morning very early to fetch may or green boughs. Or he would take the queen into the greenwood to see how Robin Hood and the outlaws lived, and to breakfast on venison. Then there were jousts and tournaments at which the king, the bravest knight of his time, always bore away the prize, happy to receive it at the gracious hands of Katherine. For it was an age of chivalry, in which the customs and titles of knighthood were still preserved; and even when the king went to war, it was but a joust fought to the death; challenges were given and received; and great captains donned their armour as much for display as for policy.

But the culmination of glory and splendour was the Field of the Cloth of Gold, whereon Henry and Francis took the sound advice of Comines, whose maxim it was that princes should not meet, except to share their pleasures. Never was so noble a spectacle seen before. The palace of gold, which sparkled in the plain of Guisnes, rose as by enchantment. Before the gate stood old Bacchus, fashioned in gold, 'birlyng the wine,' and over his head was the motto, which Rabelais adapted to his own purpose: 'faictes bonne chere quy vouldra.' To those who crossed the large court, 'fayre and beautifull' there was presented a scene of dazzling beauty.

The roofs were covered with cloth of silk, which showed like fine burned gold. Gold was the arras, 'compassed of many ancient stones'; gold the chairs, gold the cushions. The chapel was a still greater marvel. Over the altar stood twelve golden images. The crucifix in the king's closet was gold, gold were the candlesticks; even the roof was gilt 'with fine golde and Senapar and Bice.' And the trees which shone in this wondrous plain—the Hawthorn for Henry, the Raspberry for Francis— they, too, were wrought of silver and Venice gold, until nature was eclipsed by artifice, and the very flowers and fruits were golden symbols of friendship and alliance. Thus in reciting the glories of this encounter Hall sings a pæan to the precious metal, and the burden of his song is always the same—gold, gold, gold! The knights themselves did not fall below the splendour of the landscape. 'To-day the French,' as Shakespeare wrote,

'All clinquant, all in gold, like heathen gods,
Shone down the English; and to-morrow they
Made Britain India: every man that stood
Show'd like a mine.'

And the bravest sight of all was the king himself —'the moste goodliest Prince that ever reigned over the realme of Englande'—apparelled in a garment of 'Clothe of Silver, of Damaske, ribbed with Clothe of Golde, so thicke as might bee,' and bravely did he bear himself against the rufflers and gallants of the French Court. There, in the golden field, the kings ran course after course, breaking their spears like valiant princes, and presently went each his own way, eager to efface this memory of joyance in envy and hatred. Such was the pageant, which Hall, doubtless a spectator, described with all his curious knowledge of trappings, and which was the noblest spectacle of an age renowned above all others for its noble pageantry.

But not even the splendour of his life could endear Wolsey to the Chronicler, and it is evident from his first appearance in Hall's pages that the great Cardinal is to play the sinister part. He was a good philosopher, very eloquent and full of wit—so much Hall admits ; but ' for pride, covetous, and ambition he excelled all other.' No sooner, indeed, is Wolsey advanced to the Archbishopric of York, than Hall declares that henceforth he studied day and night to be a Cardinal; and in the least of his actions the historian detects a limitless, insensate ambition. The brilliant services which he rendered to the king, the respect for England which he imposed upon all Europe, were as nothing in Hall's eyes. The king's loyal worshipper could only see in the Cardinal's masks and banquets a stumbling-block of offence, for he thought that the king should engross the dignity and magnificence of his age; and he looked with a kind of jealousy upon the lavish grandeur of York Place. Moreover, while he delighted in all the golden triumphs of peace and war, which his eager eye witnessed, he flouted the

Cardinal as a thief, when he asked the people to pay the bill. In brief, he intensified in his book the fierce hatred, which the people expressed as loudly as they dared against the omnipotent Chancellor. Was it not a disgrace that this butcher's dog should lie in the Manor of Richmond?[1] And when Wolsey fell into disgrace, Hall was not content to repeat the articles in the Cardinal's indictment. He must needs turn and shift them to his victim's prejudice. From Hall, through Shakespeare, it has gone to the ends of the earth that Wolsey, in documents addressed to the Pope and foreign princes, was wont to write ' Ego et Meus Rex.' With this arrogance he was never charged, the worst hinted against him being that he added his own name to his master's—' my King and I.' Nor does the

[1] Shakespeare echoed this taunt: 'this butcher's cur is venom-mouthed,' says Buckingham in the play. Shakespeare, indeed, found not a little inspiration in Hall. The episodes of his *Henry VIII.* follow the *Chronicle* with curious fidelity. The drama gives you the same sense of pageantry and magnificence which is always present in Hall's pages, while in many a passage there is a verbal similarity which cannot be gainsaid. The clamours of the people against the Cardinal's exaction is trans-lated directly from the prose of Hall into the verse of Shake-speare, and even the king's angry speech to the faithful Wolsey is but an accurate paraphrase. Nor does the contempt which Hall hurls at the gallicised minions of the English Court lose its force in the phrase of Shakespeare. Buckingham's sad protest after his condemnation is another echo of Hall. The barge is ready and ' fitted with furniture as suits the greatness of his person.' Then says Buckingham:

Cardinal's tragic death persuade Hall to relent. He cannot find the same excuses for his enemy, as Shakespeare in his magnanimity puts in the mouth of honest Griffith. He only remembers that Wolsey was of a great stomach, that he counted himself equal with princes, and that by crafty suggestion got into his hands innumerable treasure. He did all this and more, and yet deserves our pardon and respect. Masterful as he was, he would let none master England but himself, and Henry's decay in honour and happiness began only with his minister's death.

But Hall was so jealous a champion of the king, that he could bear no rival near the throne. Henry was his only hero, and at the outset of his reign no finer hero could be found for epic or history. He was young, he was fair to look upon, he was accom-

> 'Nay, Sir Nicholas,
> Let it alone ; my state now will but mock me.
> When I came hither, I was lord high constable
> And Duke of Buckingham; now, poor Edward Bohun.'

Thus Shakespeare, and, if you turn to Hall, you will find the same thought set in prose. 'Sir Thomas Lovell'—thus runs the passage—'desired him to sytte on the cusshyns and carpet ordeined for him, he sayd nay, for when I went to Westminster I was Duke of Buckyngham, now I am but Edwarde Bowhen the moste caitiffe of the worlde.' The famous speech of Katherine too is borrowed from the *Chronicle*, even in its metaphor. 'It is you,' says the queen to Wolsey, 'have blown this coal betwixt my lord and me.' Or as Hall puts it : 'therefore of malice you have kindled thys fyre, and set this matter a broche.' These are but a few parallels of many which add not a little to the value and interest of the book.

plished. 'The features of his body,' says Hall with
the true accent of adulation, 'his goodly personage,
his amiable vysage, princely countenaunce, and the
noble qualities of his royall estate, to every man
knowen, nedeth no rehersall, consideryng that for
lacke of cunnyng I cannot express the gifts of grace,
and of nature, that God hath endowed hym with
all.' Katherine in the days of her unclouded state
assured Wolsey that 'with his health and life nothing
could come amiss to him.' In the eyes of Giustiniani,
the Venetian envoy, he was far handsomer than any
sovereign in Christendom. 'It was the prettiest
thing in the world,' said this enthusiast, 'to see him
play tennis, his fair skin glowing through a shirt of
the finest texture.' And like all the princes of his
house, Henry was infinitely vain of his appearance.
When Pasquilijo was in England the king called
him to a summer-house, and questioned him narrowly
about the French king. 'Is he as tall as I am?' he
asked first. Pasquilijo assured him there was little
difference. 'Is he as stout?' demanded Henry, and,
hearing that he was not, gravely inquired, 'What
sort of a leg has he?' 'Spare,' replied the envoy.
Then said the king, opening the front of his doublet,
and placing his hand upon his thigh, 'Look here; I
also have a fine calf to my leg.'[1] And not merely

[1] In precisely the same fashion did Henry's daughter Elizabeth
question Sir James Melville concerning Mary, the Queen of the
Scots, and in his answers Sir James proved himself a more
cunning diplomatist than the Venetian.

was Henry handsome, he excelled all the chivalry of
his time in manly exercises.   In the tournament there
was no knight who could withstand his onset, and
the many prizes which he won were not awarded
him out of mere courtesy.   As in war he knew no
fear, so in sport he knew no fatigue.   He never went
a-hunting without tiring eight or ten horses ; he
loved hawking and shooting as he loved the joust ;
and if he lost vast sums in the tennis-court, it was
when an encroaching corpulence hindered his activity.
Moreover, as has been said, he had a rare genius for
parade.   He surpassed all his contemporaries in the
lavish accoutrement of his court and person.   Nor
did this taste for grandeur leave him with the
joyousness of youth.   Even when he went to meet
Anne of Cleves, he was still magnificent.   His
courser was stately as ever ; his trappings of gold
and pearl had lost none of their splendour.   And, if
we may believe Hall, in comparison of his person,
his rich apparel was on that day little esteemed.

Yet he was no mere sportsman, proud of his
golden beard and sturdy arm.   By temperament
a scholar, he had become by training learned in all
the learning of his time.   Erasmus not merely
applauded his erudition, but hailed him as a true and
generous patron of poets, who had brought back the
golden age, and had illustrated in his own life the
splendid gifts of ancient heroes.   His speeches and
letters prove him the master of a style, vigorous and
his own ; and he possessed a power of argument

which, if in age it declined to sophistry, was the terror of all antagonists.   In the midst of his sedulous amusements, he still had time to play the statesman, and even after he was deprived of Wolsey's counsel, he was a match for the best of his contemporaries in policy.   Nor did the smallest detail escape him that might benefit his kingdom.   He suppressed vagabondage, and vastly improved the breed of horses. Above all, his zest of life was unquenchable.   There was no pursuit, either gay or serious, which could not arouse his enthusiasm.   He danced, he wrestled, he cast the bar, he leapt with a pole—a sport at which he once jeopardised his life, he made ballads, he set songs, he composed two goodly masses in five parts, ' whiche were song often times in hys chapel, and afterwards in diverse other places.'   He spoke, besides English, French, Spanish, and Latin, and he collected books.   Now it amused him to devise a new harness, such as no armourer had ever seen.   Now medicine engrossed him, and you hear that he invented a plaster, a sovereign remedy for sores.   In brief, he was the most highly gifted, most handsome, and most affable monarch that ever graced the throne of England, and, until ruin overtook his character, he deserved the most eloquent panegyric that Hall himself could indite.

And when he tired of tournaments and books, he fell to gambling, and hazarded his wealth with reckless prodigality.   His private accounts show how much he lost to his minions at dice and imperial, while the French hostages are said to have taken from him six or eight thousand ducats a day, a profit which doubtless lightened their enforced sojourn in a foreign country. His fame as a gambler even spread abroad, and certain Frenchmen and Lombards were brought to London to make wagers with him, and a rich harvest they reaped until their craft was discovered. And then, that he might leave nothing untried, he was constant in piety; he heard five masses a day, besides vespers and compline in the queen's chamber; or he would indulge that love of theological disquisition which never left him.

Such was Hall's hero in his youth, and such in Hall's fancy he remained unto the end. The faithful chronicler could discern no spot nor blemish in his king, and if the people justly cried out against him, he was still eloquent in excuse. In all simplicity of heart he believed that 'a certain scrupulosity pricked his master's conscience,' when Henry was minded to put Katherine away; and though it was murmured that the king's conscience had 'crept too near another lady,' Hall stoutly maintained that the murmur was slanderous and contrary to truth. Alas for Hall's loyalty! Long before the Universities had supported the king's cause, Henry was already buying purple velvet for Mistress Anne, who was so vastly increased in dignity that the Mayor of London deemed it prudent to send her a gift of cherries; he was already writing impassioned love-letters to his sweetheart, promising that 'shortly you and I shall have our desired End, which should be more to my Hearts Ease and more Quietnesse to my Minde, than any other Thing in this World.' The truth is that in spite of Hall's championship, a dark shadow had fallen across the brain of Henry VIII. The death of Wolsey had removed the last hindrance from his path of wilfulness, and after the divorce of Katherine, he set no restraint upon his actions. The very virtues which hitherto had distinguished him, changed, by a kind of excess, into vices. His learning turned to casuistry, his accomplishment became cunning, his bravery fell away into an implacable cruelty. He who had been open with all men, grew into a monster of suspicion. While his eyes, sunk deeper into his head, overlooked nothing, his tongue refused to speak what his eyes saw. 'If I thought that my cap knew my counsel,' said he to Cavendish, 'I would throw it in the fire and burn it.' But in nothing would he be thwarted. He ruled the Church, and overrode the law. It is said that he was better skilled in the law of divorce than any wiseacre in Christendom, and his profound knowledge of theology, which he might wisely have left to others, converted him into that worse of men—a pedant, who was also bloodthirsty and omnipotent. Grimly determined upon matrimony, yet always unfortunate in his dealings with women, he murdered the wives whom once he had loved, and decreed his children bastards. He saw the closest of his friends, such as Francis Weston, go to the scaffold without a whisper of regret. He received Anne Boleyn's eloquent letter 'from her doleful prison in the Tower,' begging him not to 'touch the innocent souls of these poor gentlemen,' and in a few days openly showed Jane Seymour as queen. With flattery and obeisance his ferocity of temper increased, and neither man nor woman was safe who thwarted his will. It was a cruel century, which did not shrink from boiling a man alive, nor from burning a child of fifteen at the stake;[1] yet Henry outdid the worst of his contemporaries in cruelty. Whoever refused to acknowledge him the supreme head of the Church, died upon the block : thus fell Fisher and Thomas More, the wisest spirits of the time. And if his enemies did not flout his theological supremacy, a frivolous pretext was always found for their destruction. So Surrey, the most accomplished poet of an accomplished age, perished, a victim to the royal displeasure, which neither genius nor grace sufficed to conciliate. In truth, history records nothing more pathetic than this ruin of a noble mind ; and through all the ruin Hall's loyalty never wavered. In his faithful eyes the king could still do no wrong, and he was able to inspire

[1] In the twenty-second year of Henry's reign, one Richard Roose was boiled alive for poisoning divers persons ; and ten years later a child named Richard Mekins perished at Smithfield for repeating what he had heard some other folks speak against the Sacrament of the Altar.

others with his own splendid fidelity. Many of the later historians were persuaded by Hall's eloquence to reject the legend that Henry VIII. was an English Bluebeard, and to regard him as an amiable and kindly monarch. 'Of persone he was tall and mightye, and in his later yeres somewhat grosse, in witte and memory excellent. Of such majestie tempered with humanitie and gentlenesse, as was comely in so great and noble a Prince. In knowledge of good letters, he farre passed all the Kings of this realme that had bene before him, and for his magnificence and liberalitie he was renowned throughout the world.' Thus writes Grafton after Hall, in recording the death of Henry VIII., and you wonder whether any king, who had not dipped his hands in innocent blood, was ever graced with a nobler epitaph.

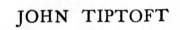
JOHN TIPTOFT

JOHN TIPTOFT

I

WHEN civil war threatened England, and the opposing forces of York and Lancaster first met in the field, John Tiptoft, Earl of Worcester, prudently betook himself to the Holy Land. So closely was his sympathy engaged on either side, that he knew not for whom he should draw the sword. If the Duke of York held the higher place in his regard, he could not persuade himself as yet to show discourtesy to Henry VI. That amiable prince had advanced him beyond the measure of his years and birth.[1] He was not far past his youth when (in 1449) he was made Earl of Worcester. At twenty-five he was Treasurer of the Exchequer, and two years later he was appointed Captain to guard the Sea. The contest between gratitude and inclination, which raged in his mind, might have had another issue, had not Somerset, the king's counsellor, dismissed him from the Court. The

---

[1] He was of noble birth, being the son of John, Baron de Tiptoft, and Joyce, his 'incomparable' wife, but not of so high a family as to justify his rapid rise to fortune.

way, then, lay open before him. Wisdom and
desire pointed to the same end. He determined,
with a moderation which presently deserted him, to
prefer peace before war, to hold himself aloof from
the strife of faction, to avoid the contamination of
turbulence and conspiracy. Thus it was that—to
cite the language of interested adulation—he imi-
tated the lofty-souled heroes whom the good ship
Argo bore eastwards, enavigated all the seas of the
earth, and conferred upon all nations the benefit of
his presence, manifesting everywhere the divinity of
his soul, and leaving behind him the immortal
memory of his name. In plainer prose, he travelled
with becoming state to Jerusalem, he visited the
holy places, as in pious duty bound, and when the
Orient had lost its hold upon him he came with
what speed he might to Venice.

II

No man of his time was better fitted to appreciate
the newly-discovered treasures of Italy. Englishman
though he was, he was the true child of the
Renaissance. He had learned at Balliol all that
Oxford could teach him, and not even his sojourn at
the Court had checked his ardent love of the
Humanities. Few scholars or Churchmen of his age
surpassed him in knowledge of the classics or in
felicity of expression; and so little did the natural
arrogance of his temper show itself in his studies,

that with all the modesty of a pupil he frequented the famous schools of Italy, and sat at the feet of the masters. He visited Ferrara, that he might hear the lectures of the renowned Guarino, whose method of discipline attracted students from every corner of Europe, even from Britain itself, a country 'situate beyond the confines of the earth.' There in Guarino's house he met many a wandering scholar, such as John Free, who with the characteristic courage of his kind, had set out from Oxford to conquer the learning of Italy with no more than ten pounds in his pocket ;[1] William Grey, erudite and disinterested as Tiptoft himself, presently appointed in Rome to the bishopric of Ely; and John Gunthorpe, who studied the Humanities with such success that he was rewarded with the deanery of Wells.

[1] The career of John Free—or Phreas as he was called —was typical of his time and class. He was a fellow of Balliol, and became, says his biographer, 'an admirable Philosopher, Lawyer, and Physician.' He was public reader of physic at Ferrara, and afterwards at Florence and Padua. He seems to have been half scholar, half pedant. His letters and odes were alike elegant. He composed a set of fluent verses, in which Bacchus expostulates with a goat for gnawing a vine, he translated Synesius' treatise concerning baldness, and dedicated both works to his patron Tiptoft. Another work, which he laid at the feet of Pope Pius ii., procured him the bishopric of Bath and Wells ; 'a month after he went to Rome, where he died before he could be consecrated but not without suspicion of poison from some competitor, 1465.' The story is wholly suitable to the Italy of the Renaissance, where the manuscript and the poisoned cup were always near neighbours.

These three he had known at Balliol—a college which did more than any other to restore in England the wisdom of the ancients, and which may still take a just pride in its nurslings, who lived, learned, and taught in the cities of Italy. Of this company John Tiptoft was the natural sovereign. He dispensed his princely favours with a large and generous hand. Whatever was asked of him he gave,—to this one his friendship, to that the support of a well-filled purse, to all sympathy and encouragement. By general consent he was acclaimed the Mæcenas of his age, and learning has rarely found a nobler patron. So for three years he wandered up and down Italy—from Ferrara to Padua, from Padua to Florence, from Florence to Rome, — gathering treasures in manuscript and storing his head with the knowledge and policy of the time. Of his life at Florence Vespasiano has left us an amiable sketch. Now Vespasiano, courtliest of booksellers, humanest of scholars, a mediæval scribe who witnessed the triumph of the black art which came from across the mountains, had the fairest opportunity of observing the character of Tiptoft, to whom he gave a place among his 'Illustrious Men,' and we accept his account in the best of good faith. 'He had a great abundance of books,' says Vespasiano, 'and in Florence he bought what more he could find, and also had a goodly number made for him. While certain books were being made which his lordship desired, he abode some days in Florence, and wished to see the whole place. Without attendants, alone and empty-handed, he went about; and if he was told to go to the right hand, he went to the left,'— an excellent method of sight-seeing truly, which may be commended to the idly obedient traveller of to-day. 'And having heard of the fame of Messer Giovanni Argiropoulo,' thus Vespasiano continues, ' he desired to hear one of his lectures at the school; and he came thither unknown, in the said manner, and he was well satisfied with the teaching of Messer Giovanni.'

A man of letters and of exceeding wisdom—thus it is that Vespasiano sums him up after his simple fashion, sending him on to Rome, where ' he visited the Pontiff and the Cardinals and the other prelates who were there.' It was at Rome, indeed, that Tiptoft won his highest triumph and gave the best proof of his eloquence. In vain would he have visited Italy if he had not seen Rome, which, says Leland, had not for many centuries received so noble and so welcome a guest, and which thought that a god had descended from heaven, so much did it marvel at his humanity, his splendour, and the Ciceronian abundance of his discourse. The effect of his oratory upon Pius II.—that learned Pontiff who, fifteen years before, had wondered that the Latin tongue had penetrated as far as Britain— was the highest tribute that could have been paid to Tiptoft's attainments. John Free who may have been a witness of the scene, describes how the Pope burst into tears of joy as he listened to Tiptoft's eloquence. If only time had spared the oration, we might form a clearer judgment. But the centuries have dealt hardly with the orator, and we must accept a verdict at second-hand.

Harshly, too, have the centuries treated the collections of books, the divers choice and rare manuscripts which Tiptoft sent to Duke Humphrey's library at Oxford. The skill wherewith he hunted for the masterpieces of ancient literature, the munificence wherewith he purchased them, were legendary in his day. Ludovico Carbo, his friend of Ferrara, whom he would have carried with him to England, adds his testimony to the sure knowledge of Vespasiano. 'He despoiled the libraries of Italy,' says Carbo, 'that he might make England a treasure-house of beautiful books.' If his books ever reached the University, they were long since dispersed. One alone has escaped in the general rout—a Commentary on Juvenal, written in an Italian hand, and bearing upon the cover the arms of the Earl of Worcester. Thus Italy was despoiled in vain, and England is the richer but by a single volume for Tiptoft's zeal and generosity.

Though much that Tiptoft wrote and said is lost, the art and diligence of Caxton have preserved for us some excellent specimens of his translations. Inspired by the Renaissance, he too did what he might to recapture the ancient classics, and to enrich

his country and his country's language with some
works of Cæsar and Cicero. His choice of originals
was wise. The treatise 'De Amicitia' is packed
with the splendid commonplaces which the revival
of learning had made already popular. And of
Cæsar's 'Commentaries' he Englished only so
'much as concernyth thys realm of England callyd
Bretanyne; which is the eldest hystoryes of all
other that can be found that ever wrote of thys
realm of England.' Thus was his patriotism as
well as his scholarship engaged. He thought at one
blow to sing the praise of England and to give Cæsar
an ampler life in another tongue. His version is
marked by a workmanlike simplicity. It is an
accurate representation in style as in sense of the
original. Free from the opulence and curiosity of
speech which was presently to stamp Elizabethan
prose with a character of its own, Tiptoft's English-
ing of Cæsar is far nearer to our modern method
than Golding's. Indeed, were it not for the use of
a word here and there—such as 'affyed' for *probabat*,
and 'brute' in the sense of noise—which suggests
the close relationship still existing between French
and English, Tiptoft's 'Cæsar' might have been
written yesterday.[1] But, apt as he was for learning,

[1] The following passage, chosen at hazard, and modernised
only in its spelling, will prove how closely Tiptoft approached
both his original and the English of our time : 'Now, the side
of the river, where his enemies stood, was pitched full of sharp
piles; and beside it, at the brink of the river, were other piles

Tiptoft regarded literature as the interlude of an active life, and he was destined soon to lay it aside for the clash of arms and the conflict of policies.

His sojourn in Italy gave him far more than a knowledge of the Humanities. He brought back to England with him those lessons of statecraft which were taught only on the other side of the Alps. He learned from the despots with how nice a cynicism cruelty and learning might be combined. He discovered from a hundred illustrious examples that it was in no disaccord with sovereignty to carry a cup of poison in one hand and a manuscript of Plato in the other. Though Machiavelli was not born until a year before Tiptoft lost his head, Machiavellism in act was already plain to see. The pitiless dramas of lust and craft, which the wise Florentine resumed in his stern theory of life and government, were enacted, many of them, before the eyes of Tiptoft. He might, perchance, have known the famous Lord of Rimini, Sigismundo Pandolfo Malatesta, who engrossed in his single person the vices and virtues of his age. Scholar and savage, Sigismundo studied the classics and listened to the

covered with water. Of the which things, when Cæsar was advertised by the report of the prisoners, and by them which had left the Britons and were come to Cæsar, he sent first his men of arms, and commanded the legions should follow them without delay.' There is not a touch of archaism in these lines. Plainness is their quality—a quality, above all others, necessary to the interpreter of Cæsar, who wrote as though his hand held not a pen but a sword.

lectures of learned men with the same ardour wherewith
he killed his wives, or betrayed, tricked, and tortured
his enemies. Trained in such a school, with such
models constantly before him, Tiptoft easily acquired
the hard, ruthless doctrines of the Renaissance. He
arrived at the same ends by the same paths as the
despots. He drove from his mind what to Malatesta
would have seemed the cant of mercy and justice.
Henceforth he knew but one god—success, and no
other methods of worship than force, pride, and
passion. The moral aspect of things no longer
attracted his vision. He approved only such courses
as flattered his own ambition or prospered his prince.
But he was no ogre—at any rate, in his own regard.
He encouraged culture and luxury like the best of
the despots, he did something no doubt to soften the
barbarity of English manners, and if, in obeying the
behests of the king, he showed himself as graciously
cynical as his Italian exemplars, he did not shirk the
reprisal which he knew must come. A terror to
others, he watched without terror his own approaching doom.

III

Tiptoft returned from Italy in the nick. The
battle of Towton, which had devastated the houses
of the nobles, had brought a grateful peace to the
kingdom. On no field had ever been poured forth
so much English blood. Victors and vanquished
were of one nation, many of them near in alliance.

As an eloquent historian says, not a single 'stranger of name was present at our battles, as if we had disdained to conquer or perish by other weapons than our own.' The carnage which had established Edward IV. firmly on the throne left many gaps in the ranks of his advisers, and Tiptoft was abundantly justified of his prudence. Absent in Italy, he had been spared the necessity of taking this side or that, he had borne no burden in council-chamber or on the field of battle. He was, therefore, free to accept the reward of abstinence without jealousy or suspicion. At a Court which he had not frequented he might expect to find few enemies. Moreover, he was called to serve a prince who, unconsciously perhaps, had formed himself upon the Italian model. If guiltless of the crimes which blackened the fame of Malatesta, Edward IV. was in other respects the fine flower of despotism. Courageous and cruel, munificent and pleasure-loving, he too held firmly by the precepts which Machiavelli was presently to formulate. He believed, at any rate in practice, that the only way to render his foes innocuous was to extirpate them, that it was no part of a king's honour to keep faith with an adversary, that promises might be given without intent of performance, and that vows might be forsworn for profit or revenge.

If Tiptoft found in Edward IV. an apt pupil for the lessons of Italian diplomacy, Edward IV. welcomed Tiptoft as a willing instrument of his schemes. He advanced him with an ominous rapidity. A bitter Nemesis could but await this sudden favourite of fortune. Honours were showered upon him. Chief-Justice for life of North Wales, Constable of the Tower, Constable of England, Knight of the Garter, Lord Steward of the King's Household, Commissioner to keep guard by Sea, Chancellor and Deputy of Ireland,—these are some of the titles conferred upon him by a generous sovereign. Above all, it was his duty to execute the summary justice of the king, and this duty he performed with a truculent severity which won him the hatred of the people, even when no fault might be found with his sentences. He was accused of substituting the Paduan for the English law, and, as he did not scruple to send many a noble rebel to the scaffold without the formality of trial before their peers, his accusers had right on their side. His long sojourn abroad, his intimate acquaintance with the practices of Italy, gave him a sinister aspect in the popular regard, and he soon became a legend of lawless ferocity.

Wherever he went, he was hailed as the Butcher of England, and though he did much to earn the title, it is not easy to separate his responsibility from the king's.[1] What he did, he did it by the king's

[1] In *The Mirror of Magistrates* the case is put as leniently as possible for Tiptoft :—

'And for my goods and livinges were not small,
The gapers for them bare the world in hand
For ten years space, that I was cause of all
The executions done within the land :

command, which he dared not disobey, and with
the king he reaped the harvest of hate, sown by the
hand of tyranny. It is not plain that he and the
king could have taken any other course. If they
spared the lives of their adversaries, these adversarie
speedily armed themselves again. If they punishee
them by death, they incurred the hatred of peaceable
men. But it was Tiptoft's fault that he passed his
sentences with alacrity and saw them carried out
with a merciless cruelty.

His first victims were the Earl of Oxford, the
Lord Aubrey, his son, and Sir Thomas Tottenham,
who, after the semblance of a trial, in 1462, were
carried to a scaffold on Tower Hill, eight feet high,
and there had 'their heads smitten off, that all men
might see.' Though there was no doubt concerning
the treachery of Oxford and his friends, the swiftness
with which justice was done, and the public ferocity
of the judge, even at that turbulent time, exasperated
the citizens, who henceforth were ready to believe
that Tiptoft was a public enemy. But for the
execution of Sir Ralph Grey not even Tiptoft could

> For this did such as did not understand
>   Mine enemies' drift, thinke all reports were true :
>   And so did hate me worse than any Jewe.
>
>   .   .   .   .   .
>
> Through this I was King Edward's butcher named,
> And bare the fame of all his cruell deedes :
> I cleare me not, I worthely was blamed,
> Though force was such I must obey him needes : '

—with much more to the same effect.

incur reproach. Sir Ralph was a traitor, who had opened the doors of Bamborough Castle to the enemy. He knew that he might expect no mercy, as he deserved none. The herald, who summoned the Castle to surrender, reserved two persons, Sir Humphrey Neville and Sir Ralph Grey, 'without any redemption,' and he reserved them justly.

Tiptoft's duty, then, was clear. When the Castle was taken by assault he had but to pass sentence, and this he did with a pomp, eloquence, and moderation which do not suggest the Butcher of England. 'Sir Ralph Grey,' said he, 'thou hast taken the order of Knighthood of the Bath, and any so taking that order ought to keep the faith the which he takes. Therefore remember thou the law!' After this impressive exordium Tiptoft proceeds to declare that Sir Ralph had drawn arms upon the king, had withstood and made fences against his Majesty, that according to the royal ordinance he should have had his spurs stricken off by the hard heels with the hand of the master cook, that his proper coat-of-arms should have been torn off his body, and that he should have been degraded of his worship, noblesse, and arms, as of his order of knighthood. Nevertheless, he was pardoned the ceremonies of degradation, 'for his noble grandfather, the which suffered trouble for the king's most noble predecessors.' And Tiptoft closed his harangue in these familiar terms. 'Then, Sir Ralph Grey,' said he, 'this shall be thy penance,—

thou shalt go on thy feet unto the town's end, and
there thou shalt be laid down and drawn to a scaffold
made for thee, and that thou shalt have thine head
smitten off thy body, to be buried in the freres ; thy
head where it pleaseth the King.'

No fault can be found either with the manner or
the justice of this sentence. Not even a partisan
could say a word in defence of the punishment which
Tiptoft meted out to the friends of Warwick, who
in 1470 fell into the hands of the king at Southampton. Commanded to sit in judgment of such
men as were taken in the ships, he ordered 'twenty
persons of gentlemen and yeomen to be hanged,
drawn, quartered, and headed ; and after that they
hanged up by the legs, and a stake was made sharp
at the both ends, whereof one end was put in at the
buttocks, and the other end their heads were put
upon.' It is not surprising that this brutality horri-
fied the people, and that ever after the Earl of Worcester was 'greatly behated.' His victims, no doubt,
deserved to die the death. They did not deserve the
outrage of impalement,—an outrage which was contrary to the law of England, and which suggested to
the popular imagination the unknown, unspeakable
cruelties of Italy.

IV

Harsh as Tiptoft showed himself in the judgment-
seat, he revealed but a slender talent on the field of
battle. He was not born to carry arms. When he

accompanied the king on his northward expedition,
his greatest service was done in the swift punishment
of offenders. Appointed in 1463 to guard the sea
and to prevent the escape of Queen Margaret, he
ordained a great army and a great navy by land and
water. And all in vain ! He and his crews did but
consume their stores and come out of the adventure
empty-handed and disgraced. 'O infelix successus
opprobrium et confusio !' exclaims the old Latin
chronicler with a shame of which Tiptoft himself
was insensible. He, indeed, rode arrogantly upon
the topmost wave of fortune, and recked not of
failure. His pride and influence increased in spite
of defeats on shore and sea. Was he not a scholar
and a statesman and the king's friend ? Had he
not travelled to the ends of the earth, gathering
knowledge and experience beyond the reach of
common men ? And yet, had he studied his own
countrymen with half the zeal which he had given
to the study of Italy, he might have escaped the
unpopularity which ever awaits upon cruelty and
insolence. Of his cruelty something has been said.
No better example of his insolence may be found
than the slight which he put upon the city of
London, and which has been described in terms
of proper solemnity by William Gregory, chronicler
and skinner. Tiptoft, in fact, was guilty of an unpardonable sin : he treated the Lord Mayor of
London with disdain ; and though there has always
been a touch of ridicule in civic pomp, how should

a noble hope to keep a head upon his shoulders who
had insulted the city's head in the very fastness of
citizenship itself? The story may be told in the
chronicler's own simple words.

'This year (1464), about mid-summer,' — thus William
Gregory,—'at a royal feast of the Sergeants of the Coif, the
Mayor of London was desired to be at that feast. And at
dinner-time he came to the feast with his officers, agreeing and
according to his degree. For within London he is next to the
King in all manner of things. And in time of waiting the
Earl of Worcester was taken before the Mayor, and set down
in the midst of the high table. And the Mayor, seeing that his
place was occupied, held him content, and went home again
without meat or drink or any thanks, but reward him he did as
his dignity required of the city. And he took with him the
substance of his brethren the aldermen to his place, and were
set and served as soon as any man could devise, both of cygnet
and other delicacies enough, that all the house marvelled how
well everything was done in so short a time, and prayed all men
to be merry and glad.'

If only Tiptoft had had the tact and humour to
decline the place of honour thus wrongfully thrust
upon him, he might have won, in the moment of
disaster, the sympathy of the citizens. But he was
the silent witness of an inexcusable affront. Without a word of protest he saw himself more highly
honoured than him to whom the chief honour was
due. And the Lord Mayor's victory was complete.
'Thus,' says the chronicler, 'the worship of the
city was kept, and not lost for him. And I trust
that never it shall, by the grace of God.'

A sojourn in Ireland, then as now, the grave of

reputations, did not mitigate the unpopularity of Tiptoft. Thither he went in 1467, as Clarence's deputy, charged to execute swift, unquestioned justice upon Thomas Earl of Desmond, the Chief of the Geraldines. It is still uncertain what was Desmond's offence. If we may believe the voice of rumour, he had incurred Edward's displeasure by urging him to divorce Elizabeth Woodville, and to strengthen the throne by a foreign alliance. Whatever was the cause, there is no doubt of the king's animosity or the stern injunction which he laid upon his well-trusted friend. Tiptoft, always alert to carry out his master's orders, seized upon Desmond, and had his head struck off at Drogheda. There is a baleful legend that he treated the Geraldine's two infant sons with savage cruelty, but the legend is unsupported, and was perchance the invention of the same Irish loyalty which in the records of the Geraldines described Thomas Earl of Desmond as 'a martyr of Christ.'

Deputy until 1468, Tiptoft was appointed Lieutenant of Ireland in 1470, upon the outlawry of Clarence, whom the Irish were commanded, on pain of death and forfeiture, not to 'comfort with meat, drink, or otherwise.' He did not assume the higher office. Already his career was drawing to its close. When Edward IV., from whose friendship and protection he derived all his power and influence, was forced into flight, Tiptoft could have had but little hope of life or pardon. His last chance

lay in concealment, and with that sense of picturesqueness and the unforeseen which accompanied him to the
end, he disguised himself, took refuge in Weybridge
Forest, and lived with the shepherds who there
tended their flocks.   Thus another was added to
the many parts which he had played.   The scholar,
the statesman, the Butcher of England prayed that
his peasant's garb might shield him from discovery,
and prayed in vain.   For one day he gave a piece of
gold to a shepherd that he might buy bread for him
at a farmhouse hard by.   And the people of the house,
seeing that the man brought more money than he
was wont to bring, fell instantly upon suspicion,
since they knew (as who did not?) that Tiptoft
was sought with the greatest diligence, and forthwith they sent certain men-at-arms into the wood,
if perchance they should there find the fugitive.
Their search was successful.   Tiptoft was discovered hiding in the top of a high tree, which,
says Habington, 'exprest the precipice of his
fortune,' and was carried with exultant speed to
London.

The pomp and pageantry of his life did not desert
him in his death.   Tried before the Earl of Oxford,
whose father and brother he had sent to the block,
he met with as little mercy as he had been wont to
give.   'And upon the fifteenth day of October'—
thus says the chronicler—'was the said Earl arraigned
at Westminster in the White Hall ; and upon the
Monday following adjudged that he should go from

the same place unto the Tower Hill, and there to have his head smitten off. But as he was coming from the said place of judgment toward his execution, the people pressed[1] so impatiently upon him for to see and behold him that the sheriff was fain to turn into the Fleet, and there to borrow gaol for him for that night. And upon the morrow after, at afternoon, being St. Luke's day, and the eighteenth day of October, he was led to the Tower Hill, where he took his death full patiently,'—so patiently, indeed, that few heroes have ever made a more comely end.

As he went along, one of the friars who accompanied him, an Italian of the order of St. Dominic, a kindly fellow and bountiful of speech, said to him, 'Sire, you are brought hither by your unheard cruelty.' To which the Earl made answer that what he had done he had done for the State. But the garrulous friar gave him no peace, saying that only just and honest things should be done for the State, and quoting, unkindly as it seems, the words of St. Jerome, that no merciful man ever dies an evil death. Tiptoft bore even the friar's impertinence with an equal mind, and when the time came for him to lose his head he bade the executioner cut it off in three strokes, as a courtesy to the Holy

[1] Or as the *Mirror of Magistrates*, with an excellent turn of slang, expresses it—

' That when I should have gone to Blockham feast,
I could not passe, so sore on me they preast.'

Trinity. Thus, in the words of Fuller, did the axe 'cut off more learning in England than any left in the heads of all the surviving nobility.' And Tiptoft's fiercest enemies could not but confess that he died like a man of courage and of exceeding great faith. Even after his shameful death Tiptoft was treated with the respect which belongs to grandeur. A dutiful sister saw his body honourably interred in the Church of the Blackfriars, a brotherhood which he had founded himself near All Hallows, Barking. And William Grey, the companion of his wanderings in Italy, set up in his own Cathedral of Ely a fair Gothic monument, whereon John Tiptoft lies between his two wives.

V

John Tiptoft was not so much a man of complex character as of two simple souls inhabiting one body. To attempt to harmonise the gentle scholar with the Butcher of England would be to lose one's labour. We must accept both as faithful portraits, and fall back for a parallel upon the despots of Italy. The men of learning are all of one mind. In Tiptoft's praise they exhaust the language of panegyric. John Free, as has been said, struck the first note of adulation. He declared, in his own ecstatic style, that Tiptoft alone among the men of his time was comparable with Alexander the Great and Lucius Lucullus, and he made it plain that it was not Tiptoft who suffered by the comparison.

He praises, in terms of eloquent enthusiasm, the magnitude of his mind, his prudence, his liberality, his piety towards God, his humanity towards all. Caxton falls not an inch behind Free in admiration. He vaunts the virtues and accomplishments of 'the noble, famous Earl of Worcester, son and heir to the Lord Tiptoft, which in his time flowered in virtue and learning, to whom I knew none like among the lords of the temporality in science and moral virtue.' These are the words of one well acquainted with Tiptoft and the recipient of his benefactions. And as Caxton praised the manner of his life, so he praised the manner of his death. 'And what worship had he at Rome,' thus he writes, 'in the presence of our holy father the Pope! And so in all other places on to his death, at which death every man that was there might learn to die and take his death patiently, wherein I hope and doubt not but that God received his soul into His everlasting bliss. . . . Thus I here recommend his soul ever to your prayers, and also that we at our departing may depart in such wise.' So he is held up as an example of kindliness and learning to all good men and to all sound scholars. Leland, a century after his death, echoes the praise of those who were his friends. Having spent all the resources of flattery, he fears that he may seem somewhat tedious to a hurried reader. 'How can I help it?' he cries. 'A peerless star such as this must not be robbed of a single ray.'

On the other side of the account stands the Butcher of England. And as catchwords govern the world, the Butcher of England has eclipsed in the general memory the amiable scholar and patron. Here is a manifest injustice, since if the two men united in Tiptoft are of equal force and energy, there is no reason why the one should survive the other. And though I would not soften the traits which give colour and interest to the character of the famous Earl of Worcester, it is worth while to ask how it is that so thick a cloud of obloquy has enveloped his name. He was a cruel man, who lived in a cruel age. At a time when a very low value was put upon human life, he sent his adversaries to the gallows without ruth, and went himself without regret. But he soiled his hands with no more blood than did Warwick and Montague, and so faithfully did he carry out the commands of his king, that he cannot be charged with the satisfaction of private revenge. Why, then, should he hold a place apart as the Butcher of England? I think because he came back to England with the imagined stain of Italy upon him,—because those who suffered from his judgments believed that there was something un-English in his procedure. They suspected, as we have seen, the bias of the Paduan Law. They took their death from Montague with a light heart. He had not wasted his years in foreign travel. While Tiptoft was studying the classics, he had stood, sword in hand, on English battlefields, and had every right to send his countrymen to the gallows. In the very aspect and manner of Tiptoft there was something exotic, and the prisoner of state or his friends resented that sentence should be passed by one who had not the bluff heartiness of his fellows. And then there was the impalement at Southampton. For this no excuse or palliation can be found,—a wanton outrage for which Tiptoft will be pilloried for all time as the Butcher of England.

VI

Thus, with his nickname to aid, Tiptoft became a kind of bogey. He has been denounced as an Italianate Englishman by many whose insular pride ascribes England's virtues to her own soil, her vices to benighted countries situate across the Channel. For more than a century after Tiptoft's death a kind of shame hung about those who betook themselves to Italy that they might learn the lessons of life. Though the Italianate Englishman went through several phases, they were all phases of dishonour, and his reproach is a commonplace of the sixteenth century. At first it was the cunning lessons of statecraft which were supposed to disgrace the anxious learner. A false reading of Machiavelli inflamed the public mind. Italy suggested nothing save intrigue, poison, and sudden death. This, the country of Tiptoft's policy, was the country also of such dramatists as Webster and Cyril Tourneur.

Nashe apostrophised it in the conventional terms.
'O Italy!' he exclaims, 'academy of manslaughter,
the sporting-place of murder, the apothecary-shop
of all nations! How many kinds of weapons hast
thou invented for malice!' Even to have sojourned
there for a while seemed a danger and a slur.
Harvey accused Nashe of travelling to Italy 'to
fetch him twopenny worth of Tuscanism.' And
then there came another class which sought instruction in the baleful country. They went in search
not of lessons in statecraft, but of Circe's enchantments. It was their purpose to kill their own souls,
not to destroy the bodies of others. They were no
Tiptofts; they were merely curious lovers of superstition and debauchery. 'Englese Italianato,' says
Roger Ascham, who has left us the best picture of
the kind, 'e un diabolo incarnato,' and the incarnate
devil loses nothing of his hideous aspect when Ascham
has finished with him. In a famous passage he
sketches him and his paltry ambitions.

'If some yet do not well understand,' says he,
'what is an Englishman Italianated, I will plainly
tell him. He, that by living and travelling in Italy,
bringeth home into England out of Italy the Religion, the learning, the policy, the experience, the
manners of Italy. That is to say, for Religion,
Papistry or worse: for learning, less commonly than
they carried out with them: for policy, a factious
heart, a discoursing head, a mind to meddle in all
men's matters: for experience, plenty of new mis-

chiefs never known in England before : for manners, variety of vanities, and change of filthy lying. These be the enchantments of Circe.'

And then Ascham passes from a general denunciation to condemn especially the merry books of Italy, which he thinks are no better than the works of chivalry composed in monasteries by idle monks or wanton nuns. The 'Morte d'Arthur' he holds to be bad enough, yet ten 'Morte d'Arthurs' do not the tenth part so much harm as one of these books made in Italy by Bandello or Boccaccio, and translated into English. The exaggeration is a clear proof of prejudice, and persuades the reader to think that the enchantments of Circe did not allure young wills and wits so wantonly as Ascham believed.

As the years went on the charges brought by zealous Englishmen against Italy became more precise and less heinous. Atheism, infidelity, vicious conversation, ambitious and proud behaviour—these are the sins which Harrison observed in the newly-returned Englishman. And presently the Italianate Briton, once a devil incarnate, was whittled down into a mere fop, a thing of frills and furbelows, of antics and gestures, of fantastic speech and affected manners, not unlike the tourist of to-day who comes back from Paris with a flat-brimmed hat on his head and broken English in his mouth. It is a strange chapter in the history of international relations, and it seems not a little stranger when we remember that the Italians were quick to return the compliment. A Venetian who visited England when Henry VII. was on the throne, was astonished at the lack of affection wherewith English parents regarded their children, and English husbands their wives. In no class could he trace real human nature or the passion of love. Thus are the insults of untravelled Englishmen avenged. Thus is a check given to over hasty condemnation. As for the Italianate Englishman, he seemed a very real monster to three generations of men, and let it not be forgotten that, under whatever guise he presently appeared, he owed his beginning to John Tiptoft, Earl of Worcester, accomplished scholar, munificent patron of learning, and the Butcher of England.

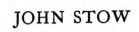

JOHN STOW

JOHN STOW—I

HIMSELF

THE history of the past is revealed to us most clearly in the highest and the lowest. Kings and rufflers, ministers and thieves, willingly surrender their secrets to the art of biography. The prowess of Sir Richard Grenville is as familiar to the world as the wisdom of Burleigh. There is none who may not read, if he will, the life of Moll Cutpurse, or delight in the fustian eloquence of many a last dying speech. It is only the simple virtue of the citizen which finds no place in the archives—of the citizen who opens his stall, follows his craft, and prays that he may become an alderman. In the career of such a one there is little chance of scandal or surprise. He does not play for the larger stakes of life. He is not asked to rescue maidens in distress, or to batter the walls of impregnable fortresses. Even if he venture beyond the limit of the law, he commits his robberies from the discreet shelter of a comfortable office. It is not strange, then, that the Elizabethan dramatists either ignore him or turn him to ridicule. In their eyes he is a fair victim for the lash of the satirist or the greed of a broken man of pleasure. The Gallipots and Yellowhammers of Middleton are extravagant caricatures. Simon Eyre, Dekker's famous shoemaker, is too nobly picturesque for truth, and even the citizen and his wife, who pleasantly interrupt 'The Knight of the burning pestal,' display so vain a simplicity as to surpass belief. Indeed were it not for the accident which made John Stow a chronicler as well as a tailor, we might lose our time in idle conjecture. But John Stow stands before us, honest, pedantic, irascible, and it is our own fault if we refuse his acquaintance. His own habit of autobiography has stimulated a general curiosity; scholars have treated him with a respect denied to others of his kind; and the last of his editors, Mr. C. L. Kingsford, has accepted the injunction of Thomas Hearne, and reprinted Stow's *Survey of London*[1] as a 'venerable original.'

Born in 1825, John Stow belonged to a family of citizens. His grandfather was an honest tallow-chandler, who supplied the Church of St. Michael in Cornhill with lamp-oil and candles, and his father, inheriting 'the great melting-pot with all instruments belonging thereto,' inherited also the same privileges. His youth, like his age, was spent in the city. The wards of London were the boundaries

---

[1] *A Survey of London* by John Stow. Reprinted from the text of 1603, with Introduction and Notes by Charles Lethbridge Kingsford. Oxford: at the Clarendon Press. To Mr. Kingsford's Introduction I am deeply indebted.

of his universe. He saw in his mind's-eye no other
river than the Thames. And London in the sixteenth
century was a real town, of narrow and absorbing
interests, the citizens of which knew one another by
sight, and joined in paying a proper deference to the
greatest of all citizens—the Lord Mayor. There was
nothing which touched the dignity and habit of this
great official, greater almost, within his limits, than the
king himself, that did not stir the imagination of his
subjects. For Stow the smallest innovation in civic
custom was a dire offence. He records sorrowfully
in 1563 that Sir Thomas Lodge, being Mayor of
London, wore a beard. He was the first that ever
ventured thus to defame his office, and hardly did
the city support the shock. That a Mayor should
leave the comely, ancient custom of a clean chin
seemed intolerable to the loyal men of London, and
the year of Lodge's office was marked by Stow with
a black stone.

And as the city was small in size and in outlook,
so also was it simple in its joys. It delighted in
pleasant shows and homely pageants. It welcomed
May-day with its masks and junketings ; it hung its
houses with holly and ivy at Christmastide ; it
shadowed its doors, on the vigil of St. John the
Baptist, with green birch, long fennel, St. John's
wort, orpin, and white lilies. Then there was
wrestling at Bartholomew Fair, and much eating of
pork, and cock-fighting and bear-baiting in their due
season. The practice of the long-bow had, alas !

been almost forsaken in Stow's time. The closing of the common grounds, so often deplored by the chroniclers, had already done its work, depraving the citizens, and weakening the national defence. 'Our Archers,' says Stow, 'for want of room to shoot abroad, creep into bowling allies and ordinary dicing-houses, nearer home, where they have room enough to hazard their money at unlawful games : and there I leave them to take their pleasures.'

And even the graver citizens, content to walk abroad in decent tranquillity, found that the city was encroaching upon their exercise. Hogg Lane, for instance, without Bishopsgate, which now bears the more pompous name of Artillery Lane, had within Stow's memory fair hedgerows of elm trees on either side, with bridges and easy stiles, such as even aldermen might climb to pass over into pleasant fields, and there to refresh their spirits, dulled with the purchase of merchandise and the counting of money, in the sweet and wholesome air. And within a few years this country lane became nothing better than one continual building of garden houses and small cottages. But even though the city was merged in the suburbs, as far as Houndsditch and Whitechapel, London was still fair and clean, seldom oppressed by poverty or exaction, and famous then, as now, for a generous hospitality. Stow remembered the time when two hundred persons were served daily at Lord Cromwell's gate, and when the Prior of Christ Church kept a bountiful house of meat and drink, both for

rich and poor. In brief, all classes seemed to be
inspired with a simple gaiety, and if there was
a reverse side to the medal, Stow takes care not to
show it to us.

Such was the quiet, provincial town in which
Stow grew up. His father's house was in Throgmorton Street, and there the old man was the victim
of an injustice which rankled in his son's breast unto
the end. Thomas Cromwell was building himself
a large and spacious house hard by, and in his
arrogance made no scruple to take down the pales
of his neighbours and to seize their land. Now,
close to William Stow's south pale there stood a
house, and this house the miscreants loosed from the
ground, with the ingenuity of modern Americans,
and moved upon rollers some twenty-two feet into
the garden, without warning, and with no other
answer, when they were taxed, than that Master
Sir Thomas had so commanded it. 'Thus much of
mine own knowledge have I thought good to note'
—such is Stow's comment—'that the sudden rising
of some men causeth them to forget themselves.'
Yet in Cromwell's despite, Throgmorton Street had
its amenity. Thence the young Stow could walk
to the Nunnery of St. Clare in the Minories, and
fetch a halfpenny worth of milk, always hot from
the kine, and never less than three ale-pints for
a halfpenny in the summer, nor less than an ale-quart
in the winter. The citizen of to-day must go
farther afield for his milk than the Minories, and

cannot hope to satisfy the farmer with so modest a coin as a halfpenny.

Of his education Stow tells us nothing. He notes only that every year on the eve of St. Bartholomew the Apostle he saw the scholars of divers grammar-schools repair into the churchyard of St. Bartholomew, where upon a bench boarded about under a tree some one scholar would oppose and answer, until he were put down by a better scholar, who in turn yielded to his superior. Though he praises this habit of disputation, Stow does not say that he took his share of the argument under the tree, and maybe he was bred at a school deemed unworthy to compete with St. Paul's in London or St. Peter's at Westminster. What is certain is that he deserted the craft of candlemaking, which his fathers had followed, was apprenticed to a tailor, was admittted to the freedom of the Merchant Tailors in 1547, and remained faithful to the trade for thirty years. That he was a good tailor seems improbable. He who, in Aubrey's phrase, ' stitched up ' so many chronicles, was not likely to be skilful with his needle. However, he kept house near Aldgate Pump, the object, no doubt, of his pious worship, and it is a strange commentary on the manners of the time that in 1549, after a commotion of the commons in the Eastern Counties, the Bailiff of Romford was hanged upon the pavement of his door. Meanwhile he performed the duties of a citizen with promptitude and loyalty. He sate upon juries, he served as a Whiffler in the pageant of two Lord Mayors, and he took as keen an interest in the affairs of the city as though he had never known what history was or had followed the devious paths of astrology.

The most loyal of his biographers tells us that he was very careless of scoffers, backbiters, and detractors, and that he lived peacefully. This tribute is wholly undeserved. Either by ill-fortune or in obedience to his temperament, John Stow was always plunged deep into the fiercest quarrels. There was nothing that did not serve him for a brawl—a book, an affront, an unjust will. Possibly he sought relief in conflict from the monotony of existence. The life of a citizen in Tudor England, amiable though it was, knew but few excitements, and when Stow's ardour was not satisfied with learning, he fell to fighting. Strife, indeed, was in his blood. He was not the only Stow that loved quarrelling. Once upon a time, for instance, there was a dispute between Thomas, his brother and Thomas Holmes, 'both brethren of this mystery,' which came before the Company of Merchant Tailors. Now, the wife of the said Holmes had used indecent words against the wife of the said Stow, and the Master and Wardens decreed that Holmes's wife should profess her sorrow, and that Holmes should solace Stow's injured feelings by twenty shillings of lawful English money.

This was a mere skirmish, if we compare it with

the far more desperate battle in which John Stow
was presently engaged with William Ditcher, *alias*
Telford, who, if we may believe Stow's own petition,
addressed to the Aldermen of the Ward, was a very
master of scurrility and abuse.   At a certain Christmas Ditcher was forbidden by the wardmote to set
'his frame with fetharbends' in the street, and
incontinently he charged Stow with lodging a complaint against him.   The charge was false, says
Stow, but its falsehood was no check to Ditcher's
ferocity.   At the outset, Ditcher and his wife were
content to rail at Stow as he passed them by, and
when that would not serve, they stood at his door
hurling at him shameful and slanderous words.
This was hard to be borne.   Still harder was it
when Ditcher told the parson of the parish, and any
other man whom he chanced to meet, that Stow
kept no company but that of rogues and rascals, who
had him from ale-house to ale-house every day and
every night till two o'clock in the morning.   The
terms of abuse chosen by Ditcher increased in
virulence as the quarrel went unassuaged, and Stow,
furious at being called 'prick-louse knave,' 'rascal
knave,' 'beggarly knave,' felt that his enemy had
reached the zenith of opprobrious injustice when he
declared that the said John had made a chronicle
of lies.

From words the miserable Ditcher went to deeds.
He challenged Stow to fight, and when the erudite
tailor declined the encounter, Ditcher scratched him

by the face, drew blood on him, and was pulled off
by the neighbours. What wonder is it, then, that
Stow appealed to the wardmote for protection from
this violent ruffian, who spared his wife and his
apprentice as little as he spared the man himself?
The apprentice, indeed, came off badly in the affair,
for when he, too, declined the combat, Ditcher said
he would provide for him, and would accuse him
of killing the man at Mile End in Whitsun Week.
And yet Stow was worthy whatever respect the
wardmote could show him. Had he not published a
worthy chronicle? And had he not, to cite his own
words, 'three daughters marriageable and in service
with right worshipful personages'?

And for all his energy and eloquence, Ditcher was
but a man of straw, set up to frighten the tailor by
the tailor's real, inveterate enemy, his brother Thomas.
Fortunately we have Stow's own account of his family
quarrel, which, as vivid in style as it is frank in expression, is a curious chapter in the history of manners,
and suggests that had Stow been minded to leave the
chronicles to such botchers as Grafton, he might have
composed a journal worthy to be set side by side with
the masterpiece of Pepys. The beginning of the strife
is hidden from us. Its end came only with the death
of the combatants, and its vigorous conduct proves
that, if John was the better scholar, Thomas was
easily superior in savagery of temper and lack of
scruple. It chanced one day in June 1568 that
old Mrs. Stow, who lived in the house of her

younger son, Thomas, came on a visit to John,
who, as in duty bound, sent for the best ale and
bread, and placed a cold leg of mutton before her,
whereof she ate very hungrily. Presently she fell
to butter and cheese, and thus heartened by meat
and drink she promised to leave John £10 in her
will, to look upon him as her eldest born, and if
any man or woman attempted to dissuade her, she
would cry out upon him, 'Avoid, devil.' And then
the best ale loosened John's tongue, who made bold
to say what he thought of his brother Thomas, and
to lament that he was matched with a harlot.

Mother and son parted well pleased with each
other, but no sooner was the good woman returned
to Thomas's house than Thomas and his wife forced
her to relate all that had passed between her and
John. When Thomas was told of the slur cast
upon his wife's character, his fury knew no bounds.
Nothing would content him than that John should
be struck out of the will altogether, and though the
overseers would not consent to this, John was bequeathed no more than a poor five pounds. 'Thus,'
says John with a grim humour, 'I was condemned
and paid five pounds for accusing Thomas his wife
a harlot, privily only to one body (who knew the
same as well as I); but if he could so punish all
men that will more openly say so much, he would
soon be richer than any Lord Mayor of London.'
The injustice thus done to John was the more
flagrant, because a few days after Thomas not

merely brought the same charge against his wife, but for her sins thrust her out of doors. And when his neighbours begged him to take her back, he refused, saying she would be his death, for she still went to witches and sorcerers.

Then came the strangest scene in this tragicomedy of middle-class life. At ten o'clock in the night the wretched woman crept back into the house, and Thomas, bare-legged and indignant, searched for her, and, having found her, fell to beating her again. Meanwhile his mother, who lay sick upon her pallet, began to look about the chamber for Thomas's hosen and shoes, and carried them downstairs, praying him to put them on lest he should catch cold. But Thomas turned a callous ear to her solicitude, and let her stand shivering for more than an hour. Nor was it Thomas who suffered in the end. He and his wife went to bed and agreed well enough. His mother took such a cold that she never rose from her pallet again.

Thus, waged with alternate cunning and fury on either side, the battle was fought to the bitter end. On St. James's Eve John sent his wife to Thomas's house with a pot of cream and a pottle of strawberries for a peace-offering. Thomas would have none of them, and drove her forth with bitter oaths and charges of witchcraft. 'I will make the villain John be handled,' cried he, 'or it shall cost me a hundred pounds. I will make all the world to know what arts he practiceth; and get ye out of my doors, or, by Peter, I will lay thee at my feet.' After this outrage a sudden calm fell upon the family. Thomas sought his brother out, sent for a pint of ale, and bade him drink, professing sorrow for the past and friendship in the future. And the dying mother murmured from her pallet : 'The Lord be praised, for now my children that were dead are alive again.' The peace, unhappily, did not last long. John, still dissatisfied, demanded once more his proper share of the inheritance, and asked his mother to cause Thomas to read the 133rd Psalm : 'Behold how pleasant and how joyful a thing it is for brethren to dwell together and be of one mind.' This was too great a demand upon the old lady's courage. She dared not argue with Thomas, evidently a ruffian of forcible character, and John would not desist from urging his claim, though she lay on her deathbed. Again the brethren fell a-quarrelling, even in her presence, and she died to the echo of oaths, threats, and foul words. On the morrow of her burial, which was Saturday, there was another reconciliation. 'I met Thomas Stow,' writes John, 'my sister, and Henry Johnson at Leadenhall. So we went to the Maiden's Head and drank a pint of wine or twain.' And then the feud broke out again more fiercely than before.

Thomas Stow's last assault upon his brother might have had a more dangerous result than the loss of a mere five pounds. Unpacified by his triumph, he laid information against him that he was a favourer of the Duke of Alva, that he practised magic, and was a friend of papistry. John Stow's books were examined by Cecil's order, and he himself was brought before the Ecclesiastical Commissioners. That he escaped does credit to the justice of the time, for Thomas was dishonest with the dishonesty of the fool, and he would have stuck at nothing to ruin his brother. As for the motives of this quarrel, unique in our annals, they are not easy to discern. It may be that differences of religion, always a fertile source of argument, kept the two men apart. It may be that Thomas was jealous of John's superiority, that he grudged him his books and the great friends that they brought him, that he hoped to put him back in what he thought his proper place—the tailor's stall. However that may be, it must be confessed that neither side conducted the dispute with dignity. There is little of the scholar and nothing of the gentleman in John's demeanour. He, too, descended into the pit, clamoured against Thomas, and embittered the last miserable days of his mother. And though he was beaten for the moment, he took a revenge which was beyond the reach of his brother. Never in his *Chronicle* nor in his *Survey* does he write of brotherly feuds without a glance at his own sad experience. With an evident zest he describes how, in 1196, William Fitz Osbert, a man of evil life and a secret murderer, and still worse, a false accuser of his elder brother, was righteously brought to the gallows, and thereto he gravely adds in the manuscript : 'Such a brother

have I.   God make him penitent.'   Thus, after
thirty years, the old man cherished his anger, and
who shall say that he was not justified?

These grimy quarrels, which set brother against
brother, this eager hankering to change an old
woman's will, were but interludes in the career of
John Stow.   Many years before he came to blows
with Thomas he had begun the process of self-
education, which gave him a place in English literature.   Studious by temperament, he had assiduously
cultivated his natural gifts.   At the outset his taste
had lain in poetry and sorcery.   He had always an
eager love of magic, and his first work was an
edition of Chaucer, the father of English poets,
whom he never quoted save with becoming reverence.
But gradually he was drawn away to the study of
history, which study he embraced with the greater
ardour because it gave him an excuse for quarrelling
with Grafton, whom he attacked sometimes with
injustice, and always with ferocity, and who in the
vigour of his hate took up almost as wide a space as
his false and avaricious brother.

Hearne, praising his industry, denies him scholarship, and Hearne, no doubt, was in the right.   On
the one hand, Stow was a late learner, and like all
late learners he was wont to take surprise at his own
erudition, and to mistrust the attainments of his
rivals.   On the other hand, his toil and energy are
beyond dispute.   He spared neither himself nor his
pocket.   That he might collect manuscripts and

books, that he might understand and transcribe what
he had collected, the honest tailor forgot his trade
and recked not of fatigue. His work cost him, as
he confessed, 'many a weary mile's travel, many a
hard-earned penny and pound, and many a cold
winter night's study.' And his labour was the
greater because he could not ride, and thus was
forced to go on foot into divers chief places of the
land to search the records. Nor was he in any
haste to gather the fruit of his toil. He was already
fifty-five before the first of his serious works, *A
Chronicle of England from Brute until the Year*
1580, was published. Twelve years afterwards
came the first edition of his *Annals*, and these two,
with his *Survey of London*, make up the literary
baggage of a busy life.

The baggage, rather heavy than various, is the
baggage not of a historian but of a chronicler. If
Stow was better than most of his kind, he was a
chronicler still. He made no pretence to combine
events or to divine their causes. He wrote from
year to year, almost from day to day, and in his
view all events were of an equal and separate
importance. If he had a preference, it was for the
trivial. Had he been alive now, he would have
made a first-rate reporter. He had learned the first
two lessons taught by the modern newspaper (1)
that the more fatuous is an episode, the more instant
is its 'appeal'; and (2) that you may discover
curiosity and even scandal in sudden changes of

the weather. I do not think that he ever found a
large gooseberry. It would have been a happy day
for him if he had. But turn his pages at random
and you will find many strange pieces of absurdity.
The specimen which follows, culled from the year
1389, will serve as well as another to illustrate the
Chronicler's sense of selection : 'A fighting among
gnats at the King's Manor of Sheen, where they were
so thick gathered, that the air was darkened with
them ; they fought and made a great battle. Two
parts of them, being slain, fell down to the ground ;
the third part, having got the victory, flew away, no
man knew whither. The number of the dead was
such, that they might be swept up with besoms,
and bushels filled with them.'

Though such an adventure, surely unparalleled
since the Battle of the Frogs and Mice, would make
the fortune of a morning paper, it may justly be
accounted beneath the dignity of history. And even
the fighting gnats faded in Stow's interest beside a
frozen river. Never, indeed, was he so happy as
when he might record a quick fall of temperature,
and seldom did he have a better chance than in
1564, when on the 21st of December there began
so hard a frost that on New Year's eve people went
over and along the ice as they would, from London
Bridge to Westminster, while some played at football
as boldly there as if it had been on dry land, and
others shot at pricks set up on the Thames. But,
despite his love of triviality, despite the fact that, as

Fuller said, ' he was such a smell-feast that he cannot
pass by Guildhall but his pen must taste of the
good cheer within,' Stow was a faithful chronicler.
' However he kept tune, he kept time very well ' ;
in other words, he was exact in chronology, and
served as an authority to many wiser historians.
He did his best, also, to gather knowledge from eye-
witnesses, and he told Sir George Buc, the biographer
of Richard III., that he had spoken with those who
had seen that king, and who pronounced him a very
comely personage. In brief, his chronicles now and
again stray into history, and his patriotism was
never at fault. If he loved London like a Londoner,
he loved England as an Englishman should love her,
and he set an example of cheerful enthusiasm which
our historians have not always followed.

And what did he get for his toil? If we may
believe him, little indeed. He rightly claimed that
those who ' have brought hidden Histories from
dusky darkness to the sight of the world ' deserve
some thanks for their pains. He had received, said
he, only ingratitude. After Stow's death, Edward
Howes, his faithful editor, hinted that the chronicler's reward was an assurance of endless reproach.
In these complaints there is an obvious exaggeration.
The rivalry of chronicler's led, no doubt, to strife.
But who loved strife better than Stow? His en-
counters with Grafton gave him more pleasure than
a Lord Mayor's feast, and he never lost a chance of
insulting his enemy. And if his toil brought him

small profit, surely he was not singular in that. His knowledge of the city should have taught him that intelligence finds its own reward. And even in pocket he was the richer for his researches. Master William Camden, 'his loving friend,' gave him £8 a year. It was not for his skill in their craft that the Company of Merchant Tailors paid John Stow, 'a loving brother of this mystery,' a yearly fee of £4, but 'for divers good considerations them specially moving.'

And Stow himself made light of his misfortunes. 'He and I walking alone,' said Ben Jonson to Drummond, 'he asked two cripples what they would take to have him of their order.' He hobbled and he was poor, and therefore in no better case than the cripples; but he could jest with them, and in the best company. Nor was the Court wholly unmindful of him. King James, recognising that his 'loving subject John Stow (a very aged and worthy member of our city of London) this five and forty years hath to his great charge, and with neglect of his ordinary means of maintenance, compiled and published divers necessary books and chronicles,' granted him Letters Patent to collect voluntary contributions and kind gratuities from whom he could. To our minds it seems a selfish kind of largesse, but it was the custom of the time, and was well understood by those to whom the appeal was made. A like privilege was given to Philemon Holland, another ill-requited man of letters, and it need have brought no shame to Stow to follow so illustrious an example.

One other reward was given to Stow by his work—the reward of friendship. He lived on terms of familiarity with the scholars and wits of his time. His geniality and his learning were such as few could withstand. He was well described as 'a merry old man,' and he was perfectly conscious of his merriment. To drink a pint of 'best ale' in an Aldgate tavern with John Stow was like cracking a bottle at the Mermaid ; and if his amiable humour, now mellowed with the years, attracted the simple, his erudition and his library brought the learned to his feet. He was among the first to join Archbishop Parker's famous Society of Antiquaries, at whose meetings he encountered the historians of either university. He was always ready to lend a manuscript or to aid in the editing of a Latin text. Among his correspondents were many honourably distinguished men. Sir Henry Savile calling him 'good old friend,' and confessing that he 'has found at all times good favour of him since their first acquaintance ; and other acquaintance in London has he none,' beseeches him to certify 'if Wigornensis is printed.' And presently, growing in intimacy, Savile sends him 'a mild sixpence to drink a quart of wine in your travel.' It is a strange relationship, and stranger still it seems if we call to mind the bare legs, the squalid household, the grim vituperation of Thomas Stow, and the three daughters in worshipful service. The Chronicler, in truth, made the best of both worlds—the world of the city, which was veritably his own, and the world of scholarship, which was his by right of conquest.

His portraits reveal what manner of man he was, and a friend has sketched him in words with a kindliness beyond the scope of portraiture. ' He was tall of stature,' wrote Howes, ' lean of body and face, his eyes small and crystalline, of a pleasant and cheerful countenance ; his sight and memory very good ; very sober, mild, and courteous to any that required his instructions ; and retained the true use of all his senses unto the day of his death, being of an excellent memory. He always protested never to have written anything for malice, fear, or favour, nor to seek his own particular gain or vainglory ; and that his only pains and care was to write truth.' He died in 1605, being four score years of age, and he was buried in his parish church of St. Andrew Undershaft. A monument was set up in his honour by Elizabeth, his wife, whom in a moment of greedy appeal he once unjustly denounced to his mother as a wife that can neither get nor save. She got or saved enough for his glory, and to her spirit of forgiveness we owe the solemn presentment of the ancient chronicler, seated at his table, and holding in his hand the goose-quill wherewith he hymned the praise of London, his native city, and celebrated in his homely style the exploits of our kings and governors.

JOHN STOW—II

WHEN John Stow sat him down to what he
called 'the discovery of London,' he approached his task in a spirit of loyal humility. 'It is
a duty,' said he, ' that I willingly owe to my native
mother and country,' and he discharged the duty
with all the zeal and intelligence that were his.
'What London hath been of ancient time,' he
claims, 'men may here see, as what it is now every
man doth beholde.' Alas, we behold it no longer,
and it is not easy to reconstruct London's vanished
beauty from Stow's record. He saw it, as we see
it, in a moment of transition. Gothic austerity was
yielding to the grace and lightness of the Tudor
style. Timber was replacing stone. Stow is quick
to record the triumph of the new material.
'Downe lower have ye Elbow lane,' says he,
'and at the corner thereof was one great stone
house, called Olde Hall, it is now taken downe and
diverse faire houses of timber placed there.' Contrary to the conservative habit of his mind he seems
to have welcomed the innovation. In a passage of
rare enthusiasm he acclaims the stately house of

brick and timber lately raised by Sir Robert Cecil, but his enthusiasm was evoked less by the elegance of the design than by the paved and levelled highway, which beautified the street and served for the great commodity of passengers. Stow, in fact, did not presume to explain or to criticise the architecture of London. He was a plain man, who dealt with facts, catalogued monuments, wrote down inscriptions, and left the work of appreciation to others. In his eyes a palace and a conduit were of equal value. A visit to St. Martin's Oteswick inspired him to this reflection, ' You had of olde time a faire well with two brackets, so fastened that the drawing up of the one let downe the other, but now of late that well is turned into a pumpe.' Herein may be discerned the true spirit of the book—a book written not merely by a citizen for citizens, but by an antiquary for antiquaries.

And Stow, being both a citizen and an antiquary, had all the limitations of his kind. He was not very observant, and he was very credulous. If he was all unconscious of the city's wonderful aspect, he was eager to believe in any legend that was brought to his ear. He is vastly interested in the strange bones that once were treasured in ancient churches. He tells us little enough of St. Lawrence, in the Jewry, but he does not forget the immense bone which he saw there, fastened to a post of timber, which most took to be the thighbone of a man, and which he attributed doubtfully to ' an oliphant.'

As to the larger specimen, preserved in the church of St. Mary, Aldermanbury, he had no doubt. 'True it is,' he writes in all simplicity, 'that this bone (from whence soever it came) being of a man, as the form showeth, must needs be monstrous, and more than after the proportion of five shanke bones of any man now living amongst us.' Again, though he pronounced Gerrard the giant and his mighty staff to be fables, perhaps because Grafton gave credit to them, and because the master of the hostelry, where the staff was kept, refused to tell him its history, but bade him consult a rival chronicle, he put implicit faith in his father's story that once, upon St. James's night, the devil appeared in the church of St. Michael's, Cornhill, and left the print of his claws on certain stones in the north window, as if they had been so much butter.

Such was Stow's temper, such the criticism of his time. He exercised his faith as he chose, accepting this fact and rejecting that, according to the whim and fancy of the moment. It is, indeed, his prejudices which give life and humour to his work. He cursed most heartily him who removed his neighbour's landmark. Living at a time when the city was greedily encroaching upon the open spaces, he lost no chance of condemning those who covered what once were pleasant walks with bricks and timber. Sorrowfully does he record that apples grew where now houses were lately built, and that from Houndsditch in the west, to

Whitechapel in the east, the fields were all turned into 'Garden plottes, teynter yardes, bowling allyes, and such like.' The truth is that, though as I have said, he smiled upon the houses of the new fashions, in all other matters he hated change with a constant heart. His sentiment was anchored securely in the past. Even the inns of London were little to his taste. He remembered with pleasure the brave days when Eastcheap was a cooks' row, and that there they cried hot ribs of beef roasted, pies well baked, and other victuals. 'Of olde time,' says he, 'when friends did meet, and were disposed to be merrie, they went not to dine and supper in taverns, but to the cookes, where they called for meate what them liked, which they alwayes found ready dressed at a reasonable rate.'

As he loves the customs, so he loves the charity and magnificence of ancient days, when the poor man found a ready welcome at the rich man's gate, and the rich man thought it no dishonour to display his wealth. He tells us, with a reflected pride, that time was when Wolsey kept 400 servants, excluding his servants' servants, who were a goodly train, and he was old enough to recall the grandeur and generosity of the religious houses. He had seen a buck brought up to the altar steps of Paul's in solemn procession, and had watched the dean and chapter, apparelled in copes and vestments, with rose-garlands on their heads, send the body of the buck to the baking. His well-stored memory carried him

back to the reign of King Henry, and as he lived to
see the first James mount the throne he had witnessed
a complete revolution in thought and manners.   He
recked not of revolutions.   He turned his eyes
resolutely backward : he sought in history what his
own age could not give him ; in pious secrecy he
deplored the evil influence of the reformation ; he
witnessed with a sad regret the influx of penurious
foreigners; and he descended to an honourable poverty
without making a single concession to the changed
world that lay about him.

If he was not quick in appreciation, if he knew
not how to describe or applaud, if he was so patient
a collector of facts, which he could neither contrast
nor combine, that he never ceased to be hampered
with his own collections, none was ever a more
constant lover of London than he.   He quotes the
testimonies to its grandeur wherever he can find
them.   He delights in the praise of Tacitus, that
London, though no colony of the Romans, was yet
most ' famous for the great multitude of merchants,
provisions, and intercourse.'   But it was not for its
beauty and romance that he loved it.   He loved it
because there he was born and bred, because it
reminded him that he was a citizen of no mean city,
because the tailor's stall, which brought him bread
and cheese, stood hard by the famous pump of Aldgate.   The brilliance and colour of its streets, the
courage of its many-coloured life, the skill of its poets,
the enterprise of its adventurers, escaped him.   And

yet the vision of its splendour might have tempted to enthusiasm even a citizen's pen. A city, noble in its simplicity, with tortuous streets, which turned and twisted by an accident of slope or stream between gabled houses of fair brick and sturdy timber—such was London in Stow's day. The brave costume and proud bearing of the rufflers and courtiers, who lived side by side with prosperous merchant or thrifty shopkeeper, were worthy so handsome a setting. There were met within a narrow compass men of a hundred crafts and a hundred talents. Travellers fresh from the wonders of the new world jostled actors from the Globe and the Curtain, or drank with soldiers fresh from the wars in the taverns of Wallbrook or on the Bankside. Like the true citizen that he was, Stow passed the traveller idly by. He had no eye for strange sights, no ear for strange stories. Give him a pageant or a Lord Mayor's Show, and he was content. Let him amuse his leisure at a bear-baiting or a fair, and he did not ask exotic pleasures.

Of architecture he made but one demand : let not the houses be too high. He deemed no censure, no punishment excessive for those who expressed their arrogance in lofty walls. The first private man that ever he heard of, who built a high tower of brick to overlook his neighbours, was Angell Dune, grocer and Alderman of London, and the delight of his eye was punished with blindness some years before his death. The second citizen, who journeyed

thus far on the path of vainglory, came to no better
end. Richard Wethell was his name, and having in
his hot youth transgressed Stow's unalterable canon,
he ' became in short time so tormented with goutes
in his joynts, of the handes and legges, that he could
neither feed himself, nor goe further than he was led,
much lesse was he able to climbe, and take the
pleasures of the height of his Tower.' Thus
a proper Nemesis overtook those who dared to ape
the impiety of Babel, and Stow's condemnation was
perfectly just. London is a true city of the
North, and cannot endure tall houses, which shut
out the light and cast long shadows. Nothing
should interrupt the rays of sun, always few and
furtive, which fall upon its streets, and Stow's
contemporaries were fortunate, in that the two
miscreants, who dared to darken the sky with
their proud roofs, were speedily overtaken by a
poetic justice. The London of to-day is less happy.
Its citizens are free to heap up mountains of bricks
and mortar, of stone and iron. This they do not
for pride but for profit, and, in order that they may
swell an over full pocket, the poor wayfarer must
walk up and down like a pigmy at the bottom of
a sightless, airless tank.

A far stranger limitation than his insensibility to
the beauty and romance of life was Stow's complete
ignorance of the drama. He lived in England's
golden age, and was all unconscious of his privilege.
His mind was as little picturesque as his style.

Devoid himself of imagination, he prized it not in others. The great ones of the earth made no impression upon his provincial mind. To read his *Survey* is to get an impression of a county town, where nothing happened of greater importance than the election of an alderman. Too old-fashioned to understand the new craft of the stage, he has no word to say of Shakespeare. Ben Jonson was his familiar friend, and he displays less interest in the poet than in last year's sheriff. The ancient plays, which two hundred years before his time took three, and even eight days to enact, aroused his curiosity. They belonged to the realm of archæology, in which he, the studious tailor of Aldgate, was a reigning monarch. The plays of his own time inspired him with no more than this simple statement : 'Of late time in place of these Stage playes, hath been used Comedies, Tragedies, Enterludes, and Histories, both true and fained : for the acting whereof certain publike places have beene erected.' And then he passes hastily to the more congenial topics of cock-pits and tennis-courts.

The omission is remarkable, even if it proves no more than that the prophet must expect no honour among his contemporaries. For Stow, though a citizen, was not unlettered. He gave many years of his life to the making and editing of books. He had done his best to bring the works of Chaucer before the eyes of his countrymen. He knew something of Gower, whose works he possessed in manuscript. He quotes Lydgate and *Piers the Plowman.* Yet he knew no more of Shakespeare than of Holbein, and it is by his limitations that we mark him : a fusty old tailor, to whom a Latin chronicle said more than *Hamlet* ; a student, who found more in the dullest records than in the sights and sounds of London ; a writer, for whom the seven deadly sins are all comprised in the one sin of inaccuracy, who has a word for Aschan the fishmonger, and none for Ascham the schoolmaster, and who mentions Sir Francis Drake, 'that famous Mariner,' for no better reason than that he once inhabited a great old house, called the Erber. In brief, worthy, affable, and merry as he was, he had closed his ears to the Sirens' song, and it is not to him that we must go for an echo of his melodious age.

Stow's London, then, is a strange dispeopled place, where no footfall is ever heard and no laugh echoes. Even his aldermen and sheriffs are but names to which neither respect nor quality is attached. For the intimacy, which divines the character of those about him, Stow had neither taste nor talent. If you could measure how far he fell short of his opportunity, turn to the more highly gifted of his contemporaries, who professed an interest in London. Instantly the honest man, so great among the chroniclers, is dwarfed to his proper stature. Thomas Nashe, for instance, understood London as well as any of his fellows, and for him it is a place of amusement or repentance, according to the

shifting of his mood and the weight of his pocket.
None knew better than he the life of the tavern and
playhouse. To none were revealed more clearly
London's ghostly dominations and the terrors of
its nights. None more eloquently deplored the
ambition and covetousness, the atheism and lust,
which beset the city to its undoing. With a
familiar touch he sketched the ostler that hath
built a goodly inn, the carman in his leather pilch,
the black-gowns and buckram bags of Westminster
Hall, the malcontents, who dined with Duke
Humphry at Paul's, the old straddling usurers, who
gave him cold comfort in his necessity. And he
made all these and many others real, because he had,
what he said the chroniclers lacked, 'the wings of
choice words to fly to heaven.'

Yet vividly as Nashe sees what lies about him, it
is denunciation which best suits his humour and his
style, and he falls upon London, like a prophet of
evil, foretelling its doom with a sinister raillery.
'London,' he cries, 'look to thyself, for the woes
that are promised to Jerusalem, are promised to thee.
. . . Fly from sin, take no pride or vainglory in it.
. . . Ah! what is sin that we should glory in it?
To glory in it is to glory that the Devil is our
father. Doth the peacock glory in his foul feet?'
Nashe's inspiration is literary, no doubt. We need
not assume that he was overcome by puritanical
zeal, or that he was a Bunyan, eager for the world's
reform. He was but painting a vision of the London

which he saw, and which was as remote from the
London of the chroniclers, who wrote of ' nothing
but mayors and sheriffs, and the dear years and the
great frost ' as the London of Elizabeth's reign was
from the well-ordered, petroleum-driven city of to-day.

As little shall we recognise the London of the
plain citizen in Dekker's masterpiece of cruel
observation : the *Gull's Horn Book*. Here, at any
rate, Dekker displayed not even a literary interest
in reformation. He was content to hold the mirror
of ridicule before the face of the Gull, who had not
the wit to see his own image reflected therein.
Irony and malice are the weapons wherewith he
attacks the insolent youth ' about town,' and we
admit the truth of his satire, because the traits
that he shows us are common to all the ages. He
takes his young gallant to an ordinary, where he
bids him discourse as loud as he can to no purpose,
to laugh in fashion, and not to doff his cap to the
gentleman, to whom, two nights since, he was
beholden for a supper. Then he sends him off to
the playhouse, and seats him on the stage, thus
giving him a conspicuous eminence, and 'a signed
patent to engross the whole commodity of censure.'
Here he tells him he shall be crowned with rich
commendation if he ' laugh aloud in the midst of
the most serious and saddest scene of the terriblest
tragedy,' and urges him, if he like not the poet, to
rise with a screwed face from his stool, and to distaste
the scenes the worse, the better they are. And so

the gallant passes from playhouse to tavern, and 'after the sound of pottle-pots is out of his ears, and that the spirit of wine and tobacco walks in his brain, the tavern door being shut upon his back, he casts about to pass through the widest and goodliest streets in the city'; he insults the watch, talks of lords if any one may approach ; and is ready at noon on the morrow to begin another day in Paul's Churchyard, censuring new books, mewing at the old, visiting the tobacco-ordinary, or breathing in a fence-school. Dekker drew from the life; we should know his gull if we met him in Piccadilly to-day ; and there is a nearer approach to truth and humanity in one of his pages than in all the folios of honest Stow.

It is not merely the types of London which endure. The ground-plan of the city still resists the shocks of time and chance. Though scarce a dwelling-house remains upon which John Stow cast his eyes, the Londoner may use a map of the sixteenth century and not find himself hopelessly at fault. With the ground-plan the ancient names of the street persist also. Cornhill and Lombard Street, Cheap and Budge Row, Aldgate Street and Poultry—there they are in Shakespeare's London as they are in ours. Other buildings have risen on their fringe and are put to other purposes, but the highway keeps the same, and by the same signs you may trace it. And the London of to-day, still breathing the air of a stern Conservatism, is confronted by the same problems

which perplexed the Elizabethans. Changed as it
is, it cherishes the same ambitions, it attempts to
suppress the same abuses as of yore.

A certain graduate of Oxford who, at Stow's
bidding, attempted to give us 'an insight' into the
city, would enter readily into our discussions, if he
came back to life. He knew full well that London's
first necessity was to find proper markets for its
merchandise. He did not think that the shortest
cut to the golden age was to buy all things cheap
and to sell nothing. He urged the city to follow
the counsel of that good old husband, Marcus Cato,
saying : 'Oportet patrem familias vendacem esse
non emacem,' since ruin lurked in a policy of bringing more merchandise from beyond the sea than we
sent over. Again, the cry of 'back to the land'
was raised as loudly in the sixteenth century as it
is raised to-day. London was already drawing to
herself all the industries of the country. Artificers
and retailers alike were leaving the ancient cities and
market towns to bring their wares to the capital,
where they found a readier sale. And as the
countryside dwindled London grew, spreading out
its arms to embrace the suburbs, more bitterly
loathed then even than now, and converting great
houses into many tenements. In vain were laws
passed to check the invading city. London heeded
no laws ; long since she claimed the outskirts for
her own ; and placed them in her giant circle with
many a country town besides.

Thus the London of Stow has disappeared, save its names and its plan. And since Stow's day there have been many Londons, each one of which has left some trace behind. No pedantry had until lately disturbed the beautiful path of accident, and if Paris may vaunt the beauty of her design, it is character which has separated the London which yesterday we knew from all the cities of the earth. The Haussmann ideal has long been reducing Europe to a meaningless uniformity. A few relics of old Spain are hidden away in corners of Madrid. The style that is only too familiar thrusts itself upon us as we travel its wider thoroughfares. It is the boast of every German capital to be a little Paris. But London has been resolutely conservative. Even when she made up her mind to replace a tangled net-work of streets with a boulevard, she was wont to do it with half a heart. How long is it since Shaftes-bury Avenue was planned? And how long will the dingy houses of Soho redeem its western side from vulgarity? In fact, London was not built; it grew at hazard. As you cross some of its streets you may still pass from century to century. You may change the Classic for the Gothic style. You may discover a masterpiece of the Adams cheek by jowl with a monstrous agglomeration of 'flats.' More fortunate still, you might, a few years ago, have strayed suddenly into an unexpected county town. West-minster was once an interlude from the provinces. Fulham and Kensington each had its High Street, and kept with the old name a corporate life of its own. But to-day reverence for the past is dead. London is the Paradise of the County Councillor, and if only the financiers are amiable, in fifty years there will be no ancient stone left standing on another. Not only will the houses of London disappear before the greed of the speculative builder ; the streets themselves will be lost in straight-cut boulevards.

Speed and avarice are the enemies. The ideal city, says the County Councillor, is that which ensures the greatest rapidity of traffic. To get from one place to another as quickly as possible is, we are told, the sole purpose of modern life. For this purpose amenity and tradition must be sacrificed without delay or excuse. The tortuous streets, which seemed to begin nowhere and to go nowhither, and which in reality followed a wise law, are being swept away, that the clerk may not be interrupted on the way to his office. The ancient inns of court, with their clean, fresh lawns and shining plane-trees, which once proved London's faculty of surprise, have been torn down to make room for—what ? A monstrous, void space, which is not fit to hold a music-hall. The ample thoroughfare, pierced at the expense of many memories, is still an ample thoroughfare flanked by nothing better than a bare hoarding. Our County Councillors, indeed, have made a wilderness, and no doubt they call it peace. They have also destroyed a fabric and a feeling, which can never be restored. Once

London was wayward, various, fantastic. Now it is
on the road to become logical, and the motor-
omnibuses exult in their freedom.

What speed begins is consummated by avarice.
The high houses, which Stow deplored, overlook
their neighbours curiously in every quarter of the
town, and they have no justification save profit.
Obviously eight stories pay more rent than four.
What matters it, then, that the eight shut out the
light of heaven? Has not America proved that the
earth pays best when the heaviest loads are laid upon
it ? And why should we not follow the example of
America ? To give one reason among many,
because London is not, like New York, a southern
city. It is not asked to cover the passenger with
its shade, while it conducts him to his destina-
tion. As I have said, it should be the hope of our
architects not to exclude the sun, but to catch every
ray that falls athwart our streets. And this hope
will never be realised so long as vast masses of
red brick and black mortar, faced at a brief interval
by other masses of equal size and sombreness, are
accepted as an adequate definition of a street.

Thus it is that London, once triumphantly in-
consistent, is brought to the uniformity of a
surveyor's office. The mysterious hiding-places
and secret corners are all uncovered. Parks are
bisected to make a short cut. The loss caused by
the accidental turns and twists of ancient days is
estimated in miles, sovereigns, or foot-pounds.

Economy is proclaimed the constant foe of character and variety. Time was when the Strand and Oxford Street had each its own aspect, its own sentiment. To-day they are so much alike that even a Cockney may be forgiven if he mistakes the one for the other. The same masses of plate-glass, the same hideous shop-windows, composed in the style once called 'the new art,' and now fortunately old-fashioned everywhere save in London, give the wayfarer the same displeasure as he might receive from travelling through an unbroken line of railway stations. The chequered window-panes, which of old gave so trim an air to our shops, survive only in half-forgotten corners. Theirs was a separate elegance, theirs was an air of an older world, and they have been abolished that the gaze of the idler may not be intercepted. So presently the last traces of pleasantness will pass from our streets. The relics of a happier time will reveal themselves only to a devout research. The London which grew by chance, and created its beauty as it went along, will be replaced by a paltry imitation of a foreign city. But even though it cherish the ambition of Paris, it will not achieve it. While it has lost the character which once belonged to it, it has not gained the sense of design which embellishes its neighbours. The Strand, the scene of our architects' loftiest aspiration, is but a museum of conflicting styles. Nothing is left us save the atmosphere, which enwraps even the masterpieces of modern architecture in a cloak of mystery, and the river, ever changing in the changing light. With these we must content ourselves, until we are crushed beneath the weight of the motor-omnibuses, stealthy and immense, for whose untrammelled progress we have sacrificed the noble city which our fathers handed down to us.

THE ADMIRABLE CRICHTON

THE ADMIRABLE CRICHTON

IN the sixteenth century, as I have said,[1] no figure was more familiar to the courts and colleges of Europe than the travelling Scot. Cameron and Blackwood, Duncan and Balfour, won a more illustrious fame abroad than at home. The glory of Dempster, who was as quick to draw his sword or to take up a quarrel as the most irascible of Brantôme's heroes, and who carried his erudition at the steel's point to Paris, Pisa, and Bologna, is still undimmed. Bordeaux, Paris, and Coimbra profited by the rugged talent of George Buchanan. And yet by a stroke of fortune it is none of these eminent and travelled Scots who holds the first place in the popular imagination. That place was usurped long since by James Crichton, a youth who, immeasurably inferior in sound scholarship to Dempster, in poetry to Buchanan, had the rare faculty of drawing the eyes of all men upon him, and by his glittering gifts of speech and person captured a renown which then, as now, appeared the child of mystery and dæmonism.

I

James Crichton, the son of Robert Crichton of Eliock, Lord Advocate, and of Elizabeth Stewart,

[1] See p. 79.

daughter of Sir James Stewart of Beath, was born in 1560, on an island, said rumour, already busy about him, in the Lake of Cluny. On either side he claimed royal descent, and his pretensions had a surer basis in fact than those of many, his compatriots, who vaunted a lofty lineage. The precocity which has made him immortal was sedulously tended. Buchanan, Hepburn, Robertson, and Rutherford share the glory of his education, and he was but thirteen when he took his first degree at St. Andrews, a boy bachelor in very truth. Two years later he became Master of Arts, and at seventeen, when he went first upon his travels, the days of his pupilage were done. By habits of invincible industry he had improved a natural aptitude until he might claim, without boasting, to be the most learned youth of his years that ever held his own in the schools of Europe. He carried in his brain all the erudition of the time. If we may believe an early document, doubtless inspired by himself, he was already the master of ten languages. Philosophy and theology held no secrets from him. He knew the works of Plato and Aristotle as the merchant knows his account-books. And he had studied profoundly all the controversies which those masters of science had inspired. There was not one of the Christian Fathers whose works he had not read and pondered; and the best proof of his sincerity in these studies is that, while his father had embraced the reformed religion, he stood steadfast in the ancient faith, for the sake of which he lived under foreign skies an exile from his fatherland. He professed a deep skill in astrology, the favourite pursuit of his age, and with that independence of mind which distinguished him, he was prepared to argue that the calculations of his contemporaries were all erroneous. In the traditional mysticism of the Cabala he was especially well versed, than which his ingenuity found few better fields of exercise. Thomas Aquinas and Duns Scotus, with their attendant trains of Thomists and Scotists, were of course his familiars, and he was ready to dispute *in utramque partem* with all comers. Of this wide and multifarious knowledge he knew how to make the best use. All the gifts of facile presentation were his. He was of a surpassing beauty, wondrous tall and fair, and the mark of a red rose (*rubea rosa*) which nature had put about his right eye marked him out as something rare among men.

In brief, his face and speech, as a devout admirer said, seemed the daughters of a noble mind. His eloquence was quick and persuasive. He could address his audiences in all languages and to all purposes, and there was that suggestion of what a later age calls hypnotism in his manner which caught and held the attention of the least sympathetic. But the most remarkable talent that the lavish gods had bestowed upon him was the talent of memory, a talent far more highly esteemed then than now. ' He knew not what it was to forget,' says his

inspired rhapsodist. Whatever he had once seen or
heard was his own intimate possession until the end
of life. Had he listened, perchance, to a long oration,
he could give it back word for word as it was
delivered. He possessed, moreover, a rapid trick of
improvisation. He could compose Latin verses on
any given subject, in any given metre. He
resembled those artists of the Music Hall who
once upon a time would sing a song on the first
man chosen from a delighted audience. And he
achieved something more which was beyond their
reach. Having improvised a poem, he could repeat
it backward, beginning at the last word,—a feat
which was hailed as none the less wonderful on
account of its uselessness.

The manifold gifts of his mind did not impede the
prowess of his body. He was as apt for arms as for
arts. His learning was nothing else than a flower to
be worn at the point of his lance or on the crest of
his helmet. He excelled in all the martial exercises
of his time. A formidable antagonist with sword
and dagger, he was invincible in the joust. Neither
his hand nor his tongue ever trembled in the presence
of any adversary. As a horseman he found few
rivals among the cavaliers of his time. There was
no steed so violently unbridled but he could break it.
The praise which Rabelais gives to his hero might
well be applied to him : ‘The voltiger of Ferrara
was but an ape compared to him. He was singularly
skilful in leaping nimbly from one horse to another,

without putting foot to ground. . . . He could likewise from either side, with a lance in his hand, leap
on horseback without stirrups, and rule the horse at
his pleasure without a bridle. . . . Another day he
exercised the battle-axe, which he so dexterously
wielded, both in the nimble, strong, and smooth
management of that weapon, and that in all the
feats practicable by it, that he passed knight of arms
in the field, and at all essays.' Moreover, he
wrestled, ran, jumped, and danced with the light,
untrammelled skill wherewith he confuted his
opponents in the schools. Not even did he disdain
to play at ball, 'making it to bound in the air, both
with fist and foot.' In brief, he set before him the
high example of Gargantua, and, if we may believe
the testimony of friends, he fell not short of that
prince's giant prowess.

II

Such was James Crichton as he appeared to the
eulogists, inspired, as I have said, by himself. Such
he seemed to the schools and courts of Paris, when
they witnessed his feats of daring and erudition. He
was no more than seventeen when first he sought
fame and fortune abroad, and surely his gifts could
have found no more fitting theatre than Paris for
their display. For the Paris to which he came was
the Paris of Henri III. and Brantôme, the Paris whose
gaiety Rabelais had enhanced, whose pedantry his
ridicule had not abolished. If, in joyousness of heart,

the Parisians took for their motto, 'Do what you will,' they still loved the combats of spear and brain which had made them famous. Learning and bravery were alike the servants of competition. Tourneys were held in the Louvre, the voice of discussion was heard at the Sorbonne. An equal chance of distinction was given to the knights-errant of pen and sword, and in Paris Crichton found himself most intimately at home. Nothing had yet availed to check the practice of disputation, of disputation on all subjects, in all forms and languages, in accordance with all rules. It was wellnigh a century since Pico della Mirandola had offered to defend nine hundred paradoxes against all comers, and the test of learning was still the same. To us the test seems pedantic and irrelevant, but it was the test of the time, and by it Crichton, like many another of sounder learning than he, was tried and found excellent.

Arrived in Paris, Crichton, boy though he was, lost no time in posting a challenge on the gates of the schools, halls, and colleges of that renowned University, inviting all comers to dispute with him in any known language, *de omni scibili*.[1] He, meanwhile, already prepared for the fray, busied himself in the sports in which he surpassed his fellows, or

[1] Our only evidence for what Crichton achieved in Paris is Sir Thomas Urquhart, a witness suspect both by time and temper. But his account, if not literally, is yet essentially true, and may be accepted as a picture of the facts, seen through Sir Thomas's romantic eyes.

diverted his leisure with singing and playing on the lute, which were always his solace and delight. And as he thus gained a reputation for an idleness of which he was never guilty, his enemies, with more malice than truth, fixed this notice upon the door of the Sorbonne: 'If you would meet this monster of perfection, to make search for him either in the tavern or bawdy-house is the readiest way to find him.' Crichton laughed at the impertinence, and took a speedy revenge. The conference which he held in Paris was a splendid triumph for the miraculous youth. He proved a quicker knowledge than the most learned professors possessed even of their own subjects. He leapt from one language to another as from his desultory horses. He turned at will from prose to verse. In fine, he entertained the nimble-witted Parisians from nine o'clock in the morning till six at night, and there was not one scholar of them all who did not acclaim him worthy of the victor's wreath. As in bodily strength he might have taken Gargantua for his model, so in the things of the mind he followed the example of Gargantua's worthy son. Of him it might have been said, as it was said of Pantagruel: 'The vivacity of his spirit among the books was like a great fire amongst dry wood, so active it was, vigorous, and indefatigable.' [1]

[1] Consciously or unconsciously the accounts which we have of Crichton's attainments are echoed from the text of Rabelais. Gargantua's celebrated letter to his son might be accepted as

Not content with his victory in the schools, Crichton lost no time in displaying his valour on what Brantôme calls the *champ clos*. 'The very next day,' thus it is that Urquhart tells the story, 'to refresh his brains, as he said, for the toil of the former day's work, he went to the Louvre in a buff suit, more like a favourite of Mars than one of the Muses' minions; where, in the presence of some Princes of the Court and great ladies that came to behold his gallantry, he carried away the ring fifteen times on end, and broke as many lances on the Saracen.'

Thus for a while all was sport to him. He lived in the mimic combat of hand and brain, basking happily under the cloudless sky of success. And then, with what motive we know not, he exchanged the tourney for the battle, lent his gallant sword to France, and fought with distinction, it is said, in the Religious Wars. The voice of fame, hushed to a whisper in these squalid conflicts, breathes no word of his achievements. For two years he disappeared in a silence as of the grave, until the scholar that was in him awoke again. He himself

a sketch of Crichton's education, and his final exhortation would not have been uttered in vain to the eloquent Scot. 'Furthermore,' wrote Gargantua, 'I will that very shortly thou try how much thou hast profited, which thou canst not better do than by maintaining publicly theses and conclusions in all arts, against all persons whatsoever, and by haunting the company of learned men, both at Paris and otherwhere.' This is precisely what Crichton did in all the cities where he sojourned in the brief course of his life.

confesses that time was when Mars held sway in him, until the peaceful arts of Apollo persuaded him to turn from the horrors of war.[1] We know not for certain the moment of conversion, but in 1579 Crichton was in Genoa deploring the narrow straits of poverty into which he had fallen, and expressing a lachrymose gratitude to those who had befriended him. In a strain of unaccustomed modesty, he confesses his youth—he was nineteen —and the weakness of his talent : he deplores his very slender skill in speaking : he declares that, if there were in him any scantlings of virtue, or any mediocrity of intelligence which might have persuaded the scholars of Genoa to look favourably on him, they skulked in secret, oppressed by grief and privation. In the lofty terms of a turgid common-place, he extols the splendour of the Republic which gave him hospitality, the limitless glory of her senators, the wisdom of her benign prince, elected by the votes of her free citizens. With these inestimable blessings he contrasts the misdeeds of tyrants, naming with a flattering unction the classic ex-amples—Tarquin and Apollodorus, Dionysius and Alexander. To justice, liberty, and virtue he pays the tribute of the obvious, and closes an oration, which nowhere shines with the spark of youth or contains a characteristic sentence, by imploring the most illustrious senators of Genoa to offer, with him, their thanks to the Eternal God. Genoa did not

[1] This is stated both in the handbill and the Aldine pamphlet.

disdain his gifts ; she saw the genius of Crichton in spite of Crichton's misery ; and she paid him so high an honour that, said he, becoming once more his arrogant self, he would not exchange it for the statues of Demetrius or the honours of a consul.

III

The first necessity of Crichton's existence was prosperity. He was like a butterfly, who could not live out of the sun. Overhead the sky must always be clear, the applause of friends must ring in his ear, he must be pointed at with an approving finger in the street. The thought of Genoa, despite the honour which he received, was soon wearisome to him. The memory of an empty pocket and hard fare irked him sorely, and he was glad to find a kindlier refuge in Venice, then, as now, the wonder of the Adriatic, then, as no longer, the meeting-place of poets and learned men. He was not yet twenty-one when he came thither, a boy still in all save experience and knowledge of the world. He was determined, at all hazards, to conquer fame and wealth, and he set about the conquest by the only method yet discovered by ambitious men—the method of bold and fearless advertisement. A handbill[1] was issued, obviously with his connivance,

---

[1] This handbill, or *affiche*, printed by the Guerras in 1580, was discovered inserted in a copy of the second Aldine edition of the *Cortegiano* of Castiglione. It sets forth facts which

in which were celebrated his handsome person, his vast learning, his invincible skill in arms and horsemanship. It is an ingenious production, brief and adulatory, a masterpiece of blatant and unashamed panegyric. Yet it is of surpassing interest, for not only is it an early specimen of the preliminary puff—it is the first solid piece of evidence upon which our knowledge of Crichton rests. Had he lived to-day he would have confided to the reporters what a very fine fellow he was. There being no reporters at his hand, he inspired a hack to compose a handbill, which declared his perfections in the simplest language. And simple as it was, it has been eagerly seized upon by his biographers, who have echoed its crude flattery to such purpose that the earliest half-dozen authorities for the life of Crichton are not six but one.

Such was the first part of Crichton's scheme for making himself known to the scholars of Venice. His next step was to address a poem,[1] composed in hexameters, to Aldus Manutius, scholar, printer, and patron of letters. The poem, like the handbill,

were known to Crichton alone in all Venice, and must necessarily have been printed with his knowledge and approval. It may be found with many other documents in the appendix to Tytler's *Life of James Crichton*, 1819.

[1] This poem, which plays so large a part in the romance of Crichton, is a pamphlet of three leaves, bearing this title : ' In appulsu ad celeberrimam urbem Venetam de proprio statu Jacobi Critonii Scoti ad Aldum Manuccium Venetiis ex typographia Guerræa.'

is contrived after a very simple pattern. Crichton
pictures himself far from his fatherland, sitting on
the shores of the Adriatic, and wondering at the
lofty city set in the midst of the waves. He
laments in his mind his unhappy lot, and often
bedews his cheeks with tears, when presently a
Naiad appears to him, a Naiad most pleasing to the
docte Muses. At first Crichton thinks she is a
dream, deceiving his eyes, but she assures him with
burning words that she is no vain image, and that
she brings with her the commands of the Muses
and of Pallas, resonant with arms, to whom he is
a peculiar care. They bid him be of good cheer,
and promise better things. And then asks the
Naiad with excellent wisdom, of what have you
come to complain? All the world has its miseries,
says she, which she enumerates in a page of much
eloquence. That is all very well, replies Crichton.
I confess I am no longer harassed by a base poverty ;
I do not bear the burden of a nameless slavery.
But who in this great town knows my wretched-
ness? Who is there to solace me as I weep by
these sandy shores? Instantly the Nymph promises
him comfort. Is it possible, she asks, that the fame
of the divine Aldus, sprung of God-like parents,
has escaped you? He is known, she tells him,
to the whole world, to the discoloured Indian as
to the fierce Cantabrian. The long-haired Apollo
has confessed himself conquered by his reed and
lyre.

Thus after a long passage of flattery, which Aldus was not slow to return, the Nymph bids Crichton seek him out, and promises that all will be well. Truly all was well. Aldus accepted the nymph-inspired praise of Crichton with an interested enthusiasm. He reprinted the handbill, with modifications, and in a limited edition of thirty copies, as a comely pamphlet of four pages. He further rewarded Crichton's interested adulation with a dedication, to be found in the tenth volume of his Cicero, which has enhanced the reputation of the Scot more generously than any other document. While it repeats the lofty panegyric of the handbill and pamphlet, it discovers in its hero a hundred other perfections, and it will remain for ever the best witness in Crichton's favour, a witness whose evidence must be received with the profound suspicion of partiality. He likens the concourse of men, who went forth to meet Crichton at Venice, to the full assembly of the Athenian citizens, who, when Plato returned from Sicily, left the spectacle of the Olympic games to salute the philosopher. He boldly calls him the miracle of the human race —*humani generis miraculum*. In brief, Crichton and Aldus addressed one another in amœbæan strains. Adulatory verse was matched with panegyric prose, until Venice was assured that not merely had she bred a man of genius, but harboured under her sheltering roof a peerless poet and philosopher. And Aldus did Crichton a far greater service than mere praise. He presented him to all the learned men of Venice. He gave him an opportunity for the display of those brilliant gifts of oratory and dialectic which shine only in the applause of vast audiences. Sperone Speroni, Laurentius Massa, the eminent Donati himself, became his familiar friends, and the Latin odes which he addressed to the last two may still be read by the curious. So under the auspices of Aldus, Crichton appeared most honourably before the Doge of Venice and the elders of the State. He disputed with all his learning and subtlety of Philosophy, Theology, and the Mathematical Sciences, and it was in Mazzoni alone that he met his match. He discussed the doctrines of Thomists and Scotists with the erudite Padre Fiamma, *e con molti altri valorosi prelati*. He gave a profound address on the Procession of the Holy Ghost, and amazed his hearers by an unexpected mastery of recondite authorities. As his skill in disputation grew, the easy confidence which he had shown in Paris decreased, and after his first success at Venice he retired to a villa on the Brenta, there to meditate in solitude and prepare himself for a contest of three days, which took place at Pentecost in 1581 in the Chiesa san Giovanni e Paolo, and in which he promised to propose and defend two thousand conclusions. Even now he was but in his twenty-first year, he had already lived through a long life of experience, and it is not wonderful that his health broke at the strain. Ill and fatigued

he retired to Padua, and there found no rest. A
dazzling rumour had preceded him, and it was in
that city, the noblest on earth, as Aldus calls it,
that he achieved his highest triumphs.

IV

It was by the advice of Aldus that Crichton took
refuge in Padua. He could not have found a worse
place of recovery or a theatre better suited to his
talents. It was but right, says his ecstatic eulogist,
that the august majesty of Padua should receive and
embrace this miracle of human kind. And Padua
lost no time in offering an appropriate welcome.
The very day after Crichton's arrival, Cornelius
Aloisius summoned to his house the most erudite
men of the city, together with the noble youths of
the University, and there and then put Crichton's
readiness and scholarship to the test. He stood
before them all prepared to accept and to embellish
any subject they might propose to him in prose or
verse. The first task they set him was to hymn
the praise of Padua. He hymned it in an improvised
poem of surpassing elegance. And then, at their
bidding, he turned in a moment from his suave
Horatian ode to a solid refutation of the errors of
Aristotle and his commentators, and he refuted them
with so fine a modesty that his hearers knew not
which to admire the more—the worth of his mind or
the suavity of his manners. Nor were the scholars

of Padua content that Crichton had performed triumphantly these heroic tasks. They wished to close the sitting with a livelier theme, and after six hours of literary colloquies, they gave him for a subject the Praise of Ignorance, which he treated with all the splendid irony of Erasmus, and illustrated with so quick and various a fancy that they believed it was no reality which passed before them but a dream. The enthusiasm of Padua suggested that Crichton should give a second performance to those who had not been happy witnesses of his first, and another day was named. But for one reason or another Crichton did not answer the call, and instantly the voice of detraction was heard. Certain *homulli*, as Aldus calls them, proving in secret hatred their savage enmity, and having the will rather than the power to strike, dared to impeach his courage.

This was the kind of provocation which aroused the Scot to his best deeds, and straightway he replied with his famous challenge, a fine specimen of the scholarly insolence of the day. 'That James Crichton, the Scot,'—thus runs the imperishable document,—'may show his immortal gratitude to those who, excelling their fellows in virtue and true nobility of mind, are wont to think well of the lovers of virtue, and that he may take away from profligate and abandoned men every chance of future boasting, he will refute the well-nigh innumerable errors of Aristotle and of all the Latin philosophers, both of those who dispute of his intellect and of those who discuss matters of theology, as well as the dreams of some professors of mathematics, and he will answer objections.' He made his appeal as widely as possible, and promised to reply in accord with the customary rules of logic, or by the secret theory of numbers, or in any one of a hundred metres. The challenge was taken up, and Crichton met his adversaries with high courage and a candid front. For three days he held his ground unvanquished, and when he had finished his great feat of oratory, so loud a shout of applause was raised that nothing more magnificent had ever been heard by human ears. So thought Aldus, who was not merely the hero's zealous counsellor, but the dazzled spectator of the marvellous combat. Truly it was a wonderful feat : yet as we picture to ourselves the valiant scholar, replying to the pedants of theology in elegiac verse or in the Sapphics of Horace, we cannot but bethink ourselves of Rabelais' stinging satire on the Schools, and remember how Thaumast the Englishman, whose name, by a whimsical co-incidence, is the Greek for Crichton's own — *Admirabilis Scotus*—was put to a *non-plus* by Panurge when he argued by signs.

V

Crichton was not one to conquer the conquered, to slay the slain. No sooner was the illustrious city of Padua at his feet than forth he went to find another battlefield. Mantua attracted him—Mantua, the

cradle of poetry, the birthplace of Virgil, Prince of
Poets.   And it was to Mars, not to the Muses, that
there he offered his earliest devotion.   At his arrival
he found the Court of Mantua lying under the
imputation of cowardice.[1]   A certain Italian gentleman, a perfect master of the sword, had challenged
all and sundry to a combat *à outrance*, the prize
whereof was a purse of 500 ducats.   In Urquhart's
phrase, he had 'changed the blunt to sharp, the
foils to tucks,' and asking no quarter, intended to
give none.   His purpose was the same as Crichton's
—to earn fame and money by his skill.   Only, while
Crichton sought to conquer by the intellect, it was
his purpose to kill by the sword.   Three courtiers
he had left dead on the field, and his ambition was
still unsated.   Then it was that Crichton took up
his gage, and the two champions met in the
presence of the whole court.   At the outset,
Crichton, respecting his adversary, thought it better
to hold himself on the defensive ; but presently, seeing the Italian's spirits damped by fatigue, he 'changed
his garb, fell to act another part, and from defender
turned assailant.'   The issue was soon beyond doubt.
With three thrusts the Scot thrice pierced his
opponent's body, and thus freed Mantua of a
dangerous pest.

[1] Sir Thomas Urquhart is our chief authority for what
Crichton achieved at Mantua.   Despite his unbridled imagination, the fantastic knight is probably a witness of truth.   It is
his form, not his matter, that is in dispute.

The Duke was loud in the expression of gratitude ;
he appointed Crichton tutor to his son, Vincenzo
Gonzaga, or, as others say, accepted him as his friend
and military adviser, and the prosperity of the Scot
seemed assured. The dread of poverty, which had
afflicted him at Genoa, and cast a shadow upon his
soul at Venice, had vanished for ever. And he took
his good fortune with all his amazing gaiety of heart.
For a while he forgot the Schools and their disputations. No longer would he defend Plato against the
attacks of the jealous Aristotelians. To prove himself
admirable in all things, he turned to the theatre
for solace. He wrote comedies, though no comedy
equalled the comedy of his life, and, if we may believe
Urquhart, he surpassed the Italians themselves in their
own arts of pantomime and the quick change. 'O
with how great liveliness,' writes Sir Thomas, ' did
he represent the conditions of all manner of men !
How naturally did he set before the eyes of all beholders the vagaries of all professions, from the over-
weening monarch to the peevish swain, through all
the intermediate degrees of the superficial courtier
or proud warrior, dissembled churchman, doting
old man, cozening lawyer, lying traveller, covetous
merchant, rude seaman, pedantick scholar, the
amorous shepherd, envious artisan, vainglorious
master, and tricky servant; he did with such
variety display the several humours of all these
sorts of people, and with a so bewitching energy,
that he seemed to be the original, they the

counterfeit.' So sincere sounds this breathless praise, that we would not have it undeserved, and we accept it for fact the more readily, because in the loftiest of his enterprises Crichton betrayed more than a spice of the true comedian.

Thus loved and feasted, Crichton fleeted the time merrily as in a golden age. He was hailed now not as a mere scholar but as an arbiter of elegances. If learned men still deferred to his judgment, beautiful women competed for his smiles. He had wealth, he had health, he was flattered by the praises of the wise. And then disaster, sudden and treacherous, overtook him. As Mantua had given him the life he loved best, so Mantua gave him death. It was at the time of Carnival, when Crichton, accompanied by the Princess whom he loved, encountered Vincenzo Gonzago and the rabble of his cup-shotten companions. Some say that a street in Mantua was the place of meeting, others declare that Crichton was holding the courtyard of the Princess's palace against the roisterers. All are agreed as to the manner of the conflict. Crichton, not knowing who were his adversaries, ran one of them through with his sword, and was on the point of dispatching the second, when a voice cried, 'Hold, hold ! kill not the prince !' In an instant Crichton recoiled, the Prince pulled off his vizard, and Crichton, sensible of his mistake, dropped on his knee like a true knight, and gave the Prince the hilt of his conquering sword. The Prince, mad with wine and rage, grasped the proferred hilt and ran the blade through the heart of the Scot.   Never was a more dastardly crime committed, and as the gallant Crichton fell, the Princess, 'rending her garments and tearing her hair, like one of the Graces possessed with a fury,' spoke thus : 'O villains, what have you done ! You vipers of men, that have thus basely slain the valiant Crichton, the sword of his own sex and the buckler of ours, the glory of his age, and the restorer of the lost honour of the Court of Mantuna : O Crichton, Crichton !'

The account of Crichton's death, given in the Gonzaga Archives, differs in detail only from Urquhart's narrative.   The Italians make no mention of a Princess, and she, perhaps, is the mere figment of an ardent brain.   For the rest, it fell out something after this guise : Crichton, having received the wound in the Via San Silvestro, walked away as far as San Tommaso, and there seated himself upon a stone, whence he was lifted to a chair and carried to the house of Hippolito Serena, where he died, well-disposed.   The Prince's anger, on the other hand, was by no means assuaged.   Not knowing that his blow had proved mortal, he hastened to the palace, and bade the warden admit five of his men by the postern-gate, that Crichton might not climb the wall or swim the lake.   The warden, already assured of the Scot's death, grimly replied that Crichton was in no case to escape by swimming, and so closed the gate.

The news of the disaster was ill-received by the

Courts of Italy, and the citizens, who loved the Admirable Scot, were no more content with the manner of his death than with the method of his burial. They murmured that he should have been carried to San Simone privately and as though abandoned, nor did they approve the humble fashion of his coffin. And so loud was the outcry, that at last the Prince was urged to defend his name, and to set forth at large his own version of the tragedy.

'One of these evenings,' thus he told the story to the Bishop of Osino, 'as I was taking the fresh air of the city at about one o'clock in the night, and having with me Messer Hippolito Lanzone, a gentleman of Mantua, in whose humour I took much pleasure, I encountered by chance James the Scot, and believing that he was the Earl of Langosco, my gentleman-in-waiting, whom he resembled in stature, I was about to jostle him as a jest; but on approaching, I knew that it was not he, and therefore, placing my buckler before my face, passed by him, leaving some suspicion in the Scot, who, seeing Lanzone following likewise with his shield before his face, turned to pass him on the side towards the wall, and when he was gone by plunged his dagger into his shoulder up to the hilt. Thereupon both the one and the other laid hold of their weapons, but as Lanzone was mortally wounded, he could not defend himself, wherefore I, hearing the noise, turned round, and pointed my sword in the direction of the turmoil. The Scot, not knowing me at the first glance, dealt me a sword-cut and thrust, which I parried with my buckler, and thereupon I aimed a stroke at the Scot, which he turned to parry with his dagger, but for sheer impetuosity could not. It wounded him in the breast, and he, having recognized me, prayed for life as a gift. I left him and turned to my companion, who, I found, could hardly support himself on his feet, and as I tried to support him he fell dead before me. The happening, in truth, was pure misadventure, and had I had to deal with any other than a barbarian, so much evil would not have ensued. It displeases me that the Illustrious Farnese, my uncle and lord, should have been vexed at this, my unexpected adventure, but I hope that, hearing my justification, he will thank God the affair ended with the safety of my life, placed in no small jeopardy by the barbarity of that wretch, whom God assoil.'

Such is the Prince's own account, which, I think, fails to justify him. In the first place it is evident that the insult to Crichton was unprovoked. In the second the mere presence of Lanzone, whom Donato denounces as ' bestiale,' a creature ill-suited for the concourse of gentlemen, is sufficient proof that the Prince was not in the right of it. It stands clearly also in the archives that Crichton made but one thrust at the Prince before he recognised him, and then it was that, handing his own sword to his adversary, he received his death-blow. Nor will those who have studied Crichton's career willingly believe that he begged his life as a gift. The Prince, moreover, destroys his own case by the violence of his speech. Crichton was no barbarian, as Vincenzo Gonzaga well knew, and he would hardly have flung so ill-deserved a taunt at him, had he not felt the weakness of his own case.

VI

On the other side may be set not a few early authorities, who support a verdict favourable to Crichton. Of them the first is Fynes Moryson, who visited Mantua as early as 1594, and found the Duke still a young man, 'having a redde bearde, a full visage, a cheareful ruddy complexion like the Germans of whom he descends.' The story, as told to Moryson, was in no sense doubtful. 'This Duke's honour was much scandaled among the Italians,' he writes, 'because in his youth while his father lived, he had in following manner killed a Scottish gentleman reported to have bene indued with extraordinary virtues. The Prince one night walked in the streets with his followers but unknowne, and by ill adventure meeting the said Scottish gentleman, well-reputed in his father's court, took a fancye to trye his valour, and to that end commanded one of his familiar friends to assault him with his drawne sword, whom he taking for an enemy, in good earnest resisted valiantly, and at the first encounter hapned to give him a deadly wounde, whereupon the Prince much lamented, and the Scottish gentleman, knowing him by his voyce, and so humbling himselfe at his feete, with tender of His Rapier, the point towards himselfe, the Prince in rage killed him with his owne weapon.'[1]

Lithgow, again, some twenty-five years after Crichton's death, tells us that 'Crichton his worth in learning and excellent memory rests admired in Italy, but especially by the noble Gonzagas, and dependent friends of the house of Mantua; for whose loss and accidental death they still heavily bemoan, acknowledging that the race of that Princely stock by God's judgment was cut off because of his untimely death.' And the worthy Thomas Wright, author of *The Passions of the Mind in Generall* (1621), gives a precise, ungrudging support to the later version of Sir Thomas Urquhart. 'The Scot perceiving well what he was,' thus he concludes the story, 'fell down upon his knees, demanding pardon at his hands, and gave the Prince his naked rapier; who, no sooner had received it, but with the same sword he ran him through to death; the which barbarous fact, as it was condemned of all men, so it sheweth the precipitation of his passionate ireful heart.'

We may take it, then, that the manner of Crichton's death is well established. Praise and regret followed him to the grave. In 1583, Aldus, still faithful in eulogy, inscribed a book of his printing

---

[1] For this quotation I am indebted to Mr. Charles Hughes, editor of Shakespeare's *Europe*.

to his memory. 'Who did not wonder at thee living,' he writes; 'who does not mourn thee dead? While thou livedst, I profited by my judgment of thee; now thou art dead, I set no limit on my grief. Thou shouldst have lived! Would that the fatherland of Virgil had never seen thee! By an unhappy chance it has fallen out that the spot, which gave him birth, has robbed thee forcibly of life. Forever shall I cherish thy memory; forever shall thy image haunt my eyes; ever shalt thou be the same to me, who shalt ever be the same to all good men.' Thus Aldus, with more to the same purpose, and Crichton being dead, he chose another scholar, one Stanilas Niegoscewski, a Pole, as fierce a disputant as the Scot, to take Crichton's place in his heart and his prefaces. To him he dedicated the verses of Aratus—*malum poetam bono poetæ*—and he confessed he knew not how to describe him. 'Shall I call you the praiser of Crichton,' he asks, 'or the rival, or the superior?' Alas for the fickleness of scholars! Aldus's trick of eulogy did not long lack an excuse. And as for Crichton, it is easy to imagine the smile wherewith he greeted in the shades this notice of his death and the name of his supplanter.

VII

The portrait of Crichton, painted by friends and by the kindly hand of tradition, is amiable rather

than characteristic. When we would know precisely
what manner of man he was, we are baffled at once
by the habit of imitation, and by the insincerity of
flattery. As I have said, the early panegyrics prove
little else than a lack of invention. The handbill
came first; the others accepted its eulogy in good
faith. Again, the voice of adulation is always in-
expressive, and no man that ever lived was so keen
an encouragement to superlatives as Crichton. To
one he is a human miracle, to another he is almost
divine. This man finds his genius stupendous, that
one acclaims him a prodigy of learning and eloquence;
all apply to him or to his gifts the epithet *Admirabilis*,[1]
which is indissolubly his. And when you have
marvelled at the store of adjectives poured forth by
the patient biographers, you are no nearer to a sane
appreciation of Crichton. You recognise that he
excelled his fellows in many arts, that his versatility
equalled his precocity, that he could turn from war
to peace with unruffled equanimity. You surmise
always that he possessed what Chesterfield called the

---

[1] There has been much discussion as to who it was that first
called Crichton 'the Admirable.' The credit has generally
been given to Urquhart, but unjustly. To Urquhart Crichton
owes the glamour and romance which hang about his name.
But he was called ' Admirable' by earlier, less eloquent writers.
Aldus uses the adjective more than once, and John Johnston
thus describes the hero in his *Heroes Scoti* (1613): 'Jacobus
Crittonius, Clunius, musarum pariter et martis alumnus, omnibus
in studiis admirabilis, Mantuæ, a Ducis Mantuani filio cæsus,
1581.'

graces, without which no man ever attained to the
mastery of an envious world.

And when all this is said, how much nearer
are we to a vision of the real Crichton? Urquhart
tells us that never was so wonderful a prodigy
witnessed since Alcibiades. Aldus, as we have seen,
gasping in admiration, can compare his apparition at
Padua with nothing less than with Plato's return to
Athens, when the whole population of the city left
the games to go forth and meet him. Obviously
Alcibiades and Plato are names which should not be
mentioned in this relation. Without underrating
Crichton's remarkable achievements, we must set
him on a far lower plane. He was, indeed, a true
child of his age, and it is by a mere accident that
he has strayed into ours. His accomplishments,
splendid as they were, are the accomplishments of
youth. He was, so to say, an undergraduate raised
to the highest power. The learning of the time
was within his reach, and he knew how to turn it
to the best account. The disputations, which at
Padua and Venice seemed miracles of genius, would
appear to our altered consciences mere exercises in
pedantry. In other words, Crichton did not stray
one inch from the fold of conventionality. He
invented nothing; he left behind him no one authentic phrase, no one imperishable line. He played
the tune of his time with a greater skill than most
of his fellows, and that is all. Had he lived to-day,
he would have played another tune, and might have

composed such verses in Greek and Latin as would
have cast even the little masterpieces of Professor
Jebb into the shade of carelessness and inelegance.

And Crichton had another quality than learning.
As I have said, he had a genius for presentation. A dozen Scots surpassed him in erudition
and originality, and are forgotten. He filled a
greater space than the most of men. He had a
talent for attracting the eyes of others to him, and
thus he achieved a result which, but for him,
might have seemed impossible : he made pedantry
romantic. Out of the dry bones of dead philo-
sophies he produced a wonderful effect. We can
well believe that neither his mind nor his tongue
weighed heavily on abstruse subjects. They touched
them, and were off. I have likened him to a
butterfly, brilliant in colour and light on wing,
but he was a butterfly who fed on cabbages. And
like a butterfly he was vain of the splendid effects
he knew how to produce. He wished to excel at
all costs. He breathed most easily in an atmosphere
of combat. His highest happiness was to pit
himself against this or that adversary, to make his
superiority visible, and he cared not whether his
hand held a sword or a book. The cause of learning
was little to him ; it was the cause of Crichton that
he had at heart. He died young, and deserves an
amiable judgment. Yet if we accept the praises
of his friends, and look kindly upon his written
words, we cannot believe that, had he lived, he could

have added a single stone to the monument of human knowledge. His genius was like a block of ice, clear and frozen, which the changing season melts to water.

The only account of him that attempts to separate him from others is Joseph Scaliger's, and Scaliger, generously admitting his miraculous gifts, stumbles on a phrase which brings us nearer to Crichton than pages of panegyric. 'Il était,' says he, 'un peu fat.' He was something of a coxcomb. There is the truth in six words. None but a coxcomb could have inspired the handbill which fashioned his reputation. None but a coxcomb could have kept himself so persistently in the eye of the world. None but a coxcomb and a coxcomb of heroic frame, could have pursued the goals of so many excellences as did Crichton. He was of those who looked upon learning as a pleasant pastime, who threw off their verses while they waited in the ring for a laggard armourer, who practised philosophy when they were tired of the fencing-school. He forgot that poetry is a jealous mistress, that humane letters are the enemies of leisure, and forgetting this he has left behind him nothing that a later generation cares to read—only a brilliant memory of daring feats daringly performed, of gallant adversaries gallantly overcome in lecture-hall and tournament.

VIII

In 1584, two years after the Admirable Crichton's death, three works—an *Epicedium* of Cardinal Borromeo, a *Gratulatio*, addressed to Gaspar Visconti and a *Carmen Nuptiale*, composed in honour of Prince Carolo Emanuele—were published, bearing the name of James Crichton on their title-pages, and a year later the same hand dedicated a collection of pieces in prose and verse, including a defence of poetry, to Sforza Brivius. These pamphlets have been generally ascribed, in catalogues and elsewhere, to the Admirable Scot. In character, or in the lack of it, they are precisely the exercises which the great Crichton would have achieved, and their author is undoubtedly named Jacobus Critonius Scotus. Whoever wrote them had a natural love of false quantities, and his lines do not always scan. That is their least defect. It is far more to their discredit that they are tasteless and mechanical. The author essays all the metres: hexameters, elegiacs, alcaics, sapphics, hendecasyllables, archilochians, all yield to his ingenuity; and all are treated in the spirit not of the poet, but of the *Gradus ad Parnassum*. What shall we think of a poet who in an *Epicedium* can be guilty of such a commonplace as this?

'Extimui, steteruntque comæ, et timor occupat artus.
Proh dolor, en veris somnia mixta noto.'

He is even less happy in a gratulatory ode, addressed to Gaspar Vincenzo :

> ' Primus in exequiis ferali carmine Scotus,
> Pastoris dolui funera mæsta pii.
> Funera mæsta pii Boromæi Præsulis ah ah,
> Deplanxit tristi nostra Thalia stylo.'

It is not for verses such as these that a scholar receives commendation, and you turn from the verse to the prose with a light heart. There, too, disappointment awaits you. The writer does not go beyond the intelligence of his time. It was his to absorb, not to foresee. It is not surprising therefore that he should condemn the fools who in their total ignorance of dialectic believe that the earth moves, or that there are more worlds than one. He is more easily intelligible when he eulogises grammar as the parent of the other arts, and sings, in a passage of genuine enthusiasm, the praise of Homer. But it is in his last work that his best page may be found—a lofty panegyric of Virgil—which persuades the reader to forget the false quantities and ineptitudes of his verse. Virgil he esteems supreme in all things. 'Would you learn,' says he, 'to argue *in utramque partem?* Consult Virgil. Would you invade the province of oratory? Approach Virgil. Would you understand the lines, forms, spaces, and magnitudes of Euclid? Devour Maro. He will discuss with you air, fire, water, earth, *ad unguem.*'

These sentiments might well have been expressed by the Admirable Crichton himself, and when they

were written he had been two years in his grave.
Here is a baffling puzzle of criticism. Nor is our
difficulty lessened by a set of verses, addressed in
1584, to James Crichton by Ludovico, Marquis of
Milan, in which you will find the lines which
follow :

> ' Ast tibi larga dedit soli, quae munera multis
>   Præbuit, et variis te dedit esse parem.
> Namque Poetarum numeros cantusque sonoros,
>   Quamque docent magni Rhetores, ipse tenes.'

That the word *soli* should be applied to any other
Crichton than the hero, who fell to the Mantuan's
sword, seems incredible. Yet there is little doubt
that at the same time two men were writing verse
and pursuing scholarship in Italy, who used the same
name, and frequented the same society. Dead men
write no elegies, and it would be easier to believe in
the existence of two James Crichtons than in the
continued activity of the murdered man, even if we
had no clear evidence of the truth.[1] Fortunately
the evidence is unmistakable. On the frontispiece
of a book, entitled *Benardini Baldini Lusus* (1586),
stand some verses addressed to Baldi by James

[1] When I first wrote of Crichton I thought that the report of
his death had been premature, that in fact Aldus and the rest
had been deceived. This opinion the precise statements of the
Gonzaga Archives make untenable. Moreover an article in *Le
Chasseur Bibliographe* (September 1863), which quotes the
verses of Bernardini Baldi, has proved clearly that there are two
Crichtons. Mr. Douglas Crichton, the author of *The Admirable
Crichton: The Real Character*, takes the same view.

Crichton, who vaunts his kinship with the hero. 'Et quia,' he writes,

> 'et quia Critoni claro mihi sanguine juncti
> Funera acerba doles, carior ipse mihi es.'

And Baldi to make assurance surer calls his friend *Jacobum Critonium Superstitem,* and does equal honour to the dead and the living Crichton.

It is a strange chapter of literary history, a not unfitting end of mystery to a mysterious career. Little as we knew of the Admirable Scot, at last we know him guiltless of much bad poetry. Though the legend will still endure, surely it was not he who hymned the death of Carlo Borromeo. Thus was he fortunate in many things—fortunate in strength, in skill, in eloquence; fortunate also in laying a burden of ineptitude upon the shoulders of a namesake. And most fortunate was he in his opportune death. 'The gods,' said Abernethy, 'wished only to show Crichton to the world, not to give him.' He died with all the laurels wreathed upon his brow; he had not time to outlive his fame; and fate in its kindly wisdom spared us the shame and regret of looking upon a Phœnix of middle age.

'A PRINCELY WOMAN'

'A PRINCELY WOMAN'

IT was by a strange chance that Margaret, Duchess of Newcastle, wandered out of her proper environment into the unquiet world of the seventeenth century. She might have played her part among the fantastical wits of Elizabeth's age. She would have been intimately at home with the Blue-stockings who met at Montagu House. She would have shone brilliantly in the social firmament of Seamore Place. She might have contributed her verselets to Lady Blessington's Book of Beauty, and taken her seat without surprise in Count D'Orsay's tilbury. Above all, she would have found in the London of our present century a gracious and sympathetic reception. She was not merely a great lady—'a princely woman,' as Charles Lamb calls her; she was also a poet and philosopher. Had she been our contemporary, she might have revived the dying salon. She might have won such laurels as popular reviews confer. She might have gathered together under one roof wit and learning, beauty and fashion. And an unkind fate bade her grow to womanhood under the iron rule of the Commonwealth, and with the return of Charles II. to frequent a Court where gallantry was pursued with simple-minded devotion, and where frivolity was mistress of all the arts. How could she sacrifice to the Muses in the perfumed atmosphere of Whitehall? How, with all her extravagance, could she hold her own against Lady Castlemaine and La Belle Stewart? It is no wonder, then, that she retired with her lord, whom she loved and worshipped, to the security of Welbeck, and cultivated, in the sunshine of his sympathy, the heaven-sent gifts which she devoutly believed to be hers.

A strayling from another time and place, she was misjudged by her own age. Pepys, strong in the prejudices of a light-hearted court, thought her 'a mad, conceited, ridiculous woman.' Later judgments have been wiser and more kind. We are far enough away to see her in a fair relation, and to refrain from condemning, even to appreciate, her pleasant foibles. Truly she might say that in all the misfortunes that pursued her, her mind still preserved its ascendency. Beset with disaster, ruined in fortune, married to a banished man, she remained always a woman of intellect. Not even poverty could tempt her into the world of common realities. She supported life and its afflictions as though they were the phantoms of a dream. Had it been her fate to live in a golden age of peace, she would not have changed her conduct a jot. Her inkpot would still have been her constant companion. The love of 'the thrice noble, high and puissant Prince, William Cavendish, Duke, Marquis, and Earl of Newcastle,' would still have engrossed her waking and her sleeping thoughts. And the very unity of her character makes it easy for us, who may contemplate the few simple actions of her life, to understand and admire her.

Born in 1620, she was the daughter of Sir Thomas Lucas, a gentleman — 'which title,' she says, 'is granted and given by merit, not by princes.' Her natural vanity persuaded her to interpret in the terms of heroism the characters of her father and mother. There was no incident or custom of her childhood that did not embellish her natural pride. Her upbringing was consonant with her exalted estate. She was bred 'virtuously, modestly, civilly, and on honest principles.' In her father's august house there was neither stint nor parsimony. 'As for plenty,' says she, 'we had not only for necessity, convenience, and decency, but for delight and pleasure to a superfluity.' The pride which she professed unto the end of her life in noble, extravagant attire, was always indulged by her mother. 'As for our garments,' she declares, 'my mother did not only delight to see us neat and cleanly, fine and gay, but rich and costly.'

With an ingenuous candour she describes the irreproachable gentility of her nurture. She and her sisters were surrounded always with respectful attendance. They were not permitted familiarity or conversation with the vulgar servants. Serving-men were never permitted 'to be in the nursery among the nursemaids, lest in their rude love-making

they might do unseemly actions, or speak unhandsome
words in the presence of children'—a prohibition
which throws a curious light on the manners of the
time. Their recreations were simple and ladylike.
In the country they would read, work, walk, and
discourse with each other. The town afforded
livelier pastimes. 'Their customs were, in winter-
time,'—thus she tells the tale,—'to go sometimes to
plays, or to ride in their coaches about the streets to
see the concourse and recourse of people; and in
the spring-time to visit the Spring Garden, Hyde
Park, and the like places; and sometimes they would
have music, and sup in barges upon the water.' It
was an innocent and sheltered life, passed by them
in full contentment with each other's virtues. No
strangers approached their felicity, and it is not surprising that pride and lack of habit afflicted the
peerless Margaret with bashfulness.

She confesses herself 'naturally bashful,' and art
and circumstance had enhanced the work of nature.
Yet the cause, she insists, lay not within her own
competence. She was not ashamed of mind or body,
birth or breeding. Conscious of her own superiority,
she trembled rather for others than for herself. Therefore she despaired of a cure, 'unless nature as well as
human governments could be civilised and brought
into a methodical order.' Before she could regard
the world with confidence, the world must be reformed, and as reform was impossible, she retained
a certain timidity to the end of her days. Her

bashfulness, however, was concerned not with qualities but with numbers. 'For were I to enter among a company of Lazaruses,' she confesses, 'I should be as much out of countenance as if they were all Cæsars or Alexanders, Cleopatras or Didos.' Thus in a curious passage of self-revelation she puts another facet upon the jewel of her pride, and in the same breath exults that she has never met with fools and unworthy persons, bold, rude, uncivil in word or action, and that naturally she has the same aversion to them as children have to spirits, or grown men and women to devils.

When civil war broke out, she made a momentary conquest of her bashfulness. Eager to prove her loyalty, she enrolled herself among the Queen's Maids of Honour, and cheerfully shared the exile of Henrietta Maria. In thus doing, she plainly obeyed the voice of fate. For it was at Paris, whither she attended her Majesty, that she met and married William Cavendish, then Earl of Newcastle. Never was woman more highly blessed than she, if we may believe her words, when she encountered this paragon of grace and virtue. He was at once the worship and inspiration of her life. His exploits and perfections she celebrated both in prose and verse. Her eloquence conferred upon them both the crown of immortality, which neither the sneers of their contemporaries nor the ribald laughter of a later age has availed to dislodge. Truly she was no common lover. Never did Muse adore hero with a purer and loftier passion. 'He was the only person I ever was in love with,' said she, and only her own words may express her triumph : 'Neither was I ashamed to own it, but gloried therein. For it was not amorous love (I never was infected there- with—it is a disease, or a passion, or both, I only know by relation, not by experience), neither could title, wealth, power, or passion entice me to love. But my love was honest and honourable, being placed upon merit, which affection joyed at the fame of his worth, pleased with delight in his wit, proud of the respects he used to me, and triumph- ing in the affections he professed for me, which affections he hath confirmed to me by a deed of time, sealed by constancy, and assigned by an un- alterable decree of his promise, which makes me happy in despite of Fortune's frowns.' Thus happily won, she faced the ruin of her lord's house and hopes with equanimity, and sought in exile such consolation as literature might bring her.

Her books are many and treat of diverse subjects. Her courage equalled her industry. Oratory and poetry, philosophy and the drama, in turn compelled her energy. She composed many comedies, in which all the characters spoke with her own proper style and accent. In a rare piece of self-criticism she defended the title of 'Plays,' which she gave to her dramatic exercises. She confessed that neither had she skill in ancient rules nor did she desire to be agreeable to modern humour. 'But,' says she, 'having pleased my fancy in writing many dialogues upon several subjects, and having afterwards ordered them into acts and scenes, I will venture in spite of the critics to call them 'Plays'; and if you like them so, well and good; if not, there is no harm done.' In the same spirit she provided the orators of her age with polished examples of their craft, and if she had had her way they would have all spoken, even 'the half-drunken gentleman,' whom her fancy pictured, with the voice of Margaret, Duchess of Newcastle.

Whatever she wrote she transfigured with the pompous imagination, which never deserted her. *Poems and Fancies, The World's Olio, Nature's Pictures by Fancy's Pencil,* are all characteristic and her own. It was not for her to check the swift facility of her mind. In quick forgetfulness of the claims of art, she let her pen dash away with her. She knew that her words 'ran stumbling out of her mouth,' yet claimed that her 'thoughts moved regularly in her brain.' With an introspection which seldom afflicted her age, she made a valiant attempt to analyse her ingenious method: 'I must tell my readers,' said she, 'that nature, which is the best and curiousest worker, hath paved my brain smoother than custom hath oiled my tongue, or vanity hath polished my senses, or art hath beaten the paper whereon I write; for my fancy is quicker than the pen with which I write, insomuch as it is many times lost through the slowness of my hand

and yet I write so fast, as I stay not so long as to make perfect letters.'

Like many other clever women, she knew not herself. The words which came so swiftly are better worth than the thoughts which she fondly believed were marshalled, like an army, in her mind. If we forget her matchless piece of biography, we shall find little save phrases that will hold the restless attention of to-day. Her experiments in philosophy, which she herself prized most highly,[1] are of an engaging triviality. She discovered the obvious with a passion of delight. It was as though in pride of heart she had found out for herself that two and two made four, and wished all the world to share her secret. Being ignorant of the works of others, writing in accord with her own natural cogitations, she produced works which have ceased to possess the interest even of curiosity. The web of nonsense, which she spun like a spider from her brain, was yet able to enmesh the fly of flattery, and it is not wonderful that she treasured her own foolish speculations, when they won the applause, feigned or real, of learned bodies and profound scholars.

The pæans that were sung in praise of her

---

[1] In her *World's Olio* (1655), she expresses her pleasure in the following lines :

'Of all my works, this work that I have writ,
My best beloved and greatest favourite,
I look upon it with a pleasing eye,
I pleasure take in its sweet company.'

philosophy are set to the tune of a magnificent insincerity. 'What shall we think of your Excellency,' wrote Bishop Pearson, 'who are both a Minerva and an Athens in yourself, the Muses as well as an Helicon, Aristotle as well as his Lycæum?' Nor did the Vice-Chancellor of the University of Cambridge lag far behind the Master of St John's: 'Most excellent Princess,' he declared, 'you have unspeakably obliged us all; but not in one respect alone, for wheresoever we find ourselves nonplussed in our studies, we repair to you as to our oracle; if we be to speak, you dictate to us; if we knock at Apollo's door, you alone open to us; if we compose a history, you are the remembrancer; if we be confused and puzzled among the philosophers, you disentangle us and assoil our difficulties.' This is of course, the language of pious and polished exaggeration. But be it remembered that Vice-Chancellors and Public Orators are not upon oath when they pronounce eulogies, and that in at least one province of literature—biography—the Duchess of Newcastle earned the praise of all wise men, not by her rank but by her achievement.

I have said that she was fantastical. A sense of splendour never deserted her. Her own description of *Nature's Pictures* shows us vividly what manner of woman she was. 'In this volume,' she claims, 'there are several feigned stories of natural descriptions, as comical, tragical, and tragi-comical, poetical, romancical, philosophical, and historical, both in prose and verse, some all verse, some all prose, some mixt, partly prose and partly verse.' Thus does she emulate the player in *Hamlet*, and attempt to convince her readers that there is no kind of literature which she has left unattempted. And as in style, so in life, she was full of pomp and circumstance. The lessons of rich and gay attire, which her mother had taught, she treasured till the end. She confesses that her serious study 'could not be much, by reason I took great delight in attiring, fine dressing, and fashions, especially in such fashions as I did invent myself. . . . Also I did dislike any should follow my fashions, for I always took delight in a singularity, even in accoutrements of habits.'

Therein lay the charm of the Duchess. In life as in books she was always picturesque. No other great lady among her contemporaries was thus authentic and of a piece. She wrote and she moved as none other wrote and moved. She gave a touch of solemn distinction to her century, which, rich in gaiety, would have lacked something without her. And her century was conscious of the obligation, though it interpreted it in more senses than one. Her follies, which were her virtues, made no appeal to Charles II. His quick sense of humour saw only what was ridiculous in the admirable Duchess. His nice conduct of life did not permit him to measure the debt that the world owes to those, who are brave enough to endure the ridicule of their fellows. '"To increase my ill-humour, I was stopped, as I was getting out of my chair," said Grammont to the king one day, " by the devil of a phantom in masquerade. . . . However, I must tell you that it is worth while to see her dress ; for she must have at least sixty ells of gauze and silver tissue about her, not to mention a sort of a pyramid upon her head, adorned with a hundred thousand baubles." . . . " I bet," said the king, " that it is the Duchess of Newcastle." '

Pepys, following his master in dispraise, could never master his curiosity. Whenever the Duchess of Newcastle went forth upon a progress, he would be there to see. His record of 1667 tells us more clearly than all the histories how bravely fantastic a figure she cut before the court of Charles. Though it affected to despise her humours, all the world was agog to gaze upon her. ' To White Hall,' writes Pepys, ' thinking there to have seen the Duchess of Newcastle's coming this night to Court to make a visit to the Queen ; the King having been with her yesterday to make her a visit since her coming to town. The whole story of this lady is a romance, and all she does romantick. Her footmen in velvet coats, and herself in an antique dress, as they say. . . . There is as much expectation of her coming to court, that so many people may come to see her, as if it were the Queen of Sheba, but I lost my labour for she did not come this night.'

In truth the chatter of the town was all of her extravagances, and her velvet cap, and her hair about her ears, 'naked-necked, without anything about it, and a black *juste-au-corps*.' Foiled again and again, Pepys was still indefatigable in pursuit: he caught a glimpse of her on April 26, when 'she seemed to me a very comely woman,' and hoped to see more of her on May-day. Once more he failed. He went forth to see her, and saw her not,—'she being followed and crowded upon by coaches all the way she went, that nobody could come near her: only I could see she was in a black coach adorned with silver instead of gold, and so white curtains, and everything black and white, and herself in a cap.' The chase, of course, could not end here. A few days later he was again in hot pursuit. 'Drove hard towards Clerkenwell,' he says, 'thinking to have overtaken my Lady Newcastle, whom I saw before us in her coach, with a hundred boys and girls running looking upon her; but I could not: and so she got home before I could come up to her. But I will get a time to see her.'

Of course he did. Pepys was not a man to be foiled of his curiosity. The occasion was the meeting of the Royal Society, the place was Arundel House. Thither came the Duchess to see and to be seen. For her entertainment the air was weighed, two cold liquors by mixture were made hot, and many other wonders performed, each of which was sufficient to excite the Duchess's ever-bubbling enthusiasm. A near view of the lady, whom he had fiercely pursued through Clerkenwell, disappointed the excellent Pepys. He confesses that she hath been a good comely woman, 'but her dress so antick, and her deportment so ordinary, that I do not like her at all, nor did I hear her say anything that was worth hearing, but that she was full of admiration, all admiration.' That he did not like her was but natural. She transcended the norm. Hers was not the ordered elegance which Pepys loved. Besides, Pepys feared that the town would soon be full of ballads concerning her visit to the Royal Society, an institution whose dignity he would have defended with his life. Yet Pepys, for all his lack of sympathy, accurately discerned her dominant qualities. 'The whole story of this lady is a romance,' said he, 'and all she does romantick.' There she is sketched in a single line. The Duchess was 'romantick,' both by conscious intent and unconscious habit. She could not move without striving after a handsome effect, and in thus striving she followed, not merely her desire, but her natural instinct. Again, how could her pose be better expressed than by the words 'all admiration'? She was ready to show an appreciative surprise at anything. In her eager eyes all was wonderful. How she would have exulted in the present age, when lion-hunting is a favourite pursuit, and when she might have packed into the same drawing-room a play-actor, a popular divine, and a German philosopher !

To compel the eyes of all men upon her was, in

truth, the first necessity of her being.   Nor was she
discriminating in applause.   'It will satisfy me,' she
says somewhere, 'if my writing please the readers,
though not the learned; for I had rather be praised
in this by the most, although not the best; for all I
desire is fame, and fame is nothing but a great noise,
and noise lives most in a multitude.'   No audience
'fit but few' for her!   She must bask in the liberal
sun of notoriety, and accept without disdain the
incense of flattery burned upon the humblest altars.
And she was furthered in the attainment of her end
by a complete lack of humour.   This is said in no
spirit of contempt.   Had she been gifted with humour
she could not have been Margaret of Newcastle.   For
humour implies self-criticism, and at the touch of
criticism the gossamer web of her fancy would have
been dissipated into nothingness.

It was essential for her genius that she should
regard herself and her husband and her enterprises
with the utmost gravity.   She never hesitates to
compare herself and her lord with the highest.   She
hopes that her readers will not find her vain for
writing her life, 'since there have been many that
have done the like as Cæsar, Ovid, and many more,
both men and women, and I know no reason I may
not do it as well as they.'   It was the same spirit
which moved her to sketch her own character in the
terms of panegyric.   She was, as she confesses,
a great emulator,—not that she wished others worse
than they are, but that she herself endeavoured to be

the best. 'I think it no crime,' she wrote, and indeed it is no crime, ' to wish myself the exactest of Nature's works, my thread of life the longest, my chain of destiny the strongest, my mind the peace-ablest, my life the pleasantest, my death the easiest, and the greatest saint in heaven.'

The wish was father to the thought. She began in hope ; she ended in belief. She was sure that the mere freshness of her philosophical speculations was a shining merit. She would be beholden to none. 'The best wits,' said she, 'have the worst memory' ; and again, 'memory is nothing but the showers of other men's wits.' Nor could she contemplate her own temper without a bland enthusiasm : 'As for my disposition,' she wrote in a characteristic passage, 'it is more inclining to be melancholy than merry, but soft, melting, solitary, and contemplating memory. And I am apt to weep rather than laugh, not that I do often either of them. Also I am tender-natured, for it humbles my conscience to kill a fly, and the groans of a dying beast strike my soul. Also where I place a particular affection, I love extraordinarily and constantly, yet not fondly, but soberly and observingly, not to hang about them as a servant. . . . Likewise I am gratefull, for I never received a courtesy,—but I am impatient and troubled until I can return it. Also I am chaste, both by nature and education, insomuch as I do abhor an unchaste thought. Likewise I am seldom angry, as my ser-vants may witness for me. . . . Neither am I apt to

be exceptious or jealous.' And so on, until she easily
persuades her readers that she engrosses the virtues.

But for all her parade, for all her assumption of
philosophic understanding, she was a very woman,
feminine in charm, feminine in vanity, feminine in
caprice. She did not approve of the bustling spirit,
which would remove the proper boundaries of sex.
The charge that she haunted committees, and came
herself to petition for a share in her husband's estate,
she repudiated with fury. She had little love of the
changed customs of England, where 'women became
pleaders, attornies, petitioners and the like, running
about all their several causes, complaining of their
several grievances, exclaiming against their several
enemies.' She stood at her lord's side in his exile;
she composed a deathless eulogy of his life and
virtues; and he in return proved his gratitude for
her eloquence and fidelity by setting up such a
monument in his own lifetime as should com-
memorate the virtues of them both.[1]

---

[1] So nobly does it celebrate the lady's genius, that we cannot
but quote it in full: 'Here lyes the Loyall Duke of Newcastle,
and his Dutches, his second wife, by whom he had no issue:
Her name was Margaret Lucas, youngest sister to the Lord
Lucas of Colchester, a noble familie; for all the Brothers were
Valiant, and all the sisters virtuous. The Dutches was a wise,
wittie, and Learned Lady, which her many books do well testifie; she was a most Virtuous and a Loveing and carefull wife,
and was with her Lord all the time of his banishment and
miseries, and when he came home never parted from him in his
solitary retirements.'

Her masterpiece, in truth, was *The life of the Thrice noble, high and puissant Prince, William Cavendish, Duke, Marquis, and Earl of Newcastle.* Published within the lifetime of them both, the biography proves the Duke as happily deficient in humour as the Duchess. Not otherwise could he have gazed complacently upon so fine a panegyric of his qualities. Pepys thought him 'an ass to suffer her to write what she writes of him and to him.' The University of Cambridge, more amiably minded, crowned her as a classic. 'Hereafter,' gravely pronounced its mouthpiece, 'if generous and high-born men shall search our library for a model of a most accomplished general, they shall find it expressed to the life, not in Xenophon's Cyrus, but in the Duchess of Newcastle's William.' She herself thought so well of her book as to set it in the same class with Cæsar's Commentaries; and Charles Lamb, whose confident applause renewed the waning fame of the fantastical Duchess, thought that a book so 'good and rare' as this deserved the most sumptuous binding. 'No casket is rich enough, no casing sufficiently durable, to honour and keep safe such a jewel.'

This praise of Lamb's subtly marks the limitations of the book. It is an exotic, a fantasy, a literary curiosity, which cannot be too highly decorated ; yet of its kind it is perfect. The subject is absolutely consonant with the style and method of the author. The Duke of Newcastle was a master of pomp and ceremony. If ever a *grand seigneur* was born into England it was he. For him life was a spectacle, and policy a show. In an age of display he displayed a genius for entertainment which was unrivalled. When King Charles I. visited Welbeck, Newcastle prepared 'such an excess of feasting as had never before been known in England.' Ben Jonson devised a Masque for the royal pleasure, and his majesty liked his entertainment so well that he bade his loyal subject repeat it a year later at Bolsover. For the delight of the king twenty thousand pounds seemed but a trivial sum, and Newcastle was presently to prove that he would spend more than money in the service of his master.

At the outbreak of the rebellion he was the first to take up arms for the king. To him was entrusted the defence of the northern part of the kingdom. Lavish with his wealth, he not merely lent money to Charles, but within a short time he raised an army of 8000 foot, horse, and dragoons. 'Thus he stood upon his guard,' says the Duchess, 'and continued them upon duty ; playing his game with much prudence, and giving the town and country great satisfaction by his noble and honourable deportment.' Deportment, perhaps, was the most suitable word for his method of warfare. In no stress did his dignity desert him, he never forgot even in the acrimony of civil war the rules of chivalry. Nor did he always choose his subordinates with a wise discretion. He valued in others the

qualities which he most esteemed in himself. It is
said that he appointed Davenant lieutenant-general
of his ordnance because he was a poet, and a learned
divine discharged for him the office of scout-master.
As Clarendon puts it : 'He liked the pomp and
absolute authority of a general well, and preserved
the dignity of it to the full ; and for the discharge of
the outward state and circumstances of it, in acts
of courtesy, affability, bounty, and generosity he
abounded ; which in the infancy of a war became
him, and made him for some time very acceptable to
men of all conditions. But the substantial part of it,
and fatigue of a general, he did not in any degree
understand (being utterly unacquainted with war),
nor could submit to.'

But it was not the advice of amateurs, nor his
own lack of knowledge, which hindered the success
of Newcastle. 'There was so much treachery,
juggling, and falsehood in my Lord's own army,'
writes the Duchess, 'that it was impossible for him
to be successful in his designs and undertakings.'
And treachery was not the worst foe which he had
to combat. Orders from London drove him at last
into the very clutch of destruction. Rupert joined
him with a positive and absolute command from the
king to fight the enemy, and the result was the
battle fought 'on that fatal moor called Hessom
Moor.' Newcastle obeyed, as he would have obeyed
Charles had the king bade him cut his throat, but
he knew that in thus putting matters to the touch

he had no hope but ruin. As long as there was a chance of victory, Newcastle fought with the valour and courage which never deserted him. In an encounter with the Scots, 'my lord himself killed three with his page's half-leaden sword, for he had no other left him ; and though all the gentlemen in particular offered him their swords, yet my lord refused to take a sword of any of them.' After the crowning defeat he made his escape as best he might, and resolved, 'and that justly and honourably,' to forsake the kingdom. General King mournfully asked Rupert and Newcastle what they would do. Rupert replied, 'I will rally my men.' 'I will go to Holland,' said Newcastle, and he kept his word.

Newcastle has been severely blamed for thus deserting the cause of his king and country, and unless we understand the limits of his character, it is difficult to excuse him. Clarendon in his history made an ironical defence, which is the most that might be expected : 'All that can be said for the Marquis,' he wrote, 'is that he was utterly tired with a condition and employment so contrary to his humour, nature, and education. . . . He was a very fine gentleman, active and full of courage, and most accomplished in those qualities of horsemanship, dancing, and fencing, which accompany a good breeding—in which his delight was. Besides that he was amorous in poetry and music, to which he indulged the greatest part of his time.'

In truth, nothing save an ardent feeling of loyalty would have ever tempted him from the paths of pleasure, and if he failed, it speaks eloquently of his devotion that he faced death and ruin in the faithful service of his king. Death he escaped. Ruin held him in its savage grasp for many a long year. Even though he were 'as fit to be a general as a bishop,' he proved in adversity an unconquerable courage. Accustomed from his youth up to the lavish expenditure of money, he crossed the seas with no more than £90 in his purse. Thenceforth until the Restoration his life was one bitter fight with poverty. Wherever he went the demon of want pursued him. To obtain money was a plain impossibility. To win the credit of his fellows was an enterprise well within his compass. In Paris, as in Antwerp, he was forced 'to live upon the courtesy of those who would trust him.' Greatly daring, he married his Margaret without a shilling in his pocket.

The story of his debts is told with perfect candour and a touch of humour by his amiable spouse. One day his steward assured him that he could provide no dinner for him, for his creditors were resolved to trust him no longer. Pleasantly he suggested that the Duchess should pawn her clothes, and the Duchess, answering that they were of small value, bade her waiting-maid pledge some 'small toys,' which she had lately given her. Thus with a light heart he found a way out of every difficulty, and driven to the worst straits of poverty he would call his

creditors together, and make so effectual a speech to
them, 'that instead of urging the payment of his debts
they promised him that he should not want anything
in whatsoever they were able to assist him.' Well
might the Duchess sing the praises of the citizens
of Antwerp, who could never resist 'his civil deportment and persuasive arguments.' The credit which
they gave him she looked upon as a special blessing
of God ; for was he not a stranger in the land, and
to all appearance a ruined man ?

For men of less spirit than the Duke of Newcastle
it would have been easy to descend in the social
scale, to lead a mean life in a humble lodging. To
this degradation he would never consent. He could
not forget that he was 'a noble, high and puissant
prince.' Though his pocket held not a penny, still
would he live in the best state he might ; still would
he keep the finest horses in his stable, 'resolving for
his own recreation and divertisement, in his banished
condition, to exercise the art of manage, which he
is a great master and lover of.' In the depth of his
poverty his horses amounted to the number of eight.
Nor would the direst distress persuade him to part
with any of them. For he would say that good
horses are so rare 'as not to be valued for money,
and he who would buy him out of his pleasure
(meaning his horses) must pay dear for it.' And
the horses repaid eagerly the affection which he
lavished on them. They showed their joy, whenever he came to the stable, by their 'trampling

action,' and when he rode them himself 'they seemed to take much pleasure and pride in it.'

Thus his fame in Antwerp grew, and no traveller who might be admitted into the presence failed to pay the Duke his respects, and to admire his manage of horses. One day, says the Duchess with delight, she counted some seventeen coaches at the door of their house, which they had hired from the widow of 'Van Ruben, the famous picture-drawer.' And then, as hope grew brighter in the breasts of the Royalists, the Duke provided for the king and all the royal race who chanced to be in Antwerp a small entertainment, which, though it paled before the glories of Welbeck and Bolsover, must surely have reminded the Duke of his gracious past. If the expense were no larger than his creditors would allow, the sentiments of loyalty expressed were worthy the most august occasion. 'The King was brought in with music,' we are told, 'and all being placed, Major Mohun, the player, in a black satin robe and garland of bays, made a speech in verse of his lordship's own poetry, complimenting the King in his highest hyperbole.' Thus was prophesied the speedy restoration of the king, and when it came none rejoiced more gratefully than the loyallest of Dukes, who declared that his love to his gracious master, King Charles the Second, 'was above the love he bore to his wife, children, and all his posterity ; nay, to his own life.' Nor did the fact that his gracious master did not reciprocate his love check his ardour for a moment. 'I care not whether his Majesty loves me again or not,' said he, 'for I am resolved to love him.'

The Duke's enthusiasm at seeing once more his native land was unbounded. 'At last,' writes the Duchess in a touching passage, 'being come so far that he was able to discern the smoke of London, which he had not seen in a long time, he merrily was pleased to desire one that was near him to jog and awake him out of his dream, for surely, said he, I have been sixteen years asleep, and am not thoroughly awake yet. My Lord lay that night at Greenwich, where his supper seemed more savoury to him than any meat he had hitherto tasted, and the noise of some scraping fiddlers he thought the pleasantest harmony that ever he had heard.'

His sojourn in London was brief. In the general joyousness of the Restoration, the services which he had rendered to the king, and the sufferings which he had undergone, a banished man with a price upon his head, were speedily forgotten. He and his Duchess were hopelessly out of fashion. It was not for them to take part in the gallantry of a flippant Court, and they retired to Welbeck without regret, cultivated the Muses with the same pomp and ceremony wherewith they had faced the sorrows of exile, and made infrequent, if brilliant, appearances in London. He shared with enthusiasm his lady's love of literature. There were many for whom the Duke of Newcastle was at once the

Mæcenas and the Horace of England. 'The best
lyric and dramatic poet of his age' is the Duchess's
description of him. Much as she vaunted her
own genius, she willingly acclaimed his infinite
superiority :

> 'A Poet I am neither born nor bred,
>   But to a witty poet married,
>   Whose brain is fresh and pleasant as the Spring,
>   Where fancies grow, and where the Muses sing ;
>   There oft I lean my head, and listening hark,
>   T' observe his words, and all his fancies mark ;
>   And from that garden flowers of fancy take,
>   Whereof a posy up in verse I make :
>   Thus I that have no garden of my own
>   There gather flowers that are newly blown.'

A noble tribute of one poet to another ; and
though the harsh world has not accepted the
Duchess's amiable estimate, the Duke of Newcastle
was a true man of letters. His *New Method to
Dress Horses* was the fruit of lifelong knowledge.
Dryden did not disdain to adapt his translation of
Molière's *L'Étourdi* into the famous comedy, *Sir
Martin Mar-All*; and though the Duke's original
pieces did not win the approval of that most
capricious of critics, Samuel Pepys, Shadwell
packed a great part of *The Triumphant Widow,
or the Medley of Humours*, into *Bury Fair*, while
The Country Captain, acted with applause in
1649, survived until 1661, to be condemned by
Pepys as the silliest play that ever he saw. But it
is not for their comedies that we delight to

remember the Duchess of Newcastle and her lord. He at any rate was greater in life than in art ; and if we still see him in the habit as he lived, it is because the skill of the Duchess equalled her devotion, and enabled her to enrich posterity with the imperishable portrait of a great gentleman.

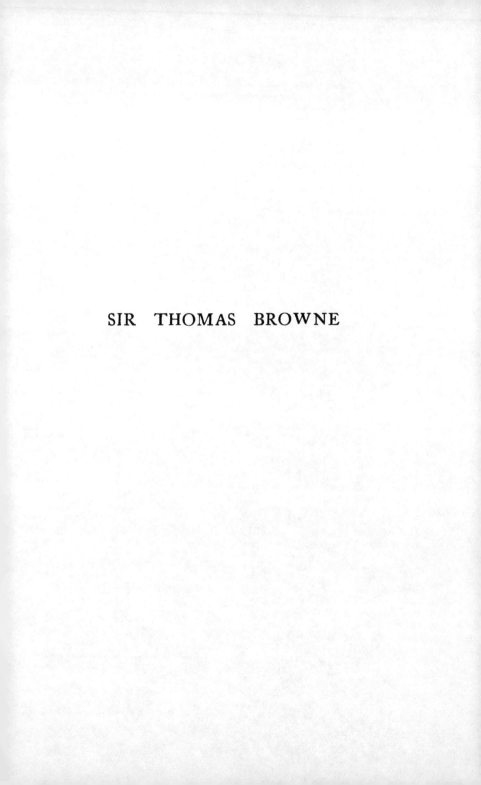

SIR   THOMAS   BROWNE

SIR THOMAS BROWNE

THOMAS BROWNE was born in 1605, the son of a mercer, who came of a good family long established in Cheshire. He was early dedicated to the love of wisdom, for 'his father,' we are told, 'used to open his breast when he was asleep, and kiss it in prayers over him, as 'tis said of Origen's father, that the Holy Ghost did take possession there.' Educated at Winchester and at Broadgate Hall, in the University of Oxford, he took his degree in 1626, and forthwith devoted himself to the study of medicine. For a while he practised his craft in Oxfordshire, and presently, being always a fervent believer in the efficacy of travel, he accompanied his step-father, Sir Thomas Dutton, on a journey to Ireland. Thereafter he sought what instruction he might at Montpellier and Padua, was made at Leyden a doctor of medicine, and after a brief sojourn at Shipden Hall, near Halifax, settled, in 1637, at Norwich, where he married Dorothy Mileham, and where he spent more than forty years in the tranquil practice of physic, in the study of antiquities, and in the pursuit of humane letters.

No man ever worked harder than he at his chosen

profession. From the tending of the sick he spared himself but a scanty leisure. He confessed that his *Popular Errors* was 'composed by snatches of time, as medical vocations and the fruitless importunity of uroscopy would permit him.' With a solemn sadness he contrasted his busy life at Norwich with the life of those 'whose quiet doors and unmolested hours offered no such distractions.' The very uniformity of his well-filled days leaves little to be told of his adventures. He wrote letters of good counsel to his sons, and received from them in exchange a full assurance of filial loyalty. To Honest Tom, as he delights to call him, he sends much sound advice, mingled with literary exhortations. When the boy, at the age of fourteen, travels into France he urges him to avoid *pudor rusticus*, to 'put on a decent boldness and learn a good garb of body,' and to 'frequent civil company.' And when Honest Tom, always a gallant fellow, chose the Navy for his profession, his father was eager to instruct him in the many sound lessons of life and letters. 'If you could quit periwigs,' says he, 'it would be more to your credit,' and then in a single sentence implores him 'not to forget French and Latin,' and insists that there is 'no such defence against extreme cold, as a woollen or flannel waistcoat next the skin.' With the literary instinct, always active in his brain, he bade his son, as a prelude to battle, read 'all the sea-fights of note, in Plutarch, the Turkish history, and others.' He was overjoyed to know

that Tom appreciated the ardour of Lucan. 'I wish
more military men would read him ; in the passage
you mention, there are noble strains and such as
may well affect generous minds.' Yet for Tom he
would temper the ardour of Lucan. Death rather than
surrender he deemed a wanton maxim. 'To be made
prisoner,' said he, 'by one unequal and over-ruling
power, after a due resistance, is no disparagement.'

And Tom proved himself an apt pupil of Plutarch
and his father. Being 'not only *Marti* but *Mercurio*,'
he read Homer and Juvenal at sea, and never forgot,
in the seduction of the classics, that it was the real
business of his life to fight. The very spirit of war
breathes in his letters. 'I thank you for your
directions,' he wrote to his father, who had advised a
remedy against the rattle of cannonades, 'but I found
that I could endure it ; nor is it so intolerable as most
conceive ; especially when men are earnest and intent
upon their business, unto whom muskets sound but
like pop-guns. It is impossible to express unto
another how a short sea-fight elevates the spirit of
a man, and makes him despise all dangers. In and
after all sea-fights I have been very thirsty.' It is
easy to imagine the dissertation upon thirst and
courage which this brave letter provoked. I would
we had many such. But suddenly Honest Tom dis-
appears from life, as though he had never been, without a word surviving of regret or explanation, and left
it to Edward, his elder brother, to take up the tale
of his father's quiet, studious life at Norwich.

And Edward, if further from the heart, was nearer to the mind, of Sir Thomas Browne. A physician like his father, and avid of curiosities, he kept a keen eye, in London or abroad, upon the doings at Norwich. Now he calls upon Guy Patin, a critic of *Religio Medici* ; now he notes with pleasure, that 'your book of Vulgar Errors is translated into Low Dutch, and is now in the press.' So under his father's care and tuition he rose high in his profession, found 'considerable practice among the higher ranks,' and attended the famous Earl of Rochester in his last illness. His letters are not significant of much, yet they help us to make the portrait of a tranquil, busy man. Nor were such excitements lacking to Browne, as his antiquarian mind would appreciate. The discovery of cinerary urns at Walsingham inspired him to his highest flight of eloquence. One day he found sixty coins of King Stephen in a grave ; another day (Sir Robert Paston, his neighbour and his friend) sent him his box of Saxon and Roman coins. A spermaceti whale, 'cast on our coast of Norfolk,' was an admirable excuse for profound research. When whales are lacking, he is content to dissect a bear, or to look for a heart without a pericardium. He marks that day with a white stone, when he hears of two ostriches brought from Tangier. ' I saw one,' he tells Edward, 'in the latter end of King James his days, at Greenwich, when I was a schoolboy. King Charles the first had a cassowary, whose fine green channelled egg I have, and you have seen.' He proved by experience that seeds found in wild-fowls' gizzards, have sprouted in the earth. Of adipocere he was the first discoverer, a 'fat concretion, where the nitre of the earth, and the salt and lixivious liquor of the body, had coagulated large lumps of fat into the consistence of the hardest Castile soap, whereof part remaineth with us.'

Thus it was that all was of interest to him. Coins, urns, lachrimatories, bones, eggs, and fossils he treasured in his house and garden, which as Evelyn said, was at once 'a paradise and cabinet of rarities.' It is no wonder, then, that thither the antiquaries of England delighted to resort. Evelyn and he exchanged many a letter before they met at Norwich. It was by the mediation of that noble person, Mr. Paston, that they were made known one to the other, and it was concerning the ornaments of gardens, ' garlands and coronary plants,' that they most willingly discoursed. Evelyn could not have found a wiser counsellor than Thomas Browne, and gladly he placed him among 'persons of ancient simplicity,—Paradisean and Hortulan saints.' Norwich, said he, ' is a place, I understand, which is very much addicted to the flowery part.' He opened his heart to Browne with discernment and eloquence. Perhaps it is not fanciful to suppose that he caught an echo of his correspondent's pomp and circumstance. He abundantly testifies his 'abhorrency of these painted and formal projections of our cockney gardens and plots, which appear like gardens of paste-board and marchpane, and smell more of paint than of verdure.' And Browne answers him with a catalogue, addressed to the Hawk and Pheasant on Ludgate Hill—a catalogue of flowers, which one is sure were speedily made to bloom at Wotton. Their friendship was already old, indeed, when Evelyn was persuaded to visit ' that famous scholar and physician, Dr. T. Browne, lately knighted.' Sir Thomas did the honours of his city with becoming gravity. ' He led me,' says Evelyn, 'to see all the remarkable places of this ancient city, being one of the largest, and certainly, after London, one of the noblest of England, for its venerable cathedral, number of stately churches, cleanness of the streets, and buildings of flint so exquisitely headed and squared, as I much astonished at, but he told me they had lost the art of squaring flints.' Hazlitt, in a famous essay, put the question which of the dead we would, if we could, recall to life. Were it given to me to live one day in the past, I could imagine no happier fate than to wander through the Norwich of the seventeenth century, already ' venerable,' with Sir Thomas Browne for guide, and John Evelyn for companion.

Though he lived always in his paradise at Norwich, no man was ever more easily accessible to his friends than Sir Thomas Browne. He is known by his associates, and they are antiquarians and men of letters. One day Dugdale writes to him for a commentary upon a passage in Tacitus, and receives a luminous

reply. Another day it is the learned Elias Ashmole,
who seeks information concerning Dr. John Dee,
and who is assured in answer that Browne had
often heard Arthur Dee, the doctor's son, 'affirm,
and sometimes with oaths, that he had seen projection made and transmutation of pewter dishes and
flagons into silver, which the goldsmiths of Prague
bought of them. And that Count Rosenberg played
at quoits with silver quoits made by projection as
before.' The insistent Aubrey, collecting facts for
Anthony à Wood, makes confident inquiry of him,
whose *Religio Medici*, in his own phrase, ' first opened
my understanding.' Ever the friend of scholars,
on whom he lavished readily his stores of erudition,
and as readily displayed the treasures of his paradise,
he let the great world go by as it would. Publicity
irked him not. He eluded the strife of factions and
the gaze of the curious. Few men have more
sternly divorced themselves from affairs than he.
When Cromwell took arms against his king, Browne,
with the greatest resolution, closed the door of his
study. The years of his greatest activity in letters
were the years of civil war. But though he knew
himself as little fit to sit in the council-chamber as
to bear arms, he was a keen partisan. No man
dared doubt his loyalty. In his eyes Cromwell was
always the Usurper. He was one of the four hundred
and thirty-two citizens, who, in 1643, the year after
the sudden appearance of *Religio Medici*, refused to
subscribe money for the recapture of Newcastle.

'Yesterday,' he tells Tom, his son, at the king's return, 'was an humiliation and fast kept to divert the judgment of God upon us and our posterity for the abominable murder of King Charles the First, and is by act of Parliament to be kept on that day for ever.' It was not strange, therefore, that, when in 1671 Charles II. visited Norwich, he should have conferred upon the physician the honour of knighthood. The king had designed to distinguish Thomas Thacker, the Mayor, but he, whose name is ever to be remembered, begged that the knighthood should be given to Thomas Browne, the philosopher, in whom Norwich already testified her pride. It is not unlikely that Charles's insatiable curiosity should have lighted upon Browne's work. Sir William Petty told Pepys that 'the three books most esteemed for wit in the world were *Religio Medici*, Osborne's *Advice to a Son*, and *Hudibras*.' And all three were doubtless familiar to the Court. But even if Browne's philosophy had escaped the king, his loyalty had long been conspicuous, and he would have earned his monarch's respect, even had he never considered the errors of the people. The spirit in which he accepted the honour is characteristic. A single reference in his *Repertorium* contents him. Among the visits paid by kings to Norwich, he mentions the visit of Charles II., 'of which,' says he, 'I had particular reason to take notice.'

Only one other public encounter disturbed the tranquillity of his life. In 1664 two women, Amy

Duny and Rose Cullender were tried for witchcraft before Sir Matthew Hale, and being found guilty were hanged. Sir Thomas Browne happened to be in court, and the judge was minded, while the trial was in progress, when, in fact, only eight witnesses had been examined, to ask his opinion. He gave it as most other intelligent men of his day would have given it, that 'the fits were natural, but heightened by the Devil's co-operating with the malice of the witches, at whose instance he did the villanies.' To condemn a scholar of the seventeenth century for a pious belief, no longer current in our age, is to make a reckless assault upon chronology. Yet it has generally been accounted to Browne's discredit that he 'believed, and did now know that there are witches.' He went further upon what to-day seems the pathway of error : he declared that those who doubted the existence of witches were not only infidels but atheists. If Browne erred, he erred in good company, and not without evidence. Though we may deplore the cruelties practised on the miserable women suspected of witchcraft, the fact that we now suppose them to have been powerless does not prove that their intention was not evil.[1] In any

---

[1] The view held by Browne and his contemporaries concerning witchcraft, is at once explained and justified by Selden. 'The law against witches does not prove there be any,' says this wise man, 'but it punishes the Malice of these people, that use such means to take away Men's lives. If one should propose that by turning his Hat thrice and crying Buz, he could take away a Man's life, though in truth he could do no such

case, a philosopher who sins with Sir Matthew Hale
and Hobbes may be acquitted, even at the bar of
modern omniscience, and Sir Thomas Browne's
memory bears no other weight of guilt than that,
being orthodox in his own day, he appears heretical
in ours.

In 1682 Sir Thomas Browne's thrice fortunate
life was brought to a close.   Happy in the affection
of his wife, happy in the loyalty of his children and
his friends, happy in his tranquil research, he lived
and died, as Johnson says, 'a zealous adherent to
the faith of Christ.'   He was buried in the Church
of St. Peter's Mancroft,[1] and it was after death that
his heaviest misfortune overtook him.   For him
there was a piety in undisturbed ashes.   'But who
knows the fate of his bones,' he asked, 'or how often
he is to be buried ?   Who hath the oracle of his
ashes, or whither they are to be scattered ?'   Not
Sir Thomas Browne surely.   'To be gnawed out
of our graves, to have our skulls made drinking-

thing, yet this was a just law made by the State, that whosoever
should turn his Hat thrice, and cry Buz, with an intention to
take away a Man's life, shall be put to death.'

[1] The monument which testifies to his death and his wife's
devotion, bears beneath the lapidary Latin the following legend :
' Near the foot of this pillar lies Sir Thomas Browne Kt. and
Doctor in Physick, Author of 'Religio Medici,' and other
Learned Books, who practis'd Physick in this City 46 yeares,
and Died Oct 19. 1682, in ye 77th year of his Age.   In Memory
of whom Dame Dorothy Browne, who had been his affectionate
wife 41 years, Caus'd this Monument to be Erected.'

bowls are tragical abominations escaped in burning burials.' He did not escape them. For nearly one hundred and sixty years he slept in peace, and then to make room for one Mary Bowman, the wife of the Rev. John Bowman, the grave of Sir Thomas was roughly attacked, the coffin was opened by a workman's pick, and the philosopher's skull was carried off by an antiquary, to be a peep-show at the hospital. Here in truth is an irony of untoward fate. 'Man is a noble animal,' said Browne, 'splendid in ashes and pompous in the grave.' And so savagely was his pomp outraged, that his stolen skull, measured as he might have measured it, aroused the curious, and not long since was fought over by anxious citizens. What an eloquent threnody might he have composed upon the pitiful adventures of his own cranium!

His life, said he in his *Religio*, 'had been a miracle of thirty years.' Whatever was marvellous lay within his heart and brain. Such adventures as he met with were the adventures of his soul. The castles whose walls he had battered were the castles of error. That he followed Erasmus and Montaigne in marvelling at the miracle of his life suggests that intelligence knows as keen a triumph as political cunning or war-like courage. His victories, like theirs, were books. And how, with *Religio Medici*, his first victory was won upon the field of letters is still a mystery. It was written, we are told, at Shibden Hall, and was ready in his wallet, when, in 1636, he came to Norwich.

'Continued in his private study,' as he said, 'and as an exercise unto himself rather than as an exercitation for any other,' it passed from his hands in a broken and imperfect shape, until one day he woke up and found it hot from the press. The first edition, the fruit of this piracy, fell into the hands of Lord Dorset, who bade Sir Kenelm Digby comment upon it. Sir Kenelm, the most fantastic of commentators, hastily put pen to paper, and composed the *Observations*, which have long shared a binding with *Religio Medici*. The episode was an occasion for the usual courtesies. Sir Thomas Browne amiably addressed Sir Kenelm, and Sir Kenelm matched the doctor's elaborate compliments. We need not make too much of this interchange of courtesies. There is no more reason to look gravely, with Dr. Johnson, upon ' the reciprocal civility of authors' as ' one of the most risible scenes in the farce of life' than to suspect Sir Thomas Browne, with the same critic, of employing a stratagem, ' by which an author panting for fame, may at once gratify his vanity, and preserve the appearance of modesty.' All that is certain is that the first copy of *Religio Medici*, the work of pirates, came in the modest guise of a chap-book, and that Sir Thomas immediately superseded it by a more accurate edition.

Sir Thomas Browne's *Religio Medici* is less a theological treatise than a work of art. Those who look to its pages for guidance in religion will be disappointed. Those whose ear is attuned to the

harmonies of our English speech will never weary of
its exquisite poetry. Its ostensible theme, indeed, is
of less interest than the style in which it is composed, or than the ingenious epigrams which give a
lustre to its pages. Though the Doctor sets out to
tell us of his religion, he very soon wanders by the
way, and discourses at hazard of all things that touch
his curiosity, and most especially of himself. The
book is various and wayward. No secure thread of
thought holds the argument together. The author
turns from martyrs to miracles, from blind fortune
to witchcraft, without difficulty or hesitation. The
tone of piety which marks the opening pages presently gives way to a subtle irony or to the mere
delight in fashioning quick and vivid sentences.
And Sir Thomas Browne is as various as his book.
By profession a scientific observer, he is a pagan
by sentiment and a Christian by faith. He is conscious that several circumstances—'as the general
scandal of my profession, the natural course of my
studies, the indifference of my behaviour and discourse'—might persuade the world that he had no
religion at all. But in the world's despite he dares
'without usurpation assume the honourable style of
a Christian.' And thus, narrowing his definition,
he confesses that he is 'of that reformed new-cast
religion, wherein he dislikes nothing but the name.'
Nor is there any Church 'whose every part so
squares unto his conscience . . . as this whereof he
holds his belief—the Church of England.' And

having once given his allegiance, he is perfect in devotion. Neither knowledge nor superstition, to both of which he was accessible, availed to disturb the constancy of his faith. He welcomed difficulties that he might prove the fidelity of his belief. A prolonged study of anatomy, the patient desire to pierce the mysteries of nature, did not shake his child-like adherence to the religion which he had chosen. 'This is no vulgar part of faith,' said he, 'to believe a thing not only above, but contrary to reason, and against the arguments of our proper senses.' With a frank simplicity he blessed himself and was thankful that he lived not in an age of miracles. 'I would not,' said he, 'have been one of those Israelites that passed the Red Sea; nor one of Christ's patients on whom he wrought his wonders; then had my faith been thrust upon me; nor should I enjoy that greater blessing pronounced to all that believe and saw not.' Sir Thomas Browne's simple faith was thus superior to the pride of knowledge and the arrogance of self. At the first word of authority, science and paganism made instant submission. Sir Thomas, being a truly learned man, was distinguished by a noble humility of soul. The 'sturdy doubts and boisterous objections,' with which his knowledge acquainted him, he conquered 'not in a martial posture, but on his knees.' The supreme knowledge that he knew nothing made belief easy to him, and thus he taught his 'haggard and unreclaimed reason to stoop to the lure of faith.'

With a fine irony he tells us how an evil spirit whispered to him that the miracles of Elias and Moses were no miracles at all. 'Thus,' says he, 'the devil played at chess with me and, yielding a pawn, sought to gain a queen of me'; but Browne was more than a match for his wily antagonist, and, strengthened by faith, had no difficulty in check-mating the Evil One.

But, as it has been said, it is not the main purpose of Sir Thomas Browne's book which enthralls us. Our curiosity is most vividly awakened when he leads us into the devious byways of speculation. To cite his own words, he 'loves to lose himself in a mystery; to pursue his reason to an *O altitudo.*' And, thus lost, he is discursive and unexpected. There, indeed, he reminds us of Montaigne, whom he had most faithfully studied, not only in manner, but in matter. Though he was free from the Frenchman's scepticism, he was engrossed with the same thoughts which held the great essayist captive in his tower. Nature and death—to these he recurs again and again. He worshipped the great mother of us all with an equal mind. In his opinion she could do nothing wrong or in vain. 'There are no grotesques in nature,' said he, 'not anything framed to fill up empty cantons and unnecessary spaces.' And though he piously confessed the perfect beauty of all nature's works, though he held that nothing was ever ugly save the chaos, he yet admitted the supremacy of art. 'Now nature is not at variance with art,' says he, in a passage which reduces the universe to a simple system, 'nor art with nature; they are both the servants of God's providence. Art is the perfection of nature. Were the world now as it was the sixth day, there were yet a chaos. Nature hath made one world, and art another. In brief, all things are artificial; for nature is the art of God.' The last phrase Hobbes transferred to the *Leviathan*. With Browne it is a recurrent theme. 'Nature hath furnished one part of the earth'—such is his variation in *Hydriotaphia*—'and man another.'

But, with Montaigne, he wondered most deeply at the life of man. 'I find,' says he, 'there are many pieces in this one fabric; this frame is raised upon a mass of antipathies.' Does not this recall Montaigne's famous epithets *ondoyant et divers*? And so, like Erasmus and many another, as I have said, he deemed his life a miracle, 'which to relate, were not a history, but a piece of poetry and would sound to common ears a fable,' and the fact that the sentiment is borrowed need not impair its sincerity. Nor, to indulge his amazement, did he need to look elsewhere than to himself. 'We carry with us,' he writes, 'the wonders we seek without us; there is all Africa and her prodigies in us'; and he was as happy in the satisfaction afforded by this undying curiosity as was the French philosopher who found an interest in life which neither ceased nor waned.

Nor did the love of life persuade him to hate death.   In truth he faced the inevitable end as bravely and simply as Montaigne himself, but for another reason.   Montaigne, sceptic as he was, had in him something of an ancient stoic.   He expected the coming of death with equanimity because he had schooled his mind to expect it.   He was always booted and spurred to take his last journey.   Sir Thomas Browne, on the other hand, looked to death as to a release.   He knew the joy of life; he had 'shaken hands,' to cite his own words, 'with delight in his warm blood and canicular days'; and yet his faith persuaded him to regard death as the only solace of life.   'When I take a full view and circle of myself,' he wrote, ' without this reasonable moderator, and equal piece of justice, death, I do conceive myself the miserablest person extant.'   And so he lived content in the conviction that we are in the power of no calamity while death is in our own.

The pagan that was within him inclined him naturally to superstition.   He could not join the others of his own Church in contemning symbols, pilgrimages and processions.   He put his faith in tutelary angels, and turned away his mind from the easy criticism of reason.   And having set forth the tenour of his belief, which, if it square not with maturer judgments he is ready to disdain, he turns, like his master Montaigne to a description of himself.   Though, when he wrote the *Religio Medici*, he was not yet thirty years of age, he

wrote as though he had long passed the boundaries
of middle life.   There is a maturity in his opinion,
an easy mastery of language, which do not consort
with youth.   He writes as one who is as far
removed from careless ardour as from vain experiment.   There is little that lies without his knowledge save himself, which he was wise enough to
accept as a mystery.   But his interest in his own
character was so great, despite its imperfections, that
he was compelled to attempt a moral portrait.   He
claimed, before all things, the virtue of charity.   He
boasted that he had ' no antipathy, or rather idiosyn-
crasy, in diet, humour, air, anything.'   His appetite
was as easily accommodating as his character, and he
could eat frogs, snails, toadstools among the French,
or locusts and grasshoppers among the Jews with
equal pleasure.   He cared not whether his salad
was gathered in a churchyard or in a garden.   Being
born in the eighth climate he was 'constellated unto
all,' and he knew no national repugnances.   He
thought it as great a madness to wound a country by
insulting all its citizens as to rail without reason
against the times.   ' I am in England everywhere,
and under any meridian,' or, in other words, he
changed his mind, and carried a fresh sympathy with
him, when he crossed the sea.

Conscious though he was of his superiority, he was
a democrat in the only wise sense.   While he acknow-
ledged that there was 'a rabble even among the gentry,'
he applauded that nobility without heraldry, that

natural dignity, 'whereby one man is ranked with another, another filed before him according to the quality of his desert, and pre-eminence of his good parts.' The charity which he would extend to all nations and to all classes he proved also in the things of the intellect. Knowing himself more deeply learned than others, he would be generous in imparting what he knew. 'I make not my head a grave,' said he, 'but a treasury of knowledge.' And he was of so rare a quality that, being a scholar, he yet disliked controversy. It pleased him rather to set forth and to illustrate his own opinions than to attack the opinions of others. He found no joy in fighting for fighting's sake. And he was content if he could discover his own image of the truth without conflict or loss of temper. 'I had rather stand in the shock of a basilisk,' said he, 'than in the fury of a merciless pen.' And his dislike of controversy is not strange when we remember the kindred dislike which he cherished of positive judgments. He would not censure nor contemn any one, because he believed that no man truly knew another. For himself, he was in the dark to all the world, and visible only through a cloud to his most intimate friends. Why then should he contemn others, or himself endure another's censure?

Being charitable and uncertain, he was perforce humble. But the expression of his humility has not always the true ring. It smacks of theological convention. 'I repute myself,' says he, 'the most abject piece of mortality'; and this familiar phrase ill accords with his conscious and declared knowledge. Nor can we believe him without question when he boasts that he has no pride. He asserts that not even his mastery of tongues, not even his familiarity with foreign countries, not even his profound knowledge of science availed to give him a good conceit of himself, but in professing this humility, he seems to vaunt his accomplishments too highly, and he would have persuaded us more easily had his design been less obvious.

It was friendship, which most easily aroused his emotion, and of friendship he writes in the same strain as Montaigne discoursing of La Boëtie. 'I love my friend,' said he, 'before myself, and yet methinks, I do not love him enough. . . . When I am from him, I am dead till I be with him.' And as he was serious in friendship, so he was easy in acquaintance. His conversation was, like the sun's, with all men ; and he looked upon all, both good and bad, with an amiable eye. But his general sympathy did not make him a boon companion. He regarded the world not as an inn, but as a hospital, and his common demeanour was like gravity itself. 'I am no way facetious,' says he, 'nor disposed for the mirth and galliardise of company.' And so with a sombre and kindly aspect he looked out upon the world, resolved already, though thirty summers had not passed over his head, that there was no happiness under the sun, and yet gaining an added happiness with every increase of knowledge.

Few books have enjoyed so swift a success and been so thoroughly misunderstood as *Religio Medici*. Sir Kenelm Digby's criticism is of little worth. Sir Thomas Browne gives him a rhapsody, and Digby urges him to read Master White's *Dialogues of the World*. In other words, he put his author's imagery upon the anvil of criticism and beat it out of shape. Dr. Alexander Ross, a fantastical Scots pedant, followed hard upon Sir Kenelm's heels with his *Medicus Medicatus*, and was no nearer to comprehension than Digby. He belaboured 'the physician's religion' with the zeal of one who scented Papistry in innocent rhetoric. Presently, John Merryweather, by translating the treatise into Latin, made it the free possession of all Europe, and contrived its easy passage into French, Dutch, and German. Then came the annotator in the person of one Keck, who attempted to explain what needed no explanation. The French philosophers followed with argument. Gui Patin was eloquent in approval, and even the ingenious Bayle condescended to a brief notice. But the early critics, from Sir Kenelm onwards, looked upon *Religio Medici* with pedantic eyes. Not one of them had the wit to consider the treatise as a work of art, as a dramatic lyric, as a clear expression of character and passion. It was left for Coleridge to perceive the truth. 'The *Religio Medici*,' says he, ' is a fine portrait of a handsome man in his best clothes,' and Browne's castigators, overlooking the elegance of his coat, have addressed him (or his portrait) in the grave language of metaphysics, and explained why he should have worn a coat of another cut.

To-day we take the juster view of Coleridge. We accept the masterpiece without argument. Inquiring not too closely into its theology, we are content to admire its noble language. And Sir Thomas himself was herein keenly conscious of his aim. 'I am naturally amorous,' says he, with perfect truth, 'of all that is beautiful,' and it was beautiful language which most easily affected him. His *Religio Medici* has survived almost alone among the treatises of the seventeenth century, because it is set to perfect music. For Sir Thomas Browne was a musician, who played upon the instrument of speech with the skill of a conscious artist. And his daring was equal to his skill. He had no fear of new forms or fresh words. By using Latin derivations he doubled the resources of our tongue, and cunningly heightened its contrasts. Thus he would always oppose a homely image to one more pompous, and by the interchange of Latin and Saxon, he could obtain effects unknown before. No literary or rhetorical artifice was beyond his reach. And, much as we admire his quiet irony, his gift of epigram, and his ingenious intelligence, it is the genius of the poet, a noble use of words, a vivid sense of metaphor, an exquisite harmony of phrase and cadence, which have given his book a gracious immortality.

His *Pseudodoxia Epidemica*, an Enquiry into Vulgar Errors, which followed *Religio Medici*, though it wore the semblance of a scientific discourse, is still a work of fancy. The real Browne is revealed in every page, with his fantastic pedantries, his strange ironies, his unquenchable love of whatever is rare and unexpected. The book is a museum of curios, arranged with the same admired disorder as he brought to the fashioning of his museum of bones, coins, and cinerary urns. Curiosity, in truth, was his constant aim; his mind was curious, his life was curious, his style was curious, he was surrounded with curiosities. Yet in this book, if anywhere, he aimed at a definite and intelligible plan. It is not unlikely that he found an inspiration in Francis Bacon, who declared in his *Use of Doubts*, that 'it would be a very profitable course to adjoin to the calendars of doubts and *non liquets* a calendar of falsehoods, and of popular errors.' If he accepted Bacon's hint, he interpreted it after his own fashion. The duty of discovering errors sat lightly on him. He was always happier in gathering flowers of fancy than in searching out the way of truth.

Nevertheless he was keenly alive to the gravity of a work, which was 'not to be performed upon one leg, and should smell of oil, if duly and deservedly handled.' And he was at first minded 'to propose it unto the Latin republic and equal judges of Europe.' Patriotism and the debt which he owed to his own country, and 'especially unto its ingenuous gentry,'

persuaded him otherwise, and he determined, fortunately for us, to throw lustre on the English tongue. He
made the resolution in no spirit of bland compliance.
' Nor have we,' said he bravely, 'addressed our pen
or style unto the people (whom books do not redress,
and who are this way incapable of reduction) but
unto the knowing and leading part of learning.' Thus
resolved, he was ' fain to wander in the America and
untravelled parts of truth.'   And for his talisman he
carried a doubt of authority.   He refused to establish
his belief upon the dictates of antiquity. He waged war
indiscriminately upon all the ancients—Herodotus,
who deserved and has at last won a more generous
faith, Aristotle, Pliny, Solinus, Athenaeus, ' a delect-
able author, and justly styled by Casaubon, *Graecorum
Plinius*,' and many others.   He tracked the common
errors of mankind through the intricate labyrinth of
their borrowings.   Here you may find pleasantly
repeated the popular beliefs that 'a pigeon hath no
gall,' ' that a salamander lives in the fire,' ' that the
chameleon lives upon air.'   The book is an encyclo-
paedia of refuted authorities.   He was minded to
sweep away all the fallacies of Pliny, Solinus, and their
imitators, and to brush from the world of research the
last speck of credulity.   He abolished the beliefs of
the Middle Ages by bringing them to the touchstone
of experiment.   And he achieved his purpose with
an irony and eloquence which never grew tired.
   Yet in our modern sense he was no true man of
science.   He had not discovered the meaning of

historical criticism. He treats his authorities with an even hand as though whatever stood in print was of an equal value. We are not surprised that he should refute Athenaeus ; we are surprised that he should have thought him worth refutation. Nor did he trouble to discriminate between history and mythology. For him Aeneas is a real person, whose words and deeds must be gravely considered. He is seriously perplexed because Aeneas feasted his followers with venison, and Aristotle affirms that neither deer nor boar are found in Africa. In a like spirit of simplicity he complains that Adam and Eve are depicted with navels 'in the authentic draughts of Urbin, Angelo, and others, which notwithstanding, cannot be allowed.' With an equal lack of humour he objects to a picture of Jerome, in the background of which there is a clock. For 'clocks or automatous organs are of late invention'—an objection which suggests that the purpose of pictorial art was veiled from him. His chapter on Satan, 'the great promoter of false opinions,' could best be considered as he considers the errors of others. He takes the Father of Evil very seriously. He browbeats him as a prosecuting attorney might browbeat a criminal. He charges him with 'endeavouring to propagate the unbelief of witches,' with deluding 'us by philtres, ligatures, charms, ungrounded amulets.' Then having accepted in good faith the activity of Satan, he willingly takes pains to disprove the vain legends of the Middle Ages, such as the fable of the

Three Kings of Cologne. And, as if to guard himself against the charge of unbelief, he cannot safely deny that there is a basilisk, and he does allow that hares may change their sex. He must not be judged by our standard. In his own age he appeared a true sceptic. There were few errors of the past which he was not resolute to examine. As resolutely he refused to accept new discoveries. 'He never mentions the motion of the earth,' says Johnson, 'but with contempt or ridicule.' In other words, he had taken up a strong position at the cross-roads, and would not be dislodged.

However, the right or the wrong of Sir Thomas Browne's scepticism need not perplex us. It is enough that he lights up his treatise with flashes of noble imagery and quick irony. 'We shall not, I hope, disparage the resurrection of our Redeemer,' says he, 'if we say that the sun doth not dance on Easter Day.' It is for such sentences as this that we take pleasure in *Vulgar Errors*. And though his fancy was never bridled, he gave it with the lapsing years an ever looser rein. *The Garden of Cyrus*, for instance, is pure fantasy. It opens discursively of gardens, 'which were before gardeners, and but some hours after the earth.' In lofty words the author celebrates 'the pensile or hanging gardens of Babylon,' and rejoices that 'the Persian gallants who destroyed this monarchy maintained their botanical bravery.' Then, in terms of pomp, he celebrates our magnified Cyrus, who 'disposed his trees like his

armies in regular ordination.'   All this is but a preface to the main argument of his singular treatise.
It is the quincunx, which engrosses him, 'that is
the rows and orders so handsomely disposed, or five
trees so set together, that a regular angularity, and
thorough prospect was left on every side.'   Henceforth he was obsessed by the quintuple number, which
makes up the letter X.   Wherever his eye was cast,
he saw 'the emphatical decussation, or fundamental
figure.'   He lays aside his humour for the moment
that he may loudly impress his ingenuity upon us.
And he detects his quincunx with so sly a vision, he
expands the results with so brave an eloquence, that
only a churl or a pedant would resent his obsession.

The enterprise is not uncommon.   I have known
a crazy philosopher who detected a form of worship
in tall hats and chimney-pots.   But by none has it
ever been carried so near to a logical conclusion as by
Sir Thomas Browne.   Art and nature conspired to
yield him quincunces.   Nothing, either dead or
living, was recalcitrant, save 'the neat retiary spider,'
whose method of weaving ' may still nettle Minerva,
the goddess of that mystery.'   The quintuple figure,
in brief, was no mere form of practice in plantation.
It dominated architecture from the floor to the roof.
There are five parts of a structure, five orders, five
intercolumniations.   The squared stones and bricks
of ancient structures were placed in hieratic quincunces.   Triumphal crowns of laurel, oak, and myrtle
were plaited in this order.   The beds of the ancients

were fine examples of the fundamental figure; and as the ancients lay in crossbeds, so they sat crosslegged upon crosslegged seats. Neither in peace nor in war can we escape 'these rhoimboidal decussations.' The Roman *batalia*, the Macedonian phalanx, the labyrinth of Crete were composed with no other end than to satisfy our quincuncial curiosity.

Nature comes to the aid of art. The proper ordination may be observed in catkins, in sainfoin, in Jupiter's beard or houseleek, and in 'the scaly composure of the oak rose.' But it is the *arbustetum* or thicket on the head of the teazel, which, in the domain of nature, most swiftly speeds his fancy. 'He that considereth that frame so regularly palisadoed,' says he, 'and stemmed with flowers of the royal colour, in the house of the solitary maggot, may find the seraglio of Solomon.' What care we, when we come upon such conceits as that, what fantasy bred them? In brief, Browne looked upon the earth, and he saw five. He gazed upon the heavens, and five still smiled at him. Truly in his eyes five, the number of justice, was all-pervading and omnipotent. Joseph designed five changes of raiment for Benjamin; David took five pebbles from the brook; it was with five barley loaves that our Saviour fed five thousand persons. It is five, ever five, in this divine piece of madness, and as Browne writes the last page late at night, he owns 'that the quincunx of heavens runs low, and 'tis time to close the five parts of knowledge.' And then with a stroke of resonant humour,

he brings his speculation to a close : ' To keep
our eyes open longer, were but to act our Antipodes.
The huntsmen are up in America, and they are
already past their first sleep in Persia.' The life and
fancy of this image will explain the hold that Browne
keeps upon our imaginations. ' Does the whimsical
knight,' asks Coleridge, ' give us thus the essence of
gunpowder tea, and call it an opiate ? '

In 1658 some urns were found in a field of Old
Walsingham. They lay, some forty or fifty, in a dry,
sandy soil, not a yard deep. Of themselves, they
were of no great worth, yet are they ever memorable,
for they inspired Sir Thomas Browne to the writing
of *Hydriotaphia*, which sets out to be a treatise
upon urn-burial, and ends as one of the greatest
poems in our language. For a discussion of ancient
burial Sir Thomas was well-equipped. He was
learned, as we know, with all the learning of his
time. None more easily than he could embellish
modern thought with ancient instances. He
marshalled his authorities with an easy confidence.
When he is compelled to state a plain fact, he does not
shirk it, even though it wofully disturb the current
of his poetry. The largest of the urns, he tells us,
not without a shock, contained ' above a gallon.'
Again, speaking of other practices, he declares that,
' how to keep the corpse seven days from corruption
by anointing and washing, without exenteration,
were an hazardable piece of art, in our choicest
practise,' and you cannot but smile as at an irrele-

vancy. But he seldom sins after this fashion, and
though he discourse by the way concerning the
burials of all the ages, he returns speedily to the
proper purpose of his work. His theme, quickened
by the sight of the ancient urns, is life, death, and
immortality, the oldest and yet the newest theme of
man. His cadences rise and fall like the cadences
of noble music. The imagery of *Hydriotaphia*
equals in magnificence and variousness its sonority.
From beginning to end the poem is a procession of
splendid phrases. With the utmost skill has Browne
interchanged passages of simple melody with the
deep notes of his organ-voice. 'These are sepul-
chral pitchers,' he writes on one page, ' which have
no joyful voices; silently expressing old mortality,
the ruins of forgotten times.' Here is a beauty of
phrase, harmonious in sound, and plain in its neat-
ness. And then turn a few pages, and you will find
by way of contrast these sentences, which Browne
alone could have written : ' to burn the bones of the
King of Edom for lime, seems no irrational ferity,
but to drink of the ashes of dead relations, a passionate
prodigality.' There we have the pomp, not un-
touched by the humour of the master, and wonder
still at the secret of his eloquence.

And then we arrive at the famous fifth chapter,
which to have written, brief as it is, were sufficient
for eternal fame. Here the world of wisdom is
packed into a little space; here is no sentence that does
not carry the weight of a folio. Shakespeare comes

to your mind as you read, for only Shakespeare has
achieved this pomp of phrase, this universality of
thought.   With incomparable amplitude of mind and
word Browne considers youth and age, the future and
the past.   His old curiosity has fallen from him like a
cloak.   He is grave and sombre, as one who deals
with large issues.   Of what profit is length of years,
if they be not well spent ?   ' If they fell by long and
aged decay, yet wrapt up in the bundle of time, they
fall into indistinction, and make one blot with
infants.'   Or maybe age overtook them prematurely.
' Many are too early old,' again 'tis Browne who
speaks, ' and before the date of age.   Adversity
stretcheth our days, misery makes Alcmena's nights,
and time hath no wings unto it.'   And if the past be
of small account, how shall we prize the future ?
' To subsist in bones, and to be pyramidally extant is
a fallacy in duration.'   Why should we take thought
of our reputation, when ' Charles v. cannot hope to
live within ten Methuselahs of Hector.'   Verily, ' 'tis
too late to be ambitious.'   Nor is there good reason
to cling eagerly to naked nominations.   ' To be
nameless in worthy deeds exceeds an infamous
history.   The Canaanitish woman lives more
happily without a name than Herodias with one.
And who had not rather have been the good thief
than Pilate ? '   And thus he comes to his conclusion
that monuments are nothing in the metaphysics of
true belief, that ' to live indeed is to be again ourselves,' that ' 'tis all one to lie in St. Innocent's

churchyard as in the sands of Egypt.   Ready to be anything, in the ecstasy of being ever, and as content with six foot as the *moles* of Adrianus.'

   To the same themes of life and death he returns in his marvellous *Letter to a Friend*, and his *Christian Morals*, showing himself serene always in the presence of death, courageous always in the presence of life. It is characteristic that, if the natural scepticism of his mind persuaded him to justify himself as a Christian in *Religio Medici*, he had no doubts concerning Christian morals.   He was firmly established upon the rock of duty.   It was not enough for him to be blameless. He aimed at the positive not the negative good. Not content with avoiding evil, he must do well. ' Be chaste in thy flaming days,' says he.   ' The sick man's sacrifice is but a lone oblation.'   He will not dally with excuses; he will admit no temptations. ' Put no names or notions,' says he, ' upon authentic virtues and vices.   Think not that morality is ambulatory.'   And thus at the end of it all he bids us with Montaigne to reckon not upon long life. ' Think every day the last,' says he, 'and live always beyond thy account.'

   As I have said, it is for his style and manner that Sir Thomas Browne ever will be memorable.   Above all, he was not merely an inventor of harmonies; he was an inventor of the words of which these harmonies are composed.   He set himself down consciously and deliberately to this work of invention. He was acutely conscious of the effect that he wished to produce. With a sly stroke at his own temerity, he anticipated the time when we shall 'be fain to learn Latin to understand English,' and by his single endeavour he brought that time sensibly nearer. Nor were his coinages natural to his temper. The letters which he wrote to his children are models of plain talk. He was not, like George Meredith, made all of one piece. It was only when he took up his pen to address the world that the artifice grew upon him. Then, indeed, he ransacked Greek and Latin to furnish him with unheard nouns and strange adjectives. His writings sparkle with exotic words, fashioned with daring, and yet in good accord with their origin. And it was not mere curiosity that prompted this research. His tissue of several languages gave him words of many lengths, and ensured the varying structure and cadence of his sentences. Thus by the deft use of synonyms, as, for instance, 'this encyclopædia and round of knowledge,' or a 'surd and earless generation,' he could play upon our speech as upon a musical instrument. Some of his new-minted coins remain in circulation,[1] others were never current save in his

---

[1] Among his inventions which have survived are hallucination, literary, umbrella, medical, antediluvian, and many another useful word. His failures have a foreign air, which suggests that they were fit only for his own management: lapidipical, coadjuvancy, pedestrious, extispicious, incremable, desumed, impennous—all made in accordance with the rules, yet fit only for one who, in Johnson's phrase, 'had very little fear of the shame of falling.'

own works.   Yet he has enriched the dictionary with more words of his own fashioning than any writer that ever lived, and the general acceptance of his discoveries proves their worth and justice.   Nor, despite his love of antiquity, was he deaf to the common speech which he heard about him in Norfolk.   Fresh from inventing that strange polysyllable, 'deoppilation,' he does not disdain to tell us that 'horses will knable at the wall,' or that 'men practise to make long-lasting snasts out of *alumen plumosum.*'

Strange words were but the bricks of his architecture.   It was in their bold use and disposition that he showed his genius.   I have already said something of the music and colour of his prose, of the constant metaphor, which gives a sort of solemn gaiety to his science and his scepticism.   He was one who thought in images.   A plain argument, a clear statement of the case could not satisfy him. He must trick his thought out in a thousand fancies and illumine his debate with an infinite variety of conceits.   And so it is that, though he writes what is called prose, he is always a poet, a poet working in careless disregard of the rules, yet never failing to achieve the effect at which he aimed.   Walter Pater complains that 'he stood in need of *technique,* of a formed taste in literature, of a literary architecture.'   He finds in his books 'words, phrases, constructions innumerable, which remind one how much the work initiated in France by Madame de Rambouillet was really needed.'   Was ever criticism more sadly irrelevant ? Happily for us, Browne found to his hand a prose that was still plastic and sincere, a prose not yet reduced to a standard by the apostles of 'good sense.' The good sense came only too soon, and made for ever impossible the sonority of *Urn-Burial*. But to wish the author of *Religio Medici* other than he was is to condemn him utterly. A true romantic, he found a keener pleasure in ornament than in structure; him the exquisites who haunted the salon of Madame de Rambouillet could have taught nothing; yet he discovered for himself a method of thought and expression far indeed from 'the reasonable transparency of Hooker,' a method which, as Pater himself admits, attained in *Hydriotaphia* a classical amplitude and serenity.